Table of Contents

SEVEN YEARS

Rightly Dividing
Daniel's 70th Week

By
Ken McDonald B.D., Th.M.

Every Word Publishing
Pensacola, Florida

SEVEN YEARS

Charts
Table of Contents

Preface

The catalyst for the information within this book was my pastor, Wesley Givens. One day we were talking Bible and going over verses on the subject of the tribulation, the AntiChrist and prophecy. We bantered back and forth over various scriptures. The more he talked and the more we studied, I began to understand some truths in the word of God that I had not understood before.

It was his leadership and belief in the preserved words of God in the Authorized Version of 1611 that initiated the study of what you are about to read. It has been a blessing to have a pastor that provokes me to study the word of God.

Thank you, Pastor Givens, for your faithfulness to our Lord Jesus Christ, and to the veracity of the words of God.

Charts
Table of Contents

Introduction

I did not grow up around the Bible, but in my later teens a book came out that grabbed the attention of my friends and was very popular at the time. The book was *The Late Great Planet Earth* by Hal Lindsey. It was a book on prophecy. Since I had never heard anything like that before, it captured my attention and turned my thoughts toward spiritual things. Up to this point in my life I had been an environmentalist. Having grown up in the Sierra Nevada Mountains of California, environmentalism was getting ready to bud out into full bloom. Consequently, with friends of mine getting saved and witnessing to me, as well as hearing about Jesus Christ returning to the earth and what was going to happen to this earth, I ended up getting saved November 29, 1977. When I heard about the Millennium, I believed what the Bible said about it and thought to myself, *"Man, I sure do not want to miss that!"* I am not going to miss it because I am now born again.

Prophecy is very interesting for it tells the future, or at least it is concerned with future events.

And because of the accuracy of past prophecies coming to pass exactly as the Bible said they would, there is great credence upon these prophecies that we are going to be studying in this book. They are going to happen, and they are going to happen soon. But you must have the Holy Spirit and the holy words of God to understand those things to come. As Jesus said in the book of John:

> [13]Howbeit when he, the Spirit of truth, is come, he will guide you into all truth: for he shall not speak of himself; but whatsoever he shall hear, *that* shall he speak: and **he will shew you things to come.** (John 16:13)

When will they happen? Well, that is knowledge that I don't have, so I am not going to be dating anything in this book, but you will get some things to look for, and when you see them you will know that it won't be long. Many writers, preachers, and Bible "scholars" have tried to date when they thought the Lord would return, and they have ended up looking like fools, because the Lord did not come back when they said He would. So, no, I am not going to to be dating anything in this book.

What you are going to get is a clearer picture of the events that are about to happen in the near future, and the order of those events that will take place. Events such as the two prophets tormenting the world, the Beast entering the Temple, the woman fleeing into the wilderness, and the anointing of the most Holy. These things are very clear from the word of God, and they will be shown from the word of God.

While I am on the subject, the word of God that I will be using is the King James 1611 Bible. It is the inerrant word of God. There are many books available today on why the King James 1611 Bible is the perfectly preserved word of God. Books by Riplinger, Hills, Grady, and Ruckman, and many more show that God has preserved His holy words for us in English. Consequently, all scripture quotes in this book will be from the King James 1611 Bible.

If we do not have, and if God has not given us, His inerrant, perfectly preserved words, then we have nothing. We might as well go get drunk or blow our brains out. Why? Because without God's words, life has no meaning whatsoever. There is no reason to do anything. No purpose in life other than to please yourself, or be an environmentalist, and it doesn't take long for that to grow old.

You have noticed lately the amount of environmentalism around the world, haven't you? It is because they do not know where the words of God are, or they do not want the words of God, so the only thing left to give them "purpose" is to preserve the world. What a wasted life!!! God is going to burn this place. They need to quit listening to man and start listening to what God said.

15

> ⁴God forbid: yea, **let God be true, but every man a liar;** as it is written, That thou mightest be justified in thy sayings, and mightest overcome when thou art judged. (Rom. 3:4)

As you read this book, I want you to know that you have the same authority that I do. It is the word of God. You and I are to view all of man's writings and words as coming from liars. That may sound harsh, but the point is that you are not to blindly trust, or believe anything that is written by man. God's word is the only thing you are to unreservedly trust and believe. I write this to you, dear reader, to make you understand that I am not the authority, and neither are you, and neither is some original manuscript that nobody alive today has ever seen.

You and I are to believe the Bible, the words of God for what they say, not what they are claimed to mean. The word of God says what it means and means what it says. When you don't understand it, then you must pray and ask Jesus Christ to show you what it means. And if you have a problem with the word of God, then there is one thing you should know. The problem is with you, not the word of God.

What you are about to read is only true as it lines up with the word of God. Young or old, educated or un-educated, we all ought to be able to be rebuked and corrected by the word of God. That will depend though, on whether you are in subjection to the word of God. There are many people alive today who think that they

16

can correct the word of God. The main reason is because they do not believe that the King James 1611 Bible is the inerrant word of God. In such a case, they become their own authority. Obviously they are wrong, and reveal their own depravity in rejecting God's authority.

Let God be true, but every man...a liar.

Seven Years

Simplified Rightly Dividing
the Word of Truth

There has been very great confusion over the centuries concerning what we will be discussing in this book: that being the Tribulation, the Antichrist, the end of the world, and the restoration of the nation of Israel. The confusion has been so great that there have been people who have discouraged others from reading the book of Revelation. Their claim is that if they read the book of Revelation they will lose their mind and go crazy. I personally have heard people say this. I even had a fairly young mother attend my church and end up getting put in the psychiatric ward after she very heavily studied end times prophecies.

It was back in the 1980's up in the Sierra Nevada mountains of California. I was attempting to build a church in my home town of Twain Harte. It is a very small, picturesque town nestled in the mountains at

3,800 ft above sea level. It is a beautiful area with tall evergreen pine, cedar and fir trees, along with black oak trees for nice color in the fall. It gets snow in the winter and clean mountain breezes in the summer with swimming in the various lakes in the area. I'm sure it's obvious that I have a very fond remembrance of the area.

One Sunday morning I had a young family show up to my church services. We were meeting in the local American Legion hall. It was a simple cement block, cement floor, building. Inside there was a bar situated in one corner of the building, but we had simple metal folding chairs set out in rows and even had an old upright piano with Sis. Hoover to play on as we sang old-fashioned hymns. To have visitors was a great encouragement to me, as well as to the handful of others who were also attending the church.

I do not remember their names, so I'll call the man John, and his wife, Leah. They came with two young children, and the family was a very nice, clean, young family. For the first month or so, things went very well, and it seemed like this new family was going to unite with our church. Leah had many questions, and it didn't take long to realize that she, and John, had grown up in a Pentecostal denominational church. We were a Baptist church so there were some very stark differences in our church from what they were used to. The main difference being the Pentecostal church denomination believes in tongues and healing, and the Baptist church believes that those "sign" gifts are for the Tribulation period. The other main difference is the Pentecostal denomination believes a Christian can lose their salvation. The Baptist denomination, as a rule, believe in eternal security, that being once a sinner is born again then they are safe and can never lose their salvation.

As I tried to gently teach the word of God, more and more questions arose from Leah about speaking in tongues, about healings, and being slain in the Spirit. I could see she was getting agitated more and more, even though I was trying to be gentle with Bible truth. I sought to spiritually nurse her along, but then things began to get weird. And I mean weird!

One of the last Sundays that she attended with her two children, the spirit in the church meeting was very strange. There was no liberty to sing, teach, or preach the word of God. Confusion and chaos were throughout the service. It was like everything was out of control, but we were all still going through the motions of singing and having church. For example, books fell off chairs that nobody was sitting in, and when they hit the hard cement floor the slap of the hymnal was very loud. I also remember when I looked at Leah, her eyes were very widely open. I mean overly wide-eyed.

After the service Leah asked me if I would be willing to come by and have a Bible study at their house, to which I agreed. I met with her and John on a Thursday night. We went over the gifts of the Spirit and what the Bible says about them. After about forty-five minutes of study, she asked me what I believe happened to someone who speaks in tongues in a Pentecostal service. I had to tell

21

her the truth, and I said that if a power was overcoming them, then they were speaking in tongues by an unclean spirit. I could tell this really bothered her, and it wasn't long after that the Bible study was over. John had listened to the study and was not at all troubled. He even seemed to enjoy the Bible answers that I gave when asked questions. I could tell though that Leah, on the other hand, was obviously troubled about what I had showed them.

Saturday morning I got a phone call from John and he said to me, "Bro. Ken, I don't know what all you were talking about Thursday night. Leah and I grew up in the same church, but I never got into all of that tongues and stuff. But after you left, she stayed up all night reading the book of Revelation. I went to work and mid morning I got a call that the neighbors had found my wife walking through the forest, getting visions and not in her right mind. She is in the psych. ward now." He then said, "I don't think she needs to do any more studying the Bible." I told him that I understood, and that I would be praying for them.

Now, do yo know what the problem is there? She grew up under preachers and people that didn't know how to rightly divide the word of God and applied everything to theirselves. They included all of the signs and wonders that are meant for the Jew in the Tribulation. The Tribulation period is when the sign gifts are properly in effect, and will be performed by the Holy Ghost through the servants of God. But in this Church Age, we are to walk by faith and not by sight. The scriptural signs and wonders are not for us today.

The counterfeit signs and wonders that are being performed in churches are done by devils and an unclean spirit. And the vast majority of those who are exercising these false gifts are women. There are some men, but the majority of "miraculous manifestations" are done by women.

So, by the grace of God, we are going to rightly divide the word of God. We will apply to the Church Age what applies to the Church Age, and what applies to the Jew in the Tribulation we will apply appropriately. Suffice it to say that the vast majority of scriptures and subject matter in this book will not apply to you and me in the Church Age. We are going to be studying what is going to take place AFTER the Church Age, so if you have been born again, you are not even going to be on the earth at the time all this takes place. If you will apply it this way, which is the way it is supposed to be applied, then you will not lose your mind. But the devils sure do have fun with those who don't rightly divide the word of truth!

> [15]Study to shew thyself approved unto God,
> a workman that needeth not to be ashamed,
> **rightly dividing the word of truth.**
> (2 Tim. 2:15)

In order for you to understand the Tribulation, then you are going to have to understand what it is to rightly divide the word of truth. You are commanded to do this, yet so many Christians today do not know what rightly

23

dividing is. One of the reasons is because in the new bibles (per-versions) this command is removed. Instead of rightly dividing, they read:

2 Tim. 2:15
ESVS ...rightly handling
ASV ...handling aright
TEV ...one who correctly teaches
NIV ...correctly handles

The command to, "**...rightly divide the word of truth**" is removed. But in the King James 1611, the inerrant words of God, you are commanded to rightly divide the word of truth. So, I am going to give you a basic proper dividing of the word of God. To begin with you can obviously see that there is a division in your Bible and it is between the Old Testament and the New Testament. This study is going to predominantly be concerned with the New Testament divisions. They are as follows:

The Church age, the Tribulation, and the Millennium. Merely three divisions is all we will be concerned with in this study.

Though not the main subject of this book, yet it will be noted how some preachers and teachers of the word of God divide the Tribulation period. They claim the first half of the Tribulation period of three and a half years took place during the earthly ministry of Jesus Christ.

One of the reasons for doing this, and in my opinion it is the main reason, is the fact that the book of Revelation never does use seven years. In the book of Revelation it always uses three and a half years, or it gives the number of days that amount to three and a half years.

In this book I will show why seven years is never used in the book of Revelation, and why there are still seven years to take place. Daniel's 70th week has yet to begin, and it still is a full seven years long. This is not hard to see as we get into this study.

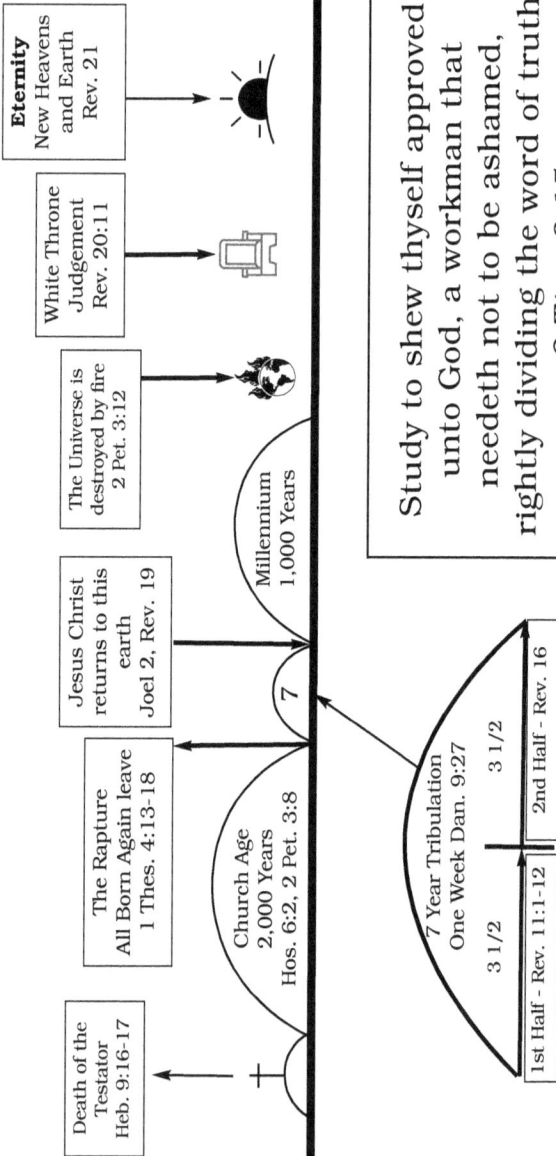

Basic Divisions in the Word of God after the Cross

Death of the Testator
Heb. 9:16-17

The Rapture
All Born Again leave
1 Thes. 4:13-18

Jesus Christ returns to this earth
Joel 2, Rev. 19

The Universe is destroyed by fire
2 Pet. 3:12

White Throne Judgement
Rev. 20:11

Eternity
New Heavens and Earth
Rev. 21

Church Age
2,000 Years
Hos. 6:2, 2 Pet. 3:8

Millennium
1,000 Years

7

7 Year Tribulation
One Week Dan. 9:27

3 1/2

3 1/2

1st Half - Rev. 11:1-12

2nd Half - Rev. 16

Study to shew thyself approved unto God, a workman that needeth not to be ashamed, rightly dividing the word of truth.
2 Tim. 2:15

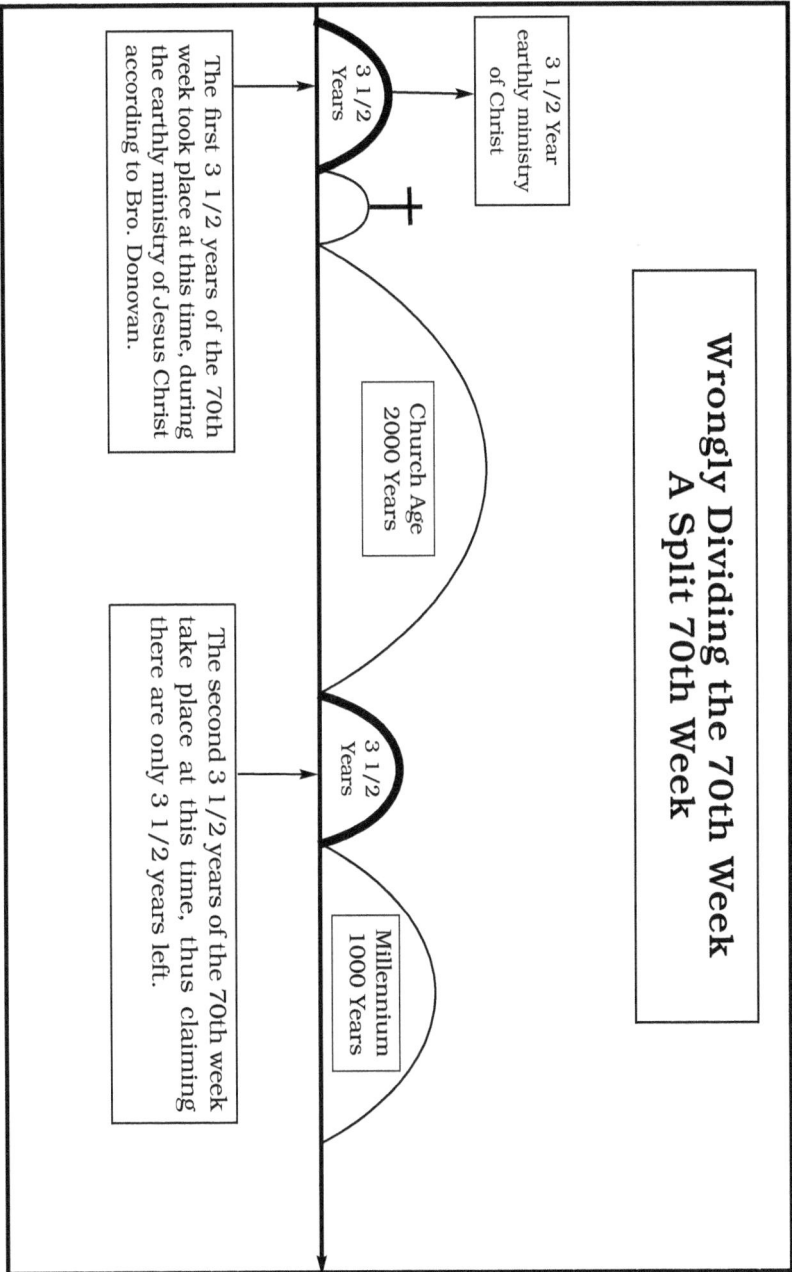

Wrongly Dividing the 70th Week
A Split 70th Week

3 1/2 Year earthly ministry of Christ

3 1/2 Years

The first 3 1/2 years of the 70th week took place at this time, during the earthly ministry of Jesus Christ according to Bro. Donovan.

Church Age 2000 Years

3 1/2 Years

The second 3 1/2 years of the 70th week take place at this time, thus claiming there are only 3 1/2 years left.

Millennium 1000 Years

Seven Years

The Seven Year Dilemma

Introduction to This Chapter

We are going to define the dilemma using quotes from a book titled, *The Revelation of the Seventy Weeks*, by Brian Donovan. Pastor Brian Donovan is the president of Pensacola Bible Institute, as well as the pastor of Bible Baptist Church, in Pensacola, Florida. The book is published by Bro. Donovan and is carried in the Bible Baptist Bookstore.

I am not attacking Pastor Brian Donovan. He loves the Lord Jesus Christ and believes the King James 1611 Bible. He has done an excellent job in the leadership position he was placed in. But I am going to discuss Bible doctrine. What you are going to read, and especially in this chapter, will have many quotes from his booklet, as well as from scripture concerning the teachings found within the pages of *The Revelation of the Seventy Weeks.* Again, I am not attacking the man.

I remember graduating from Pensacola Bible Institute in 1982. When I graduated, along with the rest of my class, we knew that the Tribulation was seven years in length and yet to be fulfilled. Since graduating, I have talked to recent graduates, and they are not sure if it is seven years. Most say that the Tribulation only has three and a half years to go once it begins. But they then say, "It could go either way, though it is not all that important." Really? It's not all that important? I believe it is important, and here is the reason why.

If you believe that half of the Tribulation has already taken place, then you have one of two positions to believe concerning the upcoming remainder of the Tribulation. Either you believe there might be some time between the Rapture and the start of the last half of the Tribulation, or if you believe the Tribulation begins right after the Rapture then you will end up looking for the Antichrist to appear. To believe there is time between the Rapture and the commencement of the last half of the Tribulation does not fit, nor does it make any sense dispensationally. A period of time from the Rapture to the start of the last half of the Tribulation is sort of a time of limbo, and there is absolutely no scripture to back it up. The problem though with all of this is the underlying uncertainty.

By the end of this book, you will know how long the Tribulation is, and when it will take place. There will be no doubt if you believe the scriptures.

The Dilemma

So what is the dilemma? It is this: if the Tribulation is yet future, and if the Tribulation is seven years long, then why does the word of God repeatedly say three and a half years in various ways. In Revelation 11:2 and 13:5, it says, "**...forty and two months,**" which equals three and a half years. Then in Revelation 12:6 and 11:3, it says, "**...a thousand two hundred and threescore days**" which equals three and a half years. Then in another place Revelation 12:14 reads, "**...a time, and times, and half a time...**" There is one thing for sure, the Lord is making it very plain that He is referencing a period of time that is three and a half years long. He mentions it in three different ways so you will get it straight. But nowhere in the book of Revelation does it ever state a time frame of seven years.

God states over and over in the book of Revelation, which is a book about events yet to come, that there are three and a half years. So why then do people believe that the future Tribulation, --the main subject of the book of Revelation -- is seven years long? To some this doesn't make any sense, and Brian Donovan is one of those influential men to whom seven years in the book of Revelation does fit. He has come up with what he believes answers this dilemma.

Here are some quotes from Bro. Donovan's book, *The Revelation of the Seventy Weeks* to illustrate the dilemma.

The results of this present study came mainly from two major points. **The first**

being the fact that the scriptures continually point to only three and one half years left after the mystery Church Age is over (Revelation 11:2-3; 12:6; 12:14; 13:5), and the second was being unable to confidently apply the sixty nine weeks "unto Messiah the Prince" as a scriptural fit for the death of Jesus Christ on Calvary. It is very interesting to study the teaching of a seven year tribulation period and note the lack of proof for it after the apostle John is caught up in Revelation 4. Almost all Bible believing dispensationalists seem to agree that John's "come up hither" to the third heaven in Revelation 4 matches a perfect picture of the pre-tribulation rapture of the Church Age saints, yet there is not a single verse from Revelation 4 (when John is caught up) through Revelation 19 (when the Lord Jesus Christ returns to earth with the church at the end of the tribulation) that even hints at a seven year period. *(Donovan, Brian, (2016), The Revelation of the Seventy Weeks, Published by Brian Donovan, 1130 Jo Jo Road, Pensacola, FL 32514, Bible Baptist Bookstore, pg 19)*

Are we to believe that John is looking down over a seven year period and repeatedly tells us that it is only three and one half years? Why does he skip over a so called "three and one half years of peace" that is supposed to precede three and one half years of great tribulation? **It would be instructive for the Bible student to go back and read Revelation chapters 4 through 19 and find this three and one half years of peace that preceded the three and one half years of great tribulation.** *(Ibid,, pg 32-33)*

The last part of this quote we will gladly accept the challenge. In essence that is the basis for the writing of this book. But these two quotes sufficiently illustrate the dilemma that was the catalyst for Bro. Donovan and others to wrest the scriptures into teaching something that the word of God does not teach. Bro. Donovan teaches that the first three and a half years of the Tribulation have already taken place. **He claims they took place during the three and a half years of the ministry of Jesus Christ.** Yes, you got that right. **He believes the three and a half years that Jesus Christ ministered in the flesh and that ended with Him dying on the Cross, that those were the first three and a half years of the Tribulation; [which is also known as] i.e. the first three and a half years of Daniel's 70th week.**

One of the six reasons for the seventy weeks is "to anoint the most holy" (Daniel 9:24) so this anointing must take place during the weeks of Daniel's prophecy. Since **the scripture points to His baptism at the beginning of His ministry for His anointing** (Acts 10:34-38), this would be the event that brings us to the conclusion of the sixty nine weeks (unto Messiah the Prince), **which would mean that during the three and one half year ministry of Jesus Christ, which followed His baptism and anointing, Daniel's seventy week prophecy clock was still running right up to the crucifixion of Christ** when Messiah was "cut off but not for himself" (Daniel 9:26). *(Ibid,, pg 23)*

There it is! He teaches that when you're reading the gospels, you're reading about the first half of the Tribulation also.

By the end of this book you will know that there are still an entire seven years left to be fulfilled of the Tribulation, which is also known as Daniel's 70th week. There will be no doubt as you will see from the scriptures.

Let God Be True

As I was reading *The Revelation of the Seventy Weeks* booklet, I came across some statements by Pastor Donovan that seemed strange to me. They had little to do with the subject of the book. The statements though did have limited application with regards to dating, and which calendar to use, at least in Bro. Donovan's opinion. He spends quite a bit of time on calendars and what should be the proper dating for the 70th week. This is to be expected in order to "prove" his teaching.

In his discussion of what he thinks are the proper dates, he mentions two men. One was Tycho Brahe, and the other was Johannes Kepler. He had glowing remarks and comments for Tycho Brahe, but a certain perceived disdain for Johannes Kepler. I found this perplexing since I did not know who these men were. In order to illustrate what I am talking about, here are some quotes.

(I have added emphasis to the places I especially want to call your attention to.)

> Pg 13
>
> After over one thousand years of using the calendar of Dionysius, a supposed error was found in the early 1600's by **a lost astronomer and astrologer named Johannes Kepler. After murdering Tycho Brahe in order to steal years of his personal astronomical calculations and take over his position as chief astronomer (See Heavenly Intrigue [Sic] by Joshua Gilder)**, Kepler proposed that the present calendar contained a four year error, and hence, Christ was actually born in 4 B.C., His "proof" of this error came from Josephus history called "The Antiquities" - page 365, where he recorded an eclipse of the moon shortly before Herod died (Matthew 2:19). Kepler dated this lunar eclipse to 4 B.C., and since that was the only observable lunar eclipse he knew of, and because Herod died shortly after the birth of Christ (Luke 2), dating that event would be a sure way to find the date for the birth of Christ. **So a lost astrologer, who was raised by a mother steeped in witchcraft,** introduced his own idea about the date for the birth of Christ for Bible believers to follow. Armed with this "absolute certainty", in 1613 Kepler calculated the birth of Jesus Christ to take place in 4 B.C., based on the eclipse mentioned by Josephus. *(Ibid.)*

Pg 17

The reader should also pray about the facts that the Roman Catholic Copernicus and this same Kepler are credited with the world accepting the idea that the earth revolves around the sun. The **saved Tycho Brahe painstakingly recorded exact astronomical calculations** to show otherwise and when Kepler wanted to use Brahe's voluminous calculations to put forth his own laws of planetary motion, **he poisoned Brahe using mercury** and took his job as court astronomer in 1601. *(Ibid.)*

It was very frustrating to me to read this part of *The Revelation of the Seventy Weeks.* There were many statements made by Bro. Donovan, and he gave no documentation whatsoever for where he obtained his information. I found it very poor work for the President of Pensacola Bible Institute. Documentation was severely lacking and almost non-existent.

In the preceding quotes there are many statements about two men. The only man of the two that I had heard of was Johannes Kepler. I knew he had something to do with astronomy, but beyond that I knew nothing. So without any documentation given for the statements about these men, I was compelled to do research myself to find out more about them. Unfortunately what I found out did not even come close to how each had been portrayed. And though this has very limited application with regards to our study at hand, I find it necessary to include my findings about these two men, and my findings will be extensively documented.

Notice the accusations given about these men:

1. Johannes Kepler was lost.
2. Johannes Kepler was an astrologer.
3. Johannes Kepler's mother was a witch, or was a woman who was "steeped in witchcraft."
4. Johannes Kepler murdered Brahe by mercury poisoning.
5. Johannes Kepler's four year error in the calendar is wrong.

6. Tycho Brahe was a saved man.
7. Tycho Brahe's calculations were exact.
8. Tycho Brahe was a Geocentrist.

To start with we will see what I found with regards to Tycho Brahe.

Tycho Brahe 12/14/1546 - 10/24/1601

Tycho, also spelled Tyge or Thico, was an astronomer who was also an astrologist and an alchemist. (Another name for alchemist is "witch doctor" or one who practices witchcraft; really! See *Aromatherapy* by Ken McDonald for documentation.) He lost part of his nose when he was drunk and got into a sword fight.

On 29 December 1566 at the age of 20, Tycho lost part of his nose in a sword duel

38

with a fellow Danish nobleman, his third cousin Manderup Parsberg. **The two had drunkenly quarreled over who was the superior mathematician** at an engagement party at the home of Professor Lucas Bachmeister on 10 December. On 29 December, **the cousins resolved their feud with a duel in the dark.** Though the two were later reconciled, in the duel Tycho lost the bridge of his nose and gained a broad scar across his forehead. He received the best possible care at the university and wore a prosthetic nose for the rest of his life. It was kept in place with paste or glue and said to be made of silver and gold. *(Benecke, Mark (2004). "The Search for Tycho Brahe's Nose" (PDF). Annals of Improbable Research. 10 (4): 6–7: As quoted from https://en.wikipedia.org/wiki/Tycho_Brahe#CITEREFHåkansson2006, viewed 5/10/2024)*

In 1571 Tycho Brahe fell in love with Kirsten Hansen, but they never married. Instead they "shacked up" for almost 30 years and had eight children, whom many people considered to be bastards.

"...The judgement of these two commissioners is not known, but in an old diocesan record it is stated that, "the minister of Hveen was dismissed in disgrace for not having kept to the ritual and prayer-book in the form of Baptism ("I adjure thee"), but acting differently; also for not having punished and

39

admonished **Tycho Brahe of Hveen, who for eighteen years had not been to the Sacrament, but lived in an evil manner with a concubine.** (*Dreyer, J. I. E., Ph. D., F.R.A.S., Tycho Brahe, A Picture of Scientific Life Work in the Sixteenth Century, , Edinburgh, Adam and Charles Black, 1890, From the University of California Library, Pg 236*)

...Tycho disposed of his portion of the family property of Knudstrup, which, since the death of his father, he had possessed jointly with his brother Stoen, **and which his sons, as born of a "bond-woman," could not have inherited.** (*ibid, Pg 223*)

The following young man named Gellius, was a young man who was dating Tycho's oldest daughter, Magdalene.

...Gellius (Sasceridos) would hardly have thought of aspiring to the hand of any other nobleman's daughter, but **the peculiar position of Tycho's children, by many people not considered to be legitimate,** may have given him courage.(*ibid, Pg 224*)

For his time Tycho was very well respected for his astronomical calculations, but since the invention of the telescope *it has been determined that much of Brahe's measurement calculations were wrong.*

According to the University of Oregon:

> Tycho's measurements were used to show that there was **no detectable parallax** (Since the invention of the telescope, stellar parallax has been repeatedly observed, thus proving the earth is orbiting the sun —my comment) with the naked eye, in support of the geocentric theory. **So, even though his observations were the best for his time, his result was wrong, a lesson in how science is done.** *(University of Oregon, Tycho Brahe, pages.uoregon.edu/jschombe/cosmo/lectures/lec03.html#:~:text=Tycho%27s%20measurements%20were%20used%20to,in%20how%20science%20is%20done., viewed on 5/10/2024)*

As an alchemist, he dabbled in the occult. He followed and adhered to the pursuits of a "mean drunk" by the name of Paracelsus, who was one of the first alchemists. Alchemists sought to find the elixir of life, also known as Chi, Ki, Prana, Aether and about 100 other names for the same demonic entity. (See my two books, *Defiled* and *Aromatherapy,* for more information on this subject.). Alchemists also sought to discover how to change lead into gold.

Tycho had a demon-possessed dwarf by the name of Jeppe, or Jep, whom Tycho claimed was clairvoyant. When Tyco was eating, he kept Jep under his dinner table and would occasionally hand the dwarf a morsel of food under the table. Jep could predict when anyone got sick, if they would live or die, and he was never wrong.

Tycho lived on Hveen, an island in Denmark. **One occupant that resided in his house was his fool, or jester, a dwarf called Jeppe or Jep, who sat at Tycho's feet when he was at table, and got a morsel now and then from his hand.** He chattered incessantly, and according to Longomontanus, was supposed to be gifted with second-sight, and his utterances were therefore listened to with some attention.

When any one was ill at Hveen, and the dwarf gave an opinion as to his chance of recovery or death, he always turned out to be right. *(Dreyer, J. I. E., Ph. D., F.R.A.S., Tycho Brahe, A Picture of Scientific Life Work in the Sixteenth Century, Edinburgh, Adam and Charles Black, 1890, From the University of California Library, Pg 127-128)*

Tycho carried out forced labor on his island which became a national scandal for Denmark. He even had his own prison and put people in it in irons.

Circa 1591

Tycho, notwithstanding the lease for life which the tenant held of his farm, had let other people plough and sow the land, and in the previous October (six months before he tried to have him legally evicted) **had taken the farm from him. Tycho had furthermore taken the law into his own hands by having**

Rasmus (Pedersen) put in irons at his own table, from whence he was carried off to Hveen, where he was detained for six weeks more. *(Ibid, pg 218)*

As to Brahe's death, his remains were exhumed in 2010 and carefully examined by Kaare Lund Rasmussen of the University of South Denmark.

We found traces of gold in Tycho Brahe's hair, and we can establish that he was exposed to gold while these hairs were still on his body," chemist Kaare Lund Rasmussen of the University of South Denmark said in a university press release. *((Eschner, Kat, Astronomer and Alchemist Tycho Brahe Died Full of Gold | Smart News| Smithsonian Magazine.pdf, December 14, 2016/https://www.smithsonianmag.com/smartnews/astronomer-and-alchemist-tycho-brahe-died-fullgold-180961447/ , viewed 5/10/2024))*

It was determined that Brahe was not murdered by mercury poisoning, for there were no concentrations of mercury found in his body. What was found was 20 to 100 times the normal level of gold, along with lesser concentrations of arsenic, silver and cobalt. He had high doses of gold the last two months of his life. Alchemists believed that was a cure for disease.

Rasmussen's team analyzed hair samples taken from the astronomer's scalp, beard and eyebrows. They found that the samples contained **a gold content of between 20-100 times higher than a normal person today,** showing that he was "excessively" exposed to gold in the last 2 months of his life, the study says. *(ibid.,)*

Brahe's remains were exhumed again in 2010 and have since led to a variety of discoveries about the man, **including that he was not murdered.** *(Ibid.)*

Tycho Brahe wrote his own epitaph:

He lived like a sage, and died like a fool. *(Weisstein, Eric W., Eric Weisstein's World of Scientific Biography, Brahe, Tycho (1546–1601), Retrieved 13 August, 2012., Tycho Brahe - Wikipedia.pdf / https://scienceworld.wolfram.com/biography/Brahe.html, viewed 5/10/2024)*

Brahe was not a true geocentrist as his model of the planets and the sun were a geo-heliocentric compromise.

In **Tycho Brahe's geo heliocentric system,** the planets moved around the sun, and the stars, sun, and moon moved around Earth, with Earth at the center of the universe," explained Mosley. "This geo heliocentric system was thought by Tycho Brahe, and by some astronomers and philosophers in the seventeenth century, to overcome some of the problems with the two alternative systems. *(Staniforth Emily, Tillman Nola Taylor, Tycho Brahe: Colorful life, accomplishments and bizarre death, last updated June 21, 2023, https://www.space.com/19623-tycho-brahe-biography.html / Future US Inc, viewed 5/10/2024)*

But what Tycho Brahe is most notably known for to this day is what is termed, Calendarium Naturale Magicum Perpetuum, commonly known as the **Magic Calendar of Tycho Brahe.** He is said to be the inventor of it.

Thico Brahae inuentor 1582:
Brahe, Tycho, 1546-1601, printer

(Digital Public Library of America, Calendarium naturale magicum perpetuum profundissimam rerum secretissimarum contemplationem totiusque Philosophiæ cognitionemcomplectens[graphic],https://dp.la/item/57 1d3c01dfd928389ac6d95279f33888/http://www.archi ve.org/details/calendariumnatur00meri, viewed 5/10/2024, This is the spelling of his name and the word "invented" in old English.)

It is a Rosicrucian (Satanic) calendar associated and still in use today with the occult's witches and warlocks. It is used for witchcraft, astrology, fortune-telling and more. Though it is disputed that Tycho invented the Magic Calendar, those who contest the claim do admit to his building some of the plates use to print the calendar. There is evidence that at least one astrological calendar was printed on Tycho's own printing press, proving that he did allow the printing of such things.

Another former University acquaintance with whom Tycho occasionally exchanged letters was Professor Bracaeus, who had been appointed to a chair of medicine in the University of Rostock in 1567 while Tycho was studying there. **He was one of the comparatively few learned men of the time who would have nothing to do with astrology, and it is therefore not to be wondered at that he expressed his disapproval on hearing about the intended printing of an astrological calendar by Elias Olsen at Hveen.** *(Dreyer, J. I. E., Ph. D., F.R.A.S., Tycho Brahe, A Picture of Scientific Life Work in the Sixteenth Century, , Edinburgh, Adam and Charles Black, 1890, From the University of California Library, Pg 133)*

The following is quoted from the website: Occult World

In Magic, he (Tycho Brahe) is known for a magical calendar of unlucky days, compiled from his astrological work for Holy Roman Emperor Rudolf II.

Another calendar, **The Magical Calendar of Tycho Brahe**, is a document of magical and occult symbolism and correspondences, important in the Rosicrucian movement. The

Magical Calendar of Tycho Brahe was designed by the engraver Theodor DeBry, who worked with Robert Fludd, Michael Meier, and other alchemists. Eliphas Levi considered the calendar to be one of the most important occult documents of the 17th century. *(Guiley, Rosemary Ellen, Occult World, The Encyclopedia of Magic and Alchemy, Brahe, Tycho, Copywrite 2006 by Visionary Living Inc., https://occult-world.com/brahe-tycho/, Viewed 5/10/2024)*

The book Bro. Donovan mentioned as documentation for the murder of Tycho Brahe by Johannes Kepler, *Heavenly Intrigue*, was written by a novelist by the name of Joshua Gilder. His wife is a journalist.

A novelist is someone who writes novels, which are book-length, fictional stories.

Here is what an advertisement for the book says in Publishers Weekly:

The writing is professional **but not noteworthy, and the Gilders occasionally stretch the inconclusive evidence into speculations too thin to persuade.** *(Vines James, Agent, Heavenly Intrigue: Johannes Kepler, Tycho Brahe, and the Murder Behind One of History's Greatest Scientific Discoveries, https://www.publishersweekly.com/9780385508445/ viewed 5/10/2024)*

There is much more that I could write, but I believe that is enough concerning this man that Bro. Donovan claims is, "The saved Tycho Brahe painstakingly recorded exact astronomical calculations ...". _(Donovan, Brian, (2016), The Revelation of the Seventy Weeks, Published by Brian Donovan, 1130 Jo Jo Road, Pensacola, FL 32514, Bible Baptist Bookstore, Pg 17)_ Really?

As Adam Scherzi's titles his article: Tycho Brahe: Wrong, but Points for Creativity. _(Scherlis Adam, Parameter Space: The Final Frontier, Tycho Brahe: Wrong, but Points for Creativity, https://adam.scherlis.com/2010/08/04/tycho-brahe/#comments , Posted on August 4, 2010: Accessed 5/10/2024)_

Now I have documented what I have written, and could have done more. But this is only Tycho Brahe, whose astronomical work is obsolete and erroneous today. That is fact!

But how about Johannes Kepler? Was he the murderer that Bro. Donovan claims he was?

Johannes Kepler 12/27/1571 - 11/15/1630

Having no reference to go on, I took it upon myself to do research on the man Johannes Kepler.

Bro. Donovan claims that Kepler was lost, an astrologer, had a mother steeped in witchcraft, and murdered Tycho Brahe in order to steal Brahe's charts and figures. If true then, Johannes Kepler was a "bad dude" for sure. So I began to research in order to see what I could find out about Johannes Kepler, since the documentation was poor in _The Revelation of the Seventy Weeks._

48

As I began to do my research on Kepler, the information that I kept coming across did not match what Bro. Donovan had written. As a matter of fact, just as his statements about Tycho Brahe were not true, so too his statements about Kepler were not true.

To begin with Johannes Kepler had studied for the Lutheran ministry when he entered college, with his studies including Hebrew, Greek, Latin, and Bible. After graduating in 1588 with his B.A., and then in 1591 with his M.A., he went on with his studies in theology intending to enter the ministry as a Lutheran minister.

> Through the Duke's continued generosity, Johannes Kepler was able to begin attending the University of Tübingen in 1587. **His studies included Latin, Hebrew, Greek, the Bible, mathematics, and astronomy.** Kepler was taught mathematics and astronomy by Michael Mästlin, one of the few astronomy professors of that time who had accepted Copernicus' idea that the planets, including the earth, revolved around the sun. Almost all scholars of that era still believed that the earth was the centre of the solar system.

> Kepler obtained his B.A. degree in 1588 and his M.A. degree in 1591. **He then continued at Tübingen, studying theology. During his youth, Kepler had become a committed Christian and dedicated himself to serving God.** As he said shortly before he died, **he**

believed 'only and alone in the service of
Jesus Christ. In Him is all refuge, all solace.'
Kepler intended to serve God as a Lutheran
minister after completing his university
education. However, God had other plans for
this uniquely gifted young man.

In 1594, Kepler was asked to go to the
Lutheran high school in Graz, Austria, to
replace the mathematics teacher who had
just died. Although close to finishing his
theological training, Kepler felt led by God to
take up this teaching position. *(Lamont Ann,
Johannes Kepler (1571-1630) Outstanding scientist and
committed Christian, https://creation.com/johannes-
kepler, Johannes Kepler, quoted in: J. H. Tiner, Johannes
Kepler-Giant of Faith and Science, Mott Media, Milford,
Michigan (USA), 1977, p. 193., Originally published in
Johannes Kepler | Answers in Genesis, Creation 15, no
1 (December 1992): 40-43., viewed 5/10/24)*

References to the scriptures are found
through out his writings such as the
following in his famous work Harmonies of
the World (in Latin, Harmonices Mundi)
begins:

I commence a sacred discourse, a most true
hymn to God the Founder, and I judge it to
be piety, not to sacrifice many hecatombs of
bulls to Him and to burn incense of

innumerable perfumes and cassia, but first to learn myself, and afterwards to teach others too, how great He is in wisdom, how great in power, and of what sort in goodness. *(Dao, Christine, 3/01/08, Man of Science, Man of God/ Johann Kepler | The Institute for CreationResearch.pdf/ https://www.icr.org/article/science-man-god-johann-kepler/, Kepler, J. 1619. "Proem." Harmonies of the World., Viewed 5/10/24)*

At the end Kepler concludes:

Purposely I break off the dream and the very vast speculation, merely crying out with the royal Psalmist: Great is our Lord and great His virtue and of His wisdom there is no number: praise Him, ye heavens, praise Him, ye sun, moon, and planets, use every sense for perceiving, every tongue for declaring your Creator...to Him be praise, honor, and glory, world without end. Amen. *(Dao, Christine, 3/01/08, Man of Science, Man of God/ Johann Kepler | The Institute for CreationResearch.pdf/ https://www.icr.org/article/science-man-god-johann-kepler/, Epilogue Concerning the Sun, By Way of Conjecture," ibid.. Viewed 5/10/24)*

As he said shortly before he died, he believed 'only and alone in the service of Jesus Christ. In Him is all refuge, all solace.' *(Lamont Ann, Johannes Kepler (1571-1630) Outstanding scientist and committed Christian,*

51

https://creation.com/johannes-kepler, Johannes Kepler, quoted in: J. H. Tiner, Johannes Kepler-Giant of Faith and Science, Mott Media, Milford, Michigan (USA), 1977, p. 193., Originally published in Johannes Kepler | Answers in Genesis, Creation 15, no 1 (December 1992): 40-43., viewed 5/10/24)

He seems pretty likely to be saved to me.

As to his use and practice of Astrology there was some, but not like Tycho Brahe, who along with his astrology used alchemy as well. Alchemy is very dark. But Kepler even published a work titled Principals of Astrology, published in 1602, "...he rails against the vanity and worthlessness of the ordinary astrology. He regards those who professed it as knaves and charlatans; and maintains that the planets and stars exercise no influence whatever over human affairs." *(Brewster David, Martyrs of Science, The, or the lives of Galileo, Tycho Brahe, and Kepler, London: John Murray, Albemarle Street. 1841, Chapter 4, downloaded from: https://www.gutenberg.org/ebooks/25992)*

What he did hold to was the effects of the stars and planets on the world and people: such as the weather, or how there is an effect on some during a full moon.

As to Kepler being raised by a mother steeped in witchcraft, from my research this is patently false. Kepler's mother was arrested for witchcraft. When this happened, Johannes Kepler quit his job as imperial mathematician and became his mother's defense lawyer, since they did not have the money to hire a lawyer.

As to Katharina Kepler being a witch the amount of evidence comes to her mixing herbal drinks for herself and occasionally giving them to help others.

Quoted from: Ulinka Rublack, Professor of Early Modern European History, Cambridge University:

> Then came the accusation against his mother. The proceedings which led to a criminal trial lasted six years. **The Imperial mathematician formally took over his mother's legal defence.** [Sic] No other public intellectual figure would have ever involved themselves in a similar role, but Kepler put his whole existence on hold, stored up his books, papers and instruments in boxes, moved his family to southern Germany and spent nearly a year trying to get his mother out of prison.

> Local records for the small town in which Katharina Kepler lived are abundant. **There is no evidence that she was brought up by an aunt who was burnt for witchcraft** – this was one of the charges which her enemies invented. **There is no evidence either that she made a living from healing** – she simply mixed herbal drinks for herself and sometimes offered her help to others, like

anyone else. A woman in her late 70s, Katharina Kepler withstood a trial and final imprisonment, **during which she was chained to the floor for more than a year.**

Kepler's defense was a rhetorical master-piece. He was able to dismantle the inconsistencies in the prosecution case, and show that the "magical" illnesses for which they blamed his mother could be explained using medical knowledge and common sense. In the autumn of 1621, Katharina was finally set free." *(Bublack Ulinka, The astronomer and the witch - how Kepler saved his mother from the stake, https://www.cam.ac.uk/research/discussion/the-as-tronomer-and-the-witch-how-kepler-saved-his-mother-from-the-stake, Published by Oxford University Press on October 22, 2015, viewed 5/10/2024)*

As to the accusation that Johannes Kepler murdered Tycho Brahe, I have already given evidence that it is not true. Before Tycho's death he —that is, Tycho Brahe— instructed Kepler to finish the Rudolphine Tables. Thus willingly Tycho gave Kepler access to his records.

According to Dreyer, whose work on Tycho Brahe is the definitive work on the man, he says:

The most important inheritance which Tycho left to Kepler and to posterity was the vast mass of observations, of which Kepler justly said that they deserved to be kept among the royal treasures, as the reform of astronomy could not be accomplished without them. He even added that there was no hope of any one ever making more accurate observations, for it was a most tedious and lengthy business! **This would have been perfectly true if the telescope had not afterwards been invented.** *(Dreyer, J. I. E., Ph. D., F.R.A.S., Tycho Brahe, A Picture of Scientific Life Work in the Sixteenth Century, , Edinburgh, Adam and Charles Black, 1890, From the University of California Library, Pg 312)*

I know this has been a rabbit trail so to speak, and it has nothing to do with the Tribulation. Yet it is relevant that in, *The Revelation of the Seventy Weeks* are found statements in the beginning of the booklet with no documentation as to the veracity of the statements. But the Bible states, **"...in the mouth of two or three witnesses shall every word be established."** (2 Cor. 13:1b)

I mention this and use the Brahe/Kepler example of what he is doing because he does the same thing when he is quoting Sir Robert Anderson and others.

In regards to Anderson, I downloaded his work, *The Coming Prince.* I'm not going to get into it, but Anderson uses much scripture, and extensively documents his conclusions.

For me, the greatest concern I have with regards to *The Revelation of the Seventy Weeks* is this statement on pg 7:

At this point, any Bible believer, even if he arrives at the correct historical command given in the Bible, **must rely on a secular calendar in order to come up with an actual historical date for the seventy week prophetic calendar to start.** _(Donovan, Brian, (2016), The Revelation of the Seventy Weeks, Published by Brian Donovan, 1130 Jo Jo Road, Pensacola, FL 32514, Bible Baptist Bookstore, Pg 7)_

Well, if that is true, then you are standing on sinking sand.

Book 1
The Scriptures

With the complexity of this subject, I have prayed about how to present the material in this book. Which is the best way to lay it all out for you, the reader, to understand what I am writing about. As I write to you, I am also aware that some of you will understand rightly dividing and all of the time lines, as well as more that is involved in this study. I am also aware that there will be some who are young in the Lord, or who have never been taught about these things. So I will write with the intention to make it simple to understand, yet interesting to read. Only the Lord able to enable anyone to write this way, but this is my goal. To write and try to impress you with big words and fancy vocabulary does not interest me in the least.

So presenting all of the information that is going to be given in this book in a way that is understandable has been a concern and prayer of mine. What I decided to do is to go through the main passages of scripture and give a commentary on the verses and how they apply. It will be a sort of Bible commentary format with comments under the verses with cross references as well.

In this day and age because so many of you have hectic schedules I have done the work for you. In other words, I have included the full text of the passages and cross references from the word of God for your ease of study. I would recommend though, that you look it all up in your own King James Bible so you will familiarize yourself with the truth in your own Bible. There is something about knowing what side of the page the certain verse is on, as well as writing your own notes in your Bible.

When I was in Bible School, I had great amounts of scripture and truth taught to me. But it wasn't until I opened my own Bible and went over the teachings myself, that I truly heard and learned what was being taught. In other words, there has to come a time when you study it all for yourself and in so many words, you digest it. I will seek to fill your plate and set it before you, but you must take it in and digest it, all the while remembering that the authority is the word of God, not man.

I am calling this section Book 1, and it will be the Bible commentary on the main passages that cover the Seven Year Tribulation. Other corresponding Bible passages will be brought in as well, instead of presenting them separately so as to avoid a lot of repeating what has already been covered.

In Book 1, there are going to be passages that cover

the same events, but I am going to go through them anyway. I am not going to combine them as sometimes there are small variations in what is written that have tremendous implications. So as you read what I have written in Daniel 9, you are going to read again elements of the same thing in Matthew 24, and again in 2 Thessalonians 2, and again in Revelation 11. I pray this is not a burden to you. I know God has repeated it, though recorded differently in each place.

For many, the doctrine of the Tribulation (which is also known as the time of Jacob's trouble, and also referred to as Daniel's 70th week), is confusing. I know for many years, even though I was a Bible School graduate with a master's degree, much of the Tribulation was confusing to me. So as you read this book, my prayer and desire is that by the end of the book you will clearly understand the layout of the Tribulation time period. With the repetition that takes place in the scriptures of the tribulation events, the order of events should become very clear to you. What also helps is the rightly dividing of the seven years. Once this is done it really does all fit together in a very understandable way.

The second, Book 2, is going to cover The Tribulation as an overview, or a running story. The scriptures will be included, but it will be more of a story format, at least that is what I will be trying to accomplish. The second book will, in a sense, be a repeat of the first. But with the two different formats, there should be a very clear understanding by the end of this book of what I am writing about. Book 2 will have more of a "poetic license," as the world calls it.

Seven Years

Daniel

Daniel 9:24-27

The foundational text for Daniel's 70th week is found in Daniel 9:24-27. These are four verses in the word of God that have probably had more disputes and commentary than any other verses in the Bible. It is here that the term, "Daniel's 70th Week" comes from. Just four verses that describe and prophesy events that will take place in the near future. What you are getting ready to study can be termed strong meat. This is not the milk of the word.

This is going to be a study of prophesy, a study of future events; they are events that are going to happen in the near future. When exactly? I don't know, and I am not going to try to date the events. You will see why as we get into the study.

Man wants to know the future. He has a craving and

earnest desire to know what is going to happen before it happens. Why? Because then man does not have to live by faith. He can plan ahead and, in a way he can plan so as to not need to rely upon God.

> [6]But **without faith** _it is_ **impossible to please** _him_: for he that cometh to God must believe that he is, and _that_ he is a rewarder of them that diligently seek him. (Heb. 11:6)

Faith requires your heart, a heart that will believe what God said and live by it. But the study of prophesy is an intellectual study. It is a study that people enjoy and follow because they never get rebuked. In the study of prophesy you can gain all kinds of knowledge that others don't have. You can learn all kinds of very interesting things, but you never get rebuked. Because of this you can get very spiritually dirty, all the while thinking that you are right with God, when you are not.

Christianity is not a mere intellectual pursuit of Bible knowledge. It ought to be a heartfelt pursuit of pleasing your Lord Jesus Christ and submitting to His will for your life. With the knowledge you gain as you study the word of God, and in order to stay right with God, you must allow the truth you get to change your daily actions and plans.

For example, in the book of Revelation, chapter 3:14-22 it talks about the conditions of saints in the last days before the Rapture. Do you know what the number one sin is during that time? Covetousness! They have all kinds of things and use those things as "proof" that they are right with God. But God says they are "wretched, miserable, poor, blind and naked." Then

He tells them what they need to do.

How about you? Is your life wrapped up in things? Is your life wrapped up in paying off your house and achieving your retirement savings goal? As you read Revelation 3, are you willing to apply it to your life? Have you sought to get rid of your entanglements in this world? Have you sought to get rid of your unnecessary things, and dedicate your life to living for and serving Jesus Christ, freed up from all of this materialistic junk? How do you live differently than an atheist, or a Mormon, or the Amish? Does God see you as spiritually bankrupt?

That is what you won't get when you study prophesy, but there is a time and a place for prophesy and that is what this book is about. Just don't end up majoring in prophesy.

"Charity rejoiceth in the truth," (1 Cor. 13:6) which includes getting rebuked from a preacher or directly from the word of God. If you have charity, then you will rejoice when getting shown where you are not right with God. Getting that message, and thus repenting, is greater than learning some prophesy. You need to remember that.

Daniel 9:24

In the chapter, Daniel has just finished fasting and praying, as he was brokenhearted and concerned for "his people," which is Israel. Gabriel appears to him and gives him the message that we are getting ready to study. The following is Gabriel talking to Daniel. You are reading Gabriel's words, which are from God, and recorded in the word of God.

> [24]Seventy weeks are determined upon **thy people** and upon **thy holy city**, to finish the transgression, and to make an end of sins, and to make reconciliation for iniquity, and to bring in everlasting righteousness, and to seal up the vision and prophecy, and **to anoint the most Holy.** (Dan. 9:24)

Seventy weeks is a reference to 490 years. Notice in Gen. 29:27-28 that the term "week" is used for a designation of seven years. Four hundred ninety years is a time frame that the Lord uses more than once in the word of God, but we will not take the time to go over them here as it is another lengthy study.

So 490 years is determined upon "thy people." Daniel was a Jew. So this has to do with Israel, and the holy city, which is Jerusalem.

> [1]¶ And the rulers of the people dwelt at Jerusalem: the rest of the people also cast lots, to bring one of ten to dwell in **Jerusalem the holy city**, and nine parts *to dwell* in *other* cities. (Neh. 11:1)

> [1]¶ Awake, awake; put on thy strength, O Zion; put on thy beautiful garments, O Jerusalem, **the holy city**: for henceforth there shall no more come into thee the uncircumcised and the unclean. (Is. 52:1)

At the very start of this study, it is important to understand that what we are going to study and deal with has nothing to do with the Church Age and born-again Christians. We are dealing with "...thy people," which is Israel, as well as the city Jerusalem. Let me repeat this. The 490 years has to do with Israel and Jerusalem. Though Jerusalem is the captial of Israel, in the prophecy each is listed as a seperate entity. The prophecy has nothing to do with born-again Christians in this Church Age.

Now, we are very close to this coming to pass because we are at the close of the Church Age. When we, the born-again Christians, leave, then God will return to deal with Israel as a nation. He will also deal with the city Jerusalem. God is going to bring Israel back into fellowship with Him, and the center of all of this will be in Jerusalem. This takes place during the seven year Tribulation.

Finish the Transgression

There are seven different events specified that are going to be fulfilled by the end Daniel's 70th week. The first of which is to finish the transgression of Israel and Jerusalem. Remember it has to do with Israel and the holy city which is Jerusalem.

As you read the Old Testament, it is astounding to read how patient and forgiving God has been with Israel, especially when you read the book of Judges! Over and over Israel rebels against God, He judges them, they repent, and He forgives and restores them.

Then you read about the same thing happening over and over in the books of 1&2 Samuel, 1&2 Kings, and 1&2 Chronicles. It is such a true statement what the Lord says about Himself:

> [4]And he hewed two tables of stone like unto the first; and Moses rose up early in the morning, and went up unto mount Sinai, as the LORD had commanded him, and took in his hand the two tables of stone.
> [5]¶ And the LORD descended in the cloud, and stood with him there, and proclaimed the name of the LORD.
> [6]And the LORD passed by before him, and proclaimed, **The LORD, The LORD God, merciful and gracious, longsuffering, and abundant in goodness and truth,**
> [7]**Keeping mercy for thousands, forgiving iniquity and transgression and sin, and that will by no means clear *the guilty*;** visiting the iniquity of the fathers upon the children, and upon the children's children, unto the third and to the fourth *generation*. (Ex. 34:4-7)

This is God describing Himself. There are nine qualities mentioned having to do with the goodness of God towards man, and only after the nine He then describes judgment placed upon those who partake in idolatry.

How many times has the Lord been merciful to you and me? Over and over we choose to sin against Him, and He patiently deals with us to bring us back to Him. Yes, there are times He chastens, and oh, how it hurts! But you know He is chastening you out of love and not anger.

> [5]And ye have forgotten the exhortation which speaketh unto you as unto children, My son, despise not thou the chastening of the Lord, nor faint when thou art rebuked of him:
> **[6]For whom the Lord loveth he chasteneth,** and scourgeth every son whom he receiveth. (Heb. 12:5-6)

Sometimes it has been the chastening hand of God that has given me comfort and demonstrable proof that God is there and loves me. I know that when I was lost those things did not happen to me. But after getting saved there has been a very real dealing in my life that was not there before.

One particular story comes to mind in this regard. At the time my son was 10, my daughter was 7, and we were living temporarily in my Grandma's house which was situated in the mountains of California, in the little town of Twain Harte. Grandma was not there at the time. My son was playing baseball, and one particular weekend I had heard that the Oakland Athletics baseball team was having a game. Before the game, the players would be meeting all the young baseball-playing kids. There was just one problem- the game and the meet were on a Sunday.

Well, since I was not pastoring at the time, and I did not know at that time that my call was evangelism, I reasoned that it would be a great family opportunity to go see the game on that Sunday. I purchased the tickets and had all things ready that Saturday evening to leave early in the morning. The drive from Twain Harte to Oakland was about three hours. The church we were attending didn't really need us to do anything, so I thought to myself, *"Alright, we are good to go."*

That night as we all attempted to rest, starting around midnight every one of us got sick to our stomachs. And then we started puking. It was so bad that we were telling the one in the restroom in front of us to hurry up as we had to get in there to puke right behind them. Then it was the dry heaves. And nothing worked to try to stop it. Our sides ached, we felt absolutely horrible, and we were worn out by morning. No, we did not go to the baseball game.

Later on about mid-morning, as I lay there worn out on the bed, I closed my eyes and began to pray as tears rolled out of my eyes. *"Thank you. Lord, for caring for us to let us know that You did not want us to skip church to go to the baseball game."* Perhaps you read that and think it was mere accident, but I know it wasn't. It was the hand of God in our lives, and I thank Him for not leaving us alone!

Over and over in the Bible, God deals with Israel. He judges them, they repent, He forgives them, brings them back, and they depart back to their rebellion and sin.

There came a point though where the patience of the Lord was done. Though it took many, many years, yet eventually He gave them up and had them taken to Babylon as prisoners. There is a verse in the Bible that to me is one of the most amazing verses in all of Scripture. After all, when I write, or when you read your Bible, you are reading about the God of all creation. There is not a God higher than the Lord Jehovah. He has all knowledge, His presence is everywhere, and He has, and is, all power. To consider how great He is and how powerful is amazing, but then notice the following verse:

> ⁹And they that escape of you shall remember me among the nations whither they shall be carried captives, because **I am broken with their whorish heart**, which hath departed from me, and with their eyes, which go a whoring after their idols: and they shall lothe themselves for the evils which they have committed in all their abominations. (Ezek. 6:9)

Have you ever been broken? Has someone ever broken your heart? The Creator of the universe understands what that is like for He has had His heart broken as well. Can you imagine almighty God, on His throne, weeping with a broken heart? I do not know, but I would guess that there is not another religious book with a description of their god like that. But God weeps over Israel. He loves them, and they love someone else. God is rejected by Israel, whom He loves, and the God of the universe is broken. That is so very amazing!

So for over 2,000 years Israel is set aside by God. He withdraws from them and turns to the Gentiles. This

To Finish The Transgression

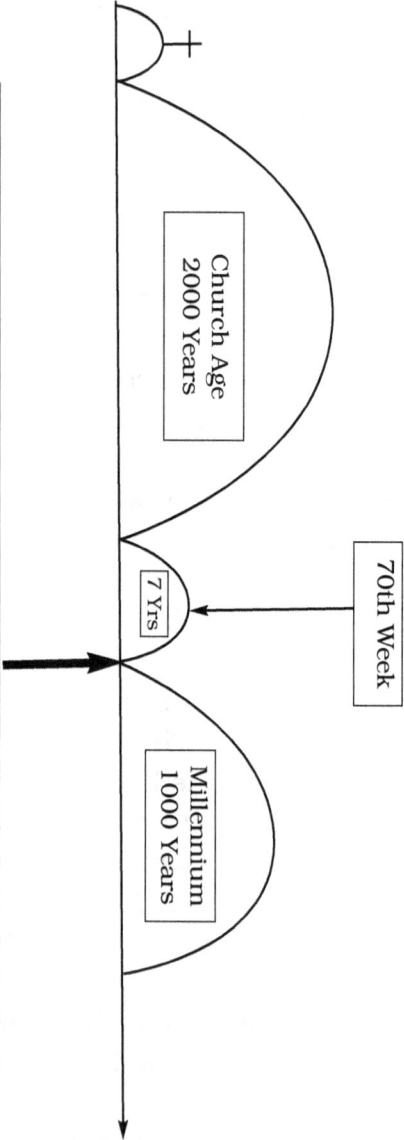

Church Age
2000 Years

70th Week

7 Yrs

Millennium
1000 Years

Daniel 9:24 prophecy concerning Israel and Jerusalem fulfilled here: **To finish the transgression:** From this point in time on Israel will never transgress against God again.

time is known as the Church age. But God is not through with Israel as many teach that He is. No, God is going to bring them back into fellowship with Him, and as I've mentioned already, He does this during the Tribulation.

By the end of the 70th week as given in Daniel 9 (also known and described as the Tribulation period, and the time of Jacob's troubles), Israel will no longer transgress against, nor leave their God. The transgressing of Israel and rebelling against their God will be over. They will be in subjection with God Himself, Jesus Christ, reigning over them for 1,000 years.

The finishing of the transgression is completed at the end of the 70th week. Not before, and not after, but at the end. Don't forget that! It's very important in order to rightly divide the 70th week.

Make an End of Sins

The second event to happen at the end of the Tribulation is for Israel and Jerusalem to no longer nationally sin against their God. This is very similar to the first prophecy.

Transgression has to do with a crossing over. "Trans" is to cross. Then to make an end of sins has to do with not breaking the law against God. For instance, over and over Israel did not keep the sabbaths which were a sign between them and God that He was their God. That was a sin and disobedience. Was it a transgression of the law? Yes. They crossed over, but it was also an outright rebellion, and thus a sin.

71

Make An End of Sins

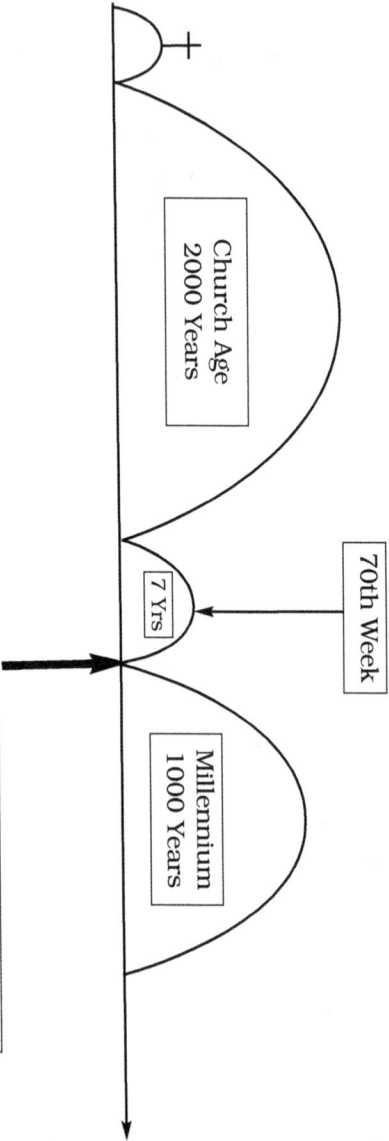

Church Age
2000 Years

70th Week

7 Yrs

Millennium
1000 Years

Daniel 9:24 prophecy concerning Israel and Jerusalem fulfilled here: "**...to make an end of sins...**" - From this point in time forward, Israel and Jerusalem will not sin against the Lord their God.

In the Millennium it will be a beautiful thing to behold Israel in fellowship with God, serving Him, and doing it joyfully. King David will be ruling over Israel. The priests will be ministering in the priesthood with the sons of Zadok ministering to Jesus Christ in the temple. It will be a time, and will last into eternity, where the people will be in unity with one another. They will be loving each other perfectly, and they will be loving the Lord God Jehovah perfectly as well. Yes, it will be a very beautiful thing to behold.

At the conclusion of the 70th week, the end of sins committed by Israel and Jerusalem against Jehovah is complete. Don't forget that, it is very important in order to rightly divide the 70th week.

Make Reconciliation for Iniquity

The next event mentioned in Daniel 9:24 is "…to **make reconciliation for iniquity**." Now there is a change in the actions listed in the verse. The first two have to do with what separated Israel from the fellowship with their God as a nation. Now it is having to do with restoration, or the reconciliation of the nation. A bringing back together of a broken relationship.

It is very, very important to observe here that the relationship between Jehovah God and His wife, Israel, had been separated by spiritual adultery and sin. Their relationship is restored after the sin and iniquity is mentioned and thus dealt with. And by the end of the Tribulation, Israel will have repented nationally.

In the middle of the Tribulation, Jerusalem is still

rejected by the Lord. Although the temple had been in operation for about three years, yet the city was idolatrous and wicked. The two witnesses of the Lord, Moses and Elijah, end up being killed in Jerusalem. And if that were not bad enough, then the inhabitants of Jerusalem, along with the rest of the world, end up rejoicing because they are dead. Many of those rejoicing are Jews by birth. God calls the city:

> [8]And their dead bodies *shall lie* in the street of the great city, **which spiritually is called Sodom and Egypt**, where also our Lord was crucified. (Rev. 11:8)

There is no doubt that in the middle of the Tribulation God the Father is still disgusted with Jerusalem, as well as the nation of Israel. And though I am getting ahead of myself, yet I will mention it anyway.

During the tribulation, the Jews in Judaea and Jerusalem who run for the wilderness, do so because they have been reading and loving the truth, the word of God. Specifically, they have been loving and included reading the New Testament. They drop the physical things of their lives, and leave their houses, jobs, positions, bank accounts, friends, and family. Why? Because they love the truth and are willing to obey the word of God. And it is in the wilderness that the Father brings that remnant of Jews into sweet fellowship and love with their husband, God the Father.

It is when the Jews are fleeing for their lives and communing with God out in the wilderness, that as the future nation Israel they repent and are reconciled to their God.

To Make Reconciliation for Iniquity

70th Week

Church Age
2000 Years

7 Yrs

Millennium
1000 Years

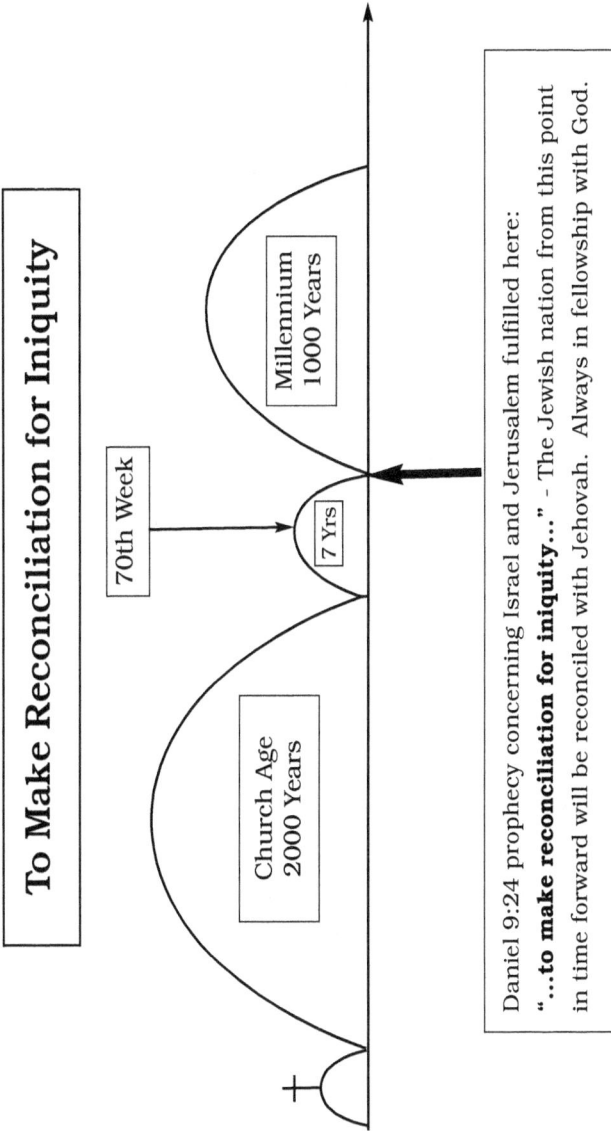

Daniel 9:24 prophecy concerning Israel and Jerusalem fulfilled here:
"...to make reconciliation for iniquity..." - The Jewish nation from this point in time forward will be reconciled with Jehovah. Always in fellowship with God.

By the end of the 70th week, Israel will be reconciled to God. They will acknowledge that Jesus Christ is their Messiah, which they do not do nationally in these last days of the Church age. But what is important to understand is that reconciliation cannot take place without repentance. The sin that separated the two, whether it is between God and Israel, or it is between you and your wife, your children or your friend, must be dealt with or there can be no reconciliation.

Often times, people will try to reconcile without any repentance. Let's let bygones be bygones and move on from here. That sounds good, but that is not what God does, and that is not how proper Biblical reconciliation takes place. Yes, there is a period of looking past transgression for the sake of seeking love and unity, but there comes a time when a person who is getting the wrong end of the stick has to stop and not take it any more. Especially if they are saved, and the other person is saved as well.

If the person is lost, you may take the wrong over and over while praying that they will get saved. But even then there comes a matter of integrity and respect where you may have to stop and go your own way.

To act like all is well and right, when all is not well and right is to live a lie. You may cover the transgression for a long while, but there may come a time when the Lord leads you to separate from them. This is hard when it is family.

> [9]¶ **He that covereth a transgression seeketh love;** but he that repeateth a matter separateth *very* friends. (Prov. 17:9)

Over and over in the Old Testament, God covered Israel's transgressions, but there came a time when He put His foot down and said enough is enough. For over 2,500 years, Israel has been out of fellowship with their God. They will not get back into fellowship with their God until they acknowledge their transgressions and repent before their God. Only then will they get reconciled to God.

During the Tribulation Israel will realize that Jesus Christ is their Messiah. A type of this is illustrated in the book of Genesis when Joseph made himself known unto his brethren. Joseph is a type of Jesus Christ, and his brethren are Israel. But He makes himself known unto them after they have repented.

> ²¹¶ And they said one to another, We *are* verily guilty concerning our brother, in that we saw the anguish of his soul, when he besought us, and we would not hear; therefore is this distress come upon us.
> ²²And Reuben answered them, saying, Spake I not unto you, saying, Do not sin against the child; and ye would not hear? therefore, behold, also his blood is required.
> ²³And **they knew not that Joseph understood** *them*; for he spake unto them by an interpreter. (Gen. 42:21-23)
>
> ²⁶¶ And when Joseph came home, they brought him the present which *was* in their hand into the house, and **bowed themselves to him to the earth.** (Gen. 43:26)

^{14}And Judah and his brethren came to Joseph's house; for he *was* yet there: and they **fell before him on the ground.**

^{15}And Joseph said unto them, What deed *is* this that ye have done? wot ye not that such a man as I can certainly divine?

^{16}And Judah said, **What shall we say unto my lord? what shall we speak? or how shall we clear ourselves? God hath found out the iniquity of thy servants: behold, we *are* my lord's servants, both we, and *he* also with whom the cup is found.** (Gen. 44:14-16)

^{1}¶ Then Joseph could not refrain himself before all them that stood by him; and he cried, Cause every man to go out from me. And **there stood no man with him, while Joseph made himself known unto his brethren.**

^{2}And he wept aloud: and the Egyptians and the house of Pharaoh heard.

^{3}And Joseph said unto his brethren, I *am* Joseph; doth my father yet live? **And his brethren could not answer him; for they were troubled at his presence.** (Gen. 45:1-3)

This is a picture of God revealing Himself to Israel in the Tribulation and they realizing that Jesus Christ is God, as well as their Messiah.

That is very important. By the end of the Tribulation,

the prophecy is fulfilled that Israel and Jehovah are reconciled. Don't forget that because it is very important to understand in order to rightly divide the 70th week.

Bring in Everlasting Righteousness

"...to bring in everlasting righteousness..." This takes place at the end of the Tribulation and in the beginning of the 1,000 year reign of Jesus Christ, Israel's Messiah. After the Millennium the heavens (first and second heavens) and the earth are burned up (2 Pet. 3:10). New ones are created with no sin in, on, nor ever shall be present in that creation. So from the end of the Tribulation and forward, Israel and the holy city Jerusalem will exist righteous, and righteously, for ever. How amazing is the Lord, and how great are His tender mercies!

Jacob was given the name "Israel" in Gen. 32:28 after he wrestled with the Angel of the Lord. That was approximately 1739 B.C., and the nation of Israel is called out of Egypt and "born" approximately 1491 B.C. in Exodus 12. Regardless of which date you use, God put up with Israel for a really long time before they attain a permanent righteousness and fellowship with their God. If you date from 1739 B.C., you are looking at well over 3700 years that God put up with a people that repeatedly rebelled against their loving, merciful and forgiving God. The omnipotent God, who could snuff them all out in a second. Yet He remained patient and restrained Himself, anticipating the time when His people, whom He loves, will be brought back into love and fellowship with Him.

In regards to you and me as born-again Christians, aren't you glad your Saviour is very patient with you? How many times have you knowingly chosen to sin against Him, confessed it, gotten right with God, only to go against Him again?   I am so thankful that He is patient with me! When I see this with Israel it truly amazes me and leaves me in awe at the tender mercies of the Lord. Israel was under the law, but we are under grace. I am so thankful for His patience and tender care of me!

Spiritually the born-again Christian is righteous, for he has been washed in the blood of Jesus Christ and then sealed with the Holy Spirit.

> [5]And from Jesus Christ, _who is_ the faithful witness, _and_ the first begotten of the dead, and the prince of the kings of the earth. **Unto him that loved us, and washed us from our sins in his own blood**... (Rev. 1:5)

> [30]And grieve not the holy Spirit of God, whereby **ye are sealed unto the day of redemption.** (Eph. 4:30)

But oh, how the old man rears up and demands his own way! We are to put him off and crucify him, but how often we do not do that and thus, the old man gets his way! We end up choosing to sin against our Saviour.

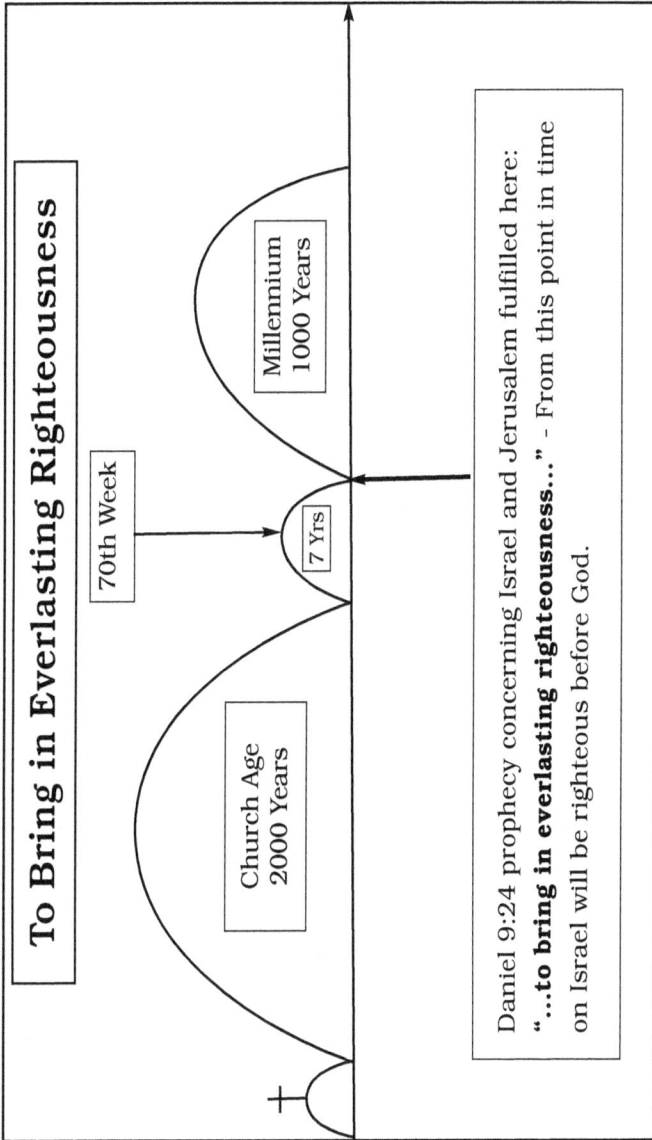

To Bring in Everlasting Righteousness

Church Age
2000 Years

70th Week

7 Yrs

Millennium
1000 Years

Daniel 9:24 prophecy concerning Israel and Jerusalem fulfilled here: **"...to bring in everlasting righteousness..."** - From this point in time on Israel will be righteous before God.

²²**That ye put off concerning the former
conversation the old man, which is corrupt**
according to the deceitful lusts; (Eph. 4:22)

¹⁹**For the good that I would I do not: but the
evil which I would not, that I do. (Rom. 7:19)**

The result is grieving the Lord, quenching the Holy
Ghost, and breaking the communion and fellowship
with God. Some Christians have gone so long with the
fellowship broken that they don't even know that they
are out of fellowship with God. Yet He patiently deals
with, and works to bring us back into fellowship with
Him. But He waits for our repentance in order for the
fellowship to be restored. That's why it is recorded in
the word of God:

⁹**If we confess our sins, he is faithful and
just to forgive us *our* sins, and to cleanse us
from all unrighteousness. (1 John 1:9)**

To confess your sins is an obvious act that shows you
know what you did was wrong, and shows your Saviour
that you don't want to do it. What's more is when you
confess your sins, you reveal to your Saviour that you
are trying to do right and that you love Him. These
actions take place from the heart, and the heart is what
the Lord is looking upon.

Well, we had better get back to Israel.

By the end of the Tribulation, Israel and Jerusalem
will be back in fellowship with Jehovah, existing

righteously in fellowship with their God. And it will be a condition, a relationship and a marriage that will never end. The Lord Jehovah will never have another broken heart over His people. But remember this is fulfilled at the end of the Tribulation.

It is at the end of the 70th week that these events which concern Jerusalem and Israel are fulfilled. Don't forget that because it is very important when it comes to rightly dividing the 70th week.

Seal Up the Vision and the Prophecy

There are two prophetical events mentioned here. The sealing of the vision, and the sealing of the prophecy. In other words it is finished. All that was foretold to happen will have happened. All that the prophets saw concerning the future events will have come to pass.

So many things in the word of God are unclear to man at this time. As we look into the word of God and try to see through the glass darkly, (1 Cor. 13:12) there are many times we cannot make out what we are looking at. As time goes by, certain things become very clear.

For instance, when man was under the law some 3000 years ago, there were very clear...to us now... passages on the crucifixion of Jesus Christ.

¹¶ My God, my God, why hast thou forsaken me?... (Psa. 22:1)

⁵But he *was* wounded for our transgressions, *he was* bruised for our iniquities: the

83

chastisement of our peace *was* upon him; and with his stripes we are healed. (Is. 53:5)

⁶I gave my back to the smiters, and my cheeks to them that plucked off the hair: I hid not my face from shame and spitting. (Is. 50:6)

³The plowers plowed upon my back: they made long their furrows. (Psa. 129:3)

There are many, many more verses that to us now in this Church age speak clearly of Calvary, and what our Lord did for us when He died and paid for our sins on the Cross. But back in the time of the writing of these verses and for many hundreds of years afterwards, these verses were not understood by Israel or others. But they are now!

So there will come a day, a time, when the vision and the prophecy will be done, finished, or "sealed up."

⁷But in the days of the voice of the seventh angel, when he shall begin to sound, **the mystery of God should be finished,** as he hath declared to his servants the prophets. (Rev. 10:7)

For now, we have the word of God as our guide, our map so to speak, to guide us through this life. But even Israel, at this time does not acknowledge the New Testament. Nor do they recognize Jesus Christ as their Messiah. One day they will nationally realize that He is their Messiah. The Jews that flee when the armies

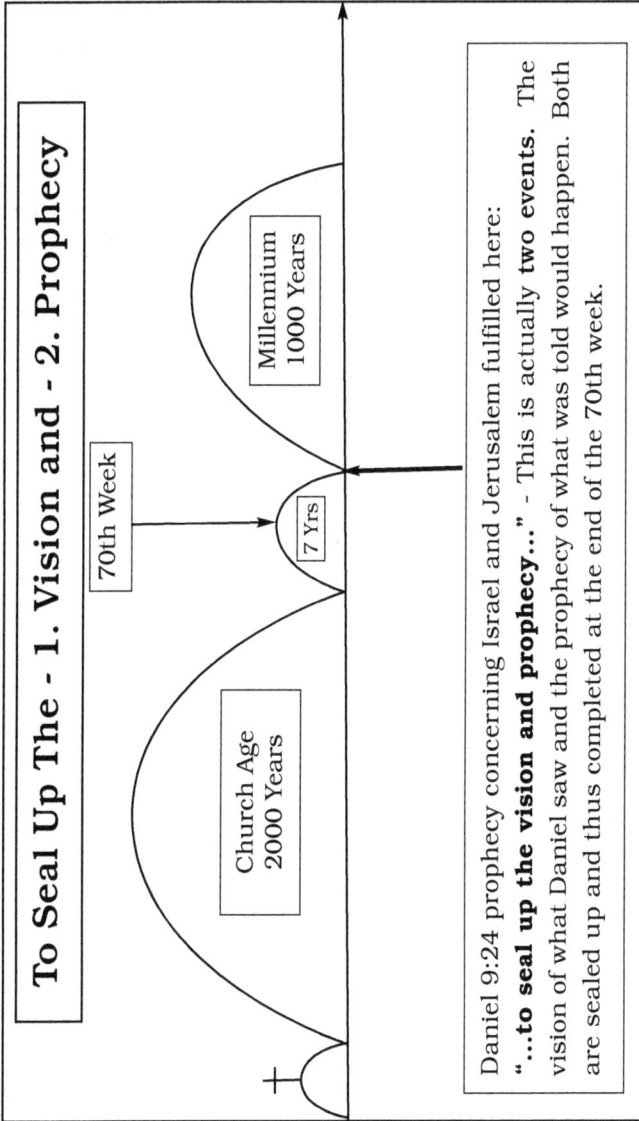

To Seal Up The - 1. Vision and - 2. Prophecy

Church Age 2000 Years

70th Week

7 Yrs

Millennium 1000 Years

Daniel 9:24 prophecy concerning Israel and Jerusalem fulfilled here: "**...to seal up the vision and prophecy...**" - This is actually **two events**. The vision of what Daniel saw and the prophecy of what was told would happen. Both are sealed up and thus completed at the end of the 70th week.

surround Jerusalem, (Luke 21:20) and then those that flee during the Tribulation when the abomination is set up in the Holy Place (Matt. 24:15) these Jews realize and understand what they need to do because they read the New Testament, or at least the gospels of Matthew and Luke. But they will not merely read those Gospels, but they will believe what they read as well. By doing so they will understand as well that Jesus Christ is their Messiah. They will have the faith of Jesus Christ, and they will keep the commandments of God. (Rev. 14:12) And by the end of the Tribulation, they will understand it all.

The prophecy and the vision are sealed up concerning Jerusalem and Israel. They are finished and sealed up at the end of the 70th week. That is very important because it has to do with rightly dividing the 70th week.

Perhaps you are tired of me writing that. I understand that I may be a bit tiresome by repeating that at the end of each event, but I do have what I consider a very, very important reason for mentioning that over and over. It is so you will understand when this last event is fulfilled as well.

Do you care to take a guess when this last event is fulfilled? Oh, and remember it is concerning Israel and Jerusalem, just like ALL of the other events were.

Yes, you guessed right! This last event is fulfilled concerning Israel and Jerusalem at the end of the 70th week. It is not fulfilled 2,000 years before the end of the 70th week. It is fulfilled at the end of the 70th week, just like the six other events mentioned in Daniel 9:24.

The last event in the list is the cherry on top of the

sundae, so to speak. It is the event and moment that God has been patiently waiting for, during the past 6,000 years.

To Anoint the Most Holy

Why have I stressed, to the point of being a burden to you, that all of these prophecies are fulfilled at the end of the 70th week? Because so many preachers, Bible teachers, and Bible commentators apply this last element of the verse to Jesus Christ at His Baptism. The following quote from Clarence Larkin is excellent:

> Some claim that by the "most Holy" Christ is meant, and that this anointing of the "Most Holy" was fulfilled when He was anointed with the Holy Spirit at His Baptism. **But the "most Holy" is a PLACE, not a person. The reference is doubtless to the "most Holy Place" of the new "Millennial Temple" as described in Ezek. 41:1--42:20,** whose erection is still future. *(Larkin Clarence, The Book of Daniel, Ch. 9, The Seventy Weeks, PDF, https://www.earnestlycontendingforthefaith.com/, viewed 5/8/2024)*

Thank you, Bro. Larkin, you are exactly correct!

Now notice the following quotes from *The Revelation of the Seventy Weeks:*

> Pg 21
> In John 1:41, immediately after **the anointing of Jesus Christ at His baptism**

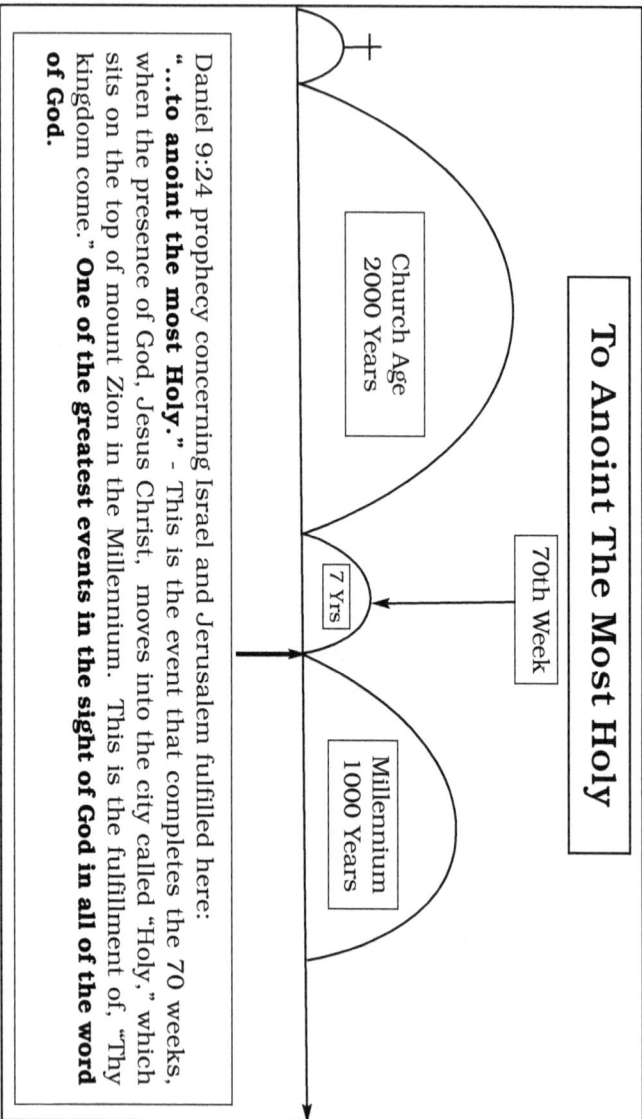

To Anoint The Most Holy

Church Age
2000 Years

70th Week

7 Yrs

Millennium
1000 Years

Daniel 9:24 prophecy concerning Israel and Jerusalem fulfilled here: **"...to anoint the most Holy."** - This is the event that completes the 70 weeks, when the presence of God, Jesus Christ, moves into the city called "Holy," which sits on the top of mount Zion in the Millennium. This is the fulfillment of, "Thy kingdom come." **One of the greatest events in the sight of God in all of the word of God.**

(John 1:29-34), Andrew tells his brother Simon Peter that they have found the "Messias", and then **the interpretation is given as "the Christ", which means "anointed".** *(Donovan, Brian, (2016), The Revelation of the Seventy Weeks, Published by Brian Donovan, 1130 Jo Jo Road, Pensacola, FL 32514, Bible Baptist Bookstore, pg 21)*

The problem here is that Jesus Christ was Christ at His birth, not when He got baptized.

¹⁶And Jacob begat Joseph the husband of Mary, of whom was born Jesus, **who is called Christ.** (Matt. 1:16)

Quote from *The Revelation of the Seventy Weeks*:

Yet there is an event in the life of Jesus Christ when He is **"anointed"** as the Messiah and it is specifically spelled out in scripture. **It is the event of His baptism by John the Baptist,** when "Jesus himself began to be about thirty years of age" (LUKE 3:23). *(Ibid,, pg 21-22)*

He plainly teaches and believes that when Jesus Christ was baptized, that it was the fulfillment of Dan. 9:24 **"...to anoint the most holy."**

The greatest problem with this teaching is that Jesus Christ is not the reference to "the most Holy." Jesus Christ is never the "most Holy." He is the most high

God, but he is never "the most Holy." Why? Because He is Holy! He is not most holy, He is Holy. Most holy implies a degree, or percentage of holiness.

It's like saying that a certain glass of water is most pure. The water may be the most pure, but by claiming "most" it proclaims that the water is not completely pure. By removing the word "most" when describing the water, it leaves the water pure. Pure water has zero impurities in it.

The same principal applies to the word "holy." God is holy. He is not most holy, He is holy. By placing most in front of holy you have lowered the claim.

What's more is that in Jn 17:11 Jesus prays and says,

> [11]¶ And now I am no more in the world, but these are in the world, and I come to thee. **Holy Father**, keep through thine own name those whom thou hast given me, that they may be one, as we _are_. (John 17:11)

If **"to anoint the most Holy"** is a reference to Jesus Christ at the start of His earthly ministry, and He calls the Father **"Holy Father,"** then Jesus Christ is more holy than the Father and the Holy Ghost, for He would be the most holy. If you want to apply the most holy to the Trinity then grammatically God is not holy, He is most holy. To claim God as holy, aside from it being right, is to declare Him with nothing unholy in Him. But when you declare God, or any one of the Godhead as most Holy, then the implication is the Godhead is not completely holy, **which is blasphemous!**

This is a scriptural and doctrinal impossibility for it would put a degree of holiness into the Godhead. But this is exactly what many Bible teachers claim the verse is a reference to. This claim is foundational to the teaching of a split seven-year Tribulation. Without **"to anoint the most Holy"** being a reference to Christ at His baptism, the teaching on the split Tribulation is destroyed.

To imply a degree of holiness is to imply a degree of sin, and we know that there is no sin in Jesus Christ, and the Godhead because They are **Holy. Holy, Holy Holy, Lord God almighty!**

Along with this attempt to apply the designation of "the most holy" to Jesus Christ, there is the fact of how out of context such a designation is.

Bro. Donovan states the following:

> One of the six reasons for the seventy weeks is "to anoint the most holy" (Daniel 9:24) so this anointing must take place during the weeks of Daniel's prophecy. **Since the scripture points to His baptism at the beginning of His ministry for His anointing** (Act 10:34-38) this would be the event that brings us to the conclusion of the sixty nine weeks (unto Messiah the Prince)... *(ibid, pg23)*

Did you notice the Daniel 9:24 reference? He thus applies **"...to anoint the most holy..."** to the baptism of Jesus Christ. And then takes it out of context once again by applying it to the sixty-nine weeks instead of the seventy weeks mentioned in verse 24. The Bible says, **"Seventy weeks are determined..."** and all of the events are fulfilled at the end of the seventy weeks. What do I mean by this?

Each one of these prophetical events mentioned in Daniel 9:24 are mentioned as the end of the prophecies. The beginning of the prophecies took place 490 years earlier. Thus, all of these prophecies are ending at "the end" of the 70th week. None of these prophecies end before the end of the seventy weeks.

There are seven prophecies, not six, given in Daniel 9:24 which concern Israel, "thy people," and "the holy city," which is Jerusalem, and they are as follows:

1. Finish transgression
2. Make an end of sins
3. Make reconciliation
4. Bring in everlasting righteousness
5. Seal up the vision
6. Seal up the prophecy
7. To anoint the most Holy

Every one of those seven prophecies **are an end** and thus **occur fulfilled at the end of the 70th week,** as I have already explained. But Bro. Donovan wants to take one of them and claim that it takes place 2000 years before the end. Or, if you want to claim it prophetically, then he is trying to apply the last one, in his mind, seven years before the end, thus putting it completely out of place and out of context. That is called wresting the scriptures. But there are more problems when you try to do this, besides Jesus not being the "most Holy," and besides placing the last

Daniel 9:24 - Not the Baptism of Jesus Christ

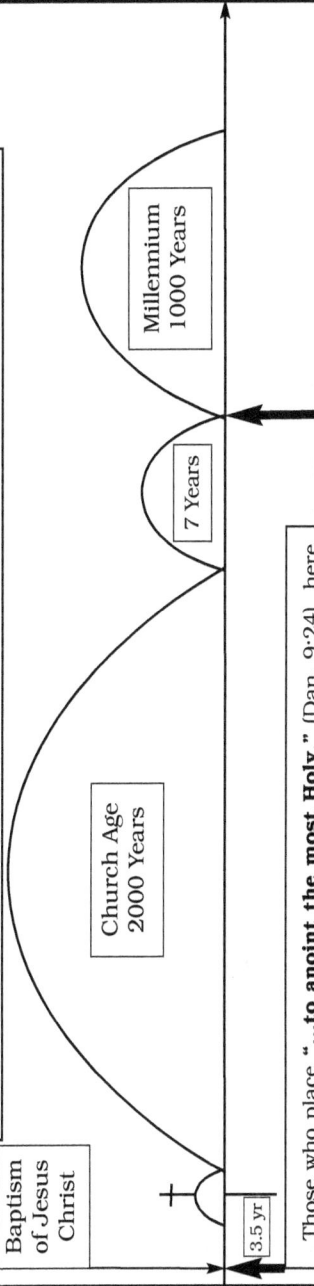

Baptism of Jesus Christ

Church Age 2000 Years

7 Years

3.5 yr

Millennium 1000 Years

All seven prophetic events of Daniel 9:24 concerning Jerusalem and Israel, are fulfilled right here at the end of the 70th week. They all are an end; never a beginning!

Daniel 9:24
1. Finish transgression
2. Make an end of sins
3. Make Reconciliation for Iniquity
4. Bring in Everlasting righteousness
5. Seal up the Vision
6. Seal up the Prophecy
7. **To anoint the most Holy**

Those who place "**...to anoint the most Holy,**" (Dan. 9:24) here and claim it was fulfilled at the baptism of Jesus Christ have to take it completely out of context; over 2000 years out of context! All seven prophetic events concern Jerusalem and Israel, NEVER an individual person. Again, this takes it out of context when applied to Jesus Christ. After doing this, they then claim that half of the 70th week took place during the ministry of Jesus Christ, thus leaving only three and a half years left of the 70th week to be fulfilled. This also places a degree of holiness within the Godhead, which is scripturally impossible. Jesus prays to the "Holy Father" in John 17:11. If Jesus is the most Holy, it implies the Father, and the Holy Ghost, are not as holy as Jesus Christ. This is borderline blasphemy.

prophecy of Daniel 9:24 out of order than what is given in the context.

And another problem is that the term "most Holy" is NEVER used in the word of God as a reference to a person or to God. Never! And the term itself is never used in the New Testament.

In the Old Testament the term "most holy" is always a reference to a place, house or things. And it is always in connection with the Temple, and the priesthood of Israel. To take one verse out of forty-four verses and claim it is a reference to something that none of the other forty-three verses apply to, is again wresting the scripture. It is taking the one verse out of context.

To anoint the most Holy takes place at the end of the Tribulation and at the beginning of the Millennium. After the Temple, at the end of the seven-year Tribulation, is defiled and left desolate and destroyed, it is going to be rebuilt and cleansed. Once it is cleansed, it will be anointed. Then when the most Holy is anointed the prophecy of Daniel 9:24 will be finished. As with the other six prophecies, so too when the most Holy is anointed in the Temple, it will be done, finished, complete. The seventy weeks will be complete. **The anointing of the most Holy is the end of all seven of the prophecies and ends with the fulfillment of the entire verse.**

Now, that is the application of the verse, and the application of **"...to anoint the most Holy,"** and it makes perfect sense. There is no way it is a reference to the baptism of Jesus Christ.

When it is claimed, **"to anoint the most Holy"** refers to the baptism of Jesus Christ, the scriptures are being distorted in their meaning to suit someone's private interpretation.

The Anointing of the Most Holy

²⁵Know therefore and understand, *that* from the going forth of **the commandment to restore and to build Jerusalem** unto the Messiah the Prince *shall be* seven weeks, and threescore and two weeks: the street shall be built again, and the wall, even in troublous times. (Dan. 9:25)

The commandment to restore and to build Jerusalem is plainly given twice. It is not hard to find. The first time it was given was:

²²¶ Now in the first year of Cyrus king of Persia, that the word of the LORD *spoken* by the mouth of Jeremiah might be accomplished, the LORD stirred up the spirit of Cyrus king of Persia, that **he made a proclamation throughout all his kingdom**, and *put it* also in writing, saying, ²³Thus saith Cyrus king of Persia, **All the kingdoms of the earth hath the LORD God of heaven given me; and he hath charged me to build him an house in Jerusalem, which** *is* **in Judah. Who** *is there* **among you of all his people? The LORD his God** *be* **with him, and let him go up.** (2 Chr. 36:22-23)

95

Here is the second time the command is given:

> ¹¶ Now in the first year of Cyrus king of Persia, that the word of the LORD by the mouth of Jeremiah might be fulfilled, the LORD stirred up the spirit of Cyrus king of Persia, that **he made a proclamation throughout all his kingdom**, and *put it* also in writing, saying,
>
> ²Thus saith Cyrus king of Persia, The LORD God of heaven hath given me all the kingdoms of the earth; and **he hath charged me to build him an house at Jerusalem, which** *is* **in Judah.**
>
> ³Who *is there* among you of all his people? his God be with him, and **let him go up to Jerusalem, which** *is* **in Judah, and build the house of the LORD God of Israel, (he** *is* **the God,) which** *is* **in Jerusalem.**
>
> ⁴And whosoever remaineth in any place where he sojourneth, let the men of his place help him with silver, and with gold, and with goods, and with beasts, beside the freewill offering for the house of God that *is* in Jerusalem. (Ezra 1:1-4)

Those two portions of scripture are plainly decrees. Now here is what Bro. Donovan uses as the decree to restore and to build Jerusalem:

> ¹¶ And it came to pass in the month Nisan, in the twentieth year of Artaxerxes the king, *that*

wine *was* before him: and I took up the wine, and gave *it* unto the king. Now I had not been *beforetime* sad in his presence.

²Wherefore the king said unto me, Why *is* thy countenance sad, seeing thou *art* not sick? this *is* nothing *else* but sorrow of heart. Then I was very sore afraid,

³And said unto the king, Let the king live for ever: why should not my countenance be sad, when the city, the place of my fathers' sepulchres, *lieth* waste, and the gates thereof are consumed with fire?

⁴Then the king said unto me, **For what dost thou make request?** So I prayed to the God of heaven.

⁵And I said unto the king, If it please the king, and if thy servant have found favour in thy sight, that thou wouldest send me unto Judah, unto the city of my fathers' sepulchres, that I may build it.

⁶And the king said unto me, (the queen also sitting by him,) For how long shall thy journey be? and when wilt thou return? **So it pleased the king to send me**; and I set him a time.

⁷Moreover I said unto the king, If it please the king, let letters be given me to the governors beyond the river, that they may convey me over till I come into Judah;

⁸And a letter unto Asaph the keeper of the king's forest, that he may give me timber to make beams for the gates of the palace which

appertained to the house, and for the wall of the
city, and for the house that I shall enter into.
**And the king granted me, according to the
good hand of my God upon me.** (Neh. 2:1-8)

The problem I have is this: where is the decree? This
is a Jew requesting permission. This is not a decree
given by a king. This is a Jew getting favor from God to
perform the decree given in 2 Chronicles 36. By the
way, did you know that the verses in 2 Chronicles
36:22-23 are the last two verses of a Jewish Bible?
Hello? The end of a Jewish Bible commands God's
people to go home and rebuild Jerusalem.

The scholars then belch out, "But the time doesn't
work out, you're crazy, it doesn't work..."

But God counts time differently than we do, and you
need to remember that. **To go to secular calendars to
try to prove and figure out the timing doesn't work
because God has His own schedule.**

For instance, this book is about Daniel's 70th week,
thus making a total of 490 years. Right? But inserted
into the time frame is a period of 2000 years. Hello?
And then there are the fourteen generations found in the
first chapter of Matthew. Have you ever studied those
fourteen generations? In Matthew 1:8 there are three
kings removed. Poof! They are not there and have been
removed by God, probably due to the sin of incest under
Athalia. (2 Chron. 21:6 cf 2 Chron. 22:2). But then you
read this:

[17]So all the generations from Abraham to
David *are* **fourteen generations**; and from

David until the carrying away into Babylon *are* **fourteen generations**; and from the carrying away into Babylon unto Christ *are* **fourteen generations**. (Matt. 1:17)

That's how God records that time frame. I have heard or read somewhere that God counts time only when Israel is in fellowship with God. Whether that is true or not, I am not sure, but the statement might have some merit to it.

What I am saying is this: talk and study about the time frame and the calendars is all smoke and mirrors, as well as very confusing. Hello! It is not important in light of Daniel 9:25. Just believe the verse! That is so simple, and it solves so much. Just believe the text, accept it, and move on. Or as the Lord commands, **"Know therefore, and understand..."** That is so easy. Unless you are trying to prove something that the scriptures do not, and are wresting the scriptures.

25Know therefore and understand, *that* from the going forth of the commandment to restore and to build Jerusalem unto the Messiah the Prince *shall be* seven weeks, and threescore and two weeks: the street shall be built again, and the wall, even in troublous times. (Dan. 9:25)

There is no doubt who Messiah the Prince is, for it is Jesus Christ. So from the commandment given in 2 Chronicles 36 unto Jesus Christ is 69 weeks, or 483 years. That's what God said so I believe it. It is not all that hard. As a matter of fact, I now KNOW and understand that by faith in what God said. It is the same as what is found in Hebrews 11. Thus I am standing upon the solid rock of scripture and NOT standing on the uncertain sand of secular calendars.

> [3]**Through faith we understand** that the worlds were framed by the word of God, so that things which are seen were not made of things which do appear. (Heb. 11:3)

I love that verse because I grew up in a home where evolution was believed as fact, and had to be believed by faith with no real authority for it. The result was a lot of confusion and doubt. But when I got saved and realized I had the holy words of God, then by faith I now UNDERSTAND where all this creation came from and how it got here. It is the same with this verse. "**Know therefore, and UNDERSTAND...**" by faith in what God is saying in this verse. The result is you will know and understand the time frame for the sixty-nine weeks. Isn't that simple? Yes, it is!

The street and the wall are built again in the book of Ezra and Nehemiah. You can read all about it by reading those books. But the salient point in the whole verse is not the time frame. The point that you need to realize is that Messiah the Prince has already come therefore 69 weeks have already taken place. Got it? There is one week to go in order to make up the 70 weeks. Got it? There are seven years to go in order to fulfill 490 years. That's all you need to know about Daniel 9:25.

²⁶And after threescore and two weeks **shall Messiah be cut off, but not for himself:** and the people of the prince that shall come shall destroy the city and the sanctuary; and the end thereof *shall be* with a flood, and unto the end of the war desolations are determined. (Dan. 9:26)

So, after the threescore and two weeks, which means it is after the total of 69 weeks, "**...shall Messiah be cut off, but not for himself...**" This is a reference to Jesus Christ, the Messiah, being crucified at Calvary. The great chapter that covers this being cut off but not for himself is Isaiah 53.

⁸He was taken from prison and from judgment: and who shall declare his generation? for **he was cut off out of the land of the living:** for the transgression of my people was he stricken. (Is. 53:8)

At the end of, "**...but not for himself...**" there is a colon. That colon represents approximately 2,000 years from the time of Calvary to the time of the Antichrist. That 2,000 years is the Church age and represents two days in the overall time frame from Genesis to Revelation.

"**The people of the prince that shall come**" is a reference to the people who will be following the Antichrist during the 70th week. The city is a reference to Jerusalem, the holy city, as in vs 24. Notice what they do to the city and the sanctuary. They destroy it. But it shows that the sanctuary is present, meaning the Jewish temple is to be rebuilt. It also shows that the events referred to in the verse take place around Jerusalem, and not out in the wilderness. Why do I say this?

Because there is a flood that comes out of the Dragon's mouth to attempt to thwart the remnant of Jews as they run for their lives into the wilderness, but this flood takes place half way through the Tribulation. So the flood referenced here (**...the end thereof shall be with a flood,** Dan. 9:26) is not the same one, contrary to *The Revelation of the Seventy Weeks.*

> "**...the flood of the verse is found in Revelation 12:15,** when during the tribulation, Satan tries to drown out the Jewish remnant fleeing his wrath, but this does not come till "the end." *(Donovan, Brian, (2016), The Revelation of the Seventy Weeks, Published by Brian Donovan, 1130 Jo Jo Road, Pensacola, FL 32514, Bible Baptist Bookstore, pg 40)*

Bro. Donovan is not correct here. The flood of Revelation 12:15 takes place in the middle of the Tribulation as the remnant of Jews flee because the abomination has just been set up in the holy place of the Jewish temple. This is when the Man of Sin walks into the temple, sits down on a throne in the most holy place, and declares himself to be God. This is not "the end." It is the middle. How do you know this?

> ⁶And the woman fled into the wilderness, where she hath a place prepared of God, that they should feed her there **a thousand two hundred and threescore days.** (Rev. 12:6)

Because the woman, who is the remnant of Israel, hides out in the wilderness for three and a half years. Therefore it could not possibly be the end. Bro. Donovan is not rightly dividing the 70th week.

"The end of the war" is a reference to the battle that takes place at the second advent of Jesus Christ. He comes back to the earth and delivers the remnant of Jews, as well as takes over the whole world.

Notice the term **"...the end."** This is a reference to the end of the 70th week. **"Desolations are determined,"** because around Jerusalem, as well as in the temple, Satan has been reigning and promoting idolatry. The entire area is desolate in the sense of God is nowhere to be found. He has deserted the place and thus refers to it as desolate.

> ²⁷And **he shall confirm the covenant with many for one week:** and in the midst of the week he shall cause the sacrifice and the oblation to cease, and for the overspreading of abominations he shall make *it* desolate, even until the consummation, and that determined shall be poured upon the desolate. (Dan. 9:27)

Here is the verse that causes much consternation amongst many of the brethren. Many books have been written on this verse and this subject.

"**...he shall confirm the covenant with many for one week...**" The "he" is a reference to "**the prince that shall come**" and thus is a reference to the Antichrist. The covenant is not a reference to the land grant given to Abraham. David Rowley taught that and a few others, and it is what is taught in *The Revelation of the Seventy Weeks*. But it doesn't make sense. That covenant was already confirmed.

> [17]And this I say, *that* **the covenant, that was confirmed** before of God in Christ, the law, which was four hundred and thirty years after, cannot disannul, that it should make the promise of none effect. (Gal. 3:17)

Here in Daniel 9:27 is the Antichrist confirming a covenant with many. *Exactly* what the covenant will be is conjecture, though I am sure the answer is found in the word of God. I do know that when the Antichrist comes in, he comes in peaceably. And, in light of Dan. 9:24, the covenant involves Israel and the holy city, Jerusalem.

> [21]¶ And in his estate shall stand up a vile person, to whom they shall not give the honour of the kingdom: but **he shall come in peaceably, and obtain the kingdom by flatteries.** (Dan. 11:21)

So it is likely that the Antichrist will make an agreement with many Jews, and it will be something to the effect of letting them live in the land and worship their God in the temple. That is very important. You see, one very important key to rightly dividing the 70th week is the Jewish temple. The temple is the key to understanding the 70th week.

Remember that the city and the sanctuary are destroyed by the people of the prince that shall come. So the city and the sanctuary are in full operation for a period of time at the beginning of the Tribulation, or Daniel's 70th week. The sanctuary is present, and Jewish oblations and sacrifices are being offered in the temple during the first half of the Tribulation, though they don't begin until sometime after six months of the covenant being made. (Dan. 8:14)

Sixty-nine weeks of the prophecy take place up to verse 26, so there is one week to go. The one week of Daniel 9:27 is the final 70th week to fulfill the 70 weeks of verse 24.

According to *The Revelation of the Seventy Weeks* when it says, **"And he shall confirm the covenant with many for one week..."** the "he" refers to Judas Iscariot. The **"confirmation of the covenant"** takes place when Judas goes out with the disciples in Matthew 10. Here is the quote:

> **"It is the belief of this author that Judas is the antichrist** and that he performs a dual fulfillment of the prophecy. As one of the twelve apostles (Matthew 10:1-7), as well as being the great imitator of the true Christ, **Judas was sent out and he confirmed the**

covenant with signs and wonders (Matthew 10:8). Notice that he did not make the covenant, but confirmed it. The scriptures indicate that the covenant was confirmed both "in Christ" (Gal. 3:17-18) **and by Judas."**
(Ibid, Pg41)

[5]¶These twelve **Jesus sent forth, and commanded them**, saying, Go not into the way of the Gentiles, and into *any* city of the Samaritans enter ye not:
[6]But go rather to the lost sheep of the house of Israel.
[7]And as ye go, preach, saying, The kingdom of heaven is at hand.
[8]Heal the sick, cleanse the lepers, raise the dead, cast out devils: freely ye have received, freely give.
[9]Provide neither gold, nor silver, nor brass in your purses,
[10]Nor scrip for *your* journey, neither two coats, neither shoes, nor yet staves: for the workman is worthy of his meat. (Matt. 10:5-10)

One of the first problems I have with this teaching is the time frame when it takes place. In Daniel 9:27, the covenant is confirmed with many for one week. There is no doubt the confirming takes place **at the beginning of the week.** That only makes sense. But the sending out of the disciples **takes place after a year into the ministry of Christ.**

It is not until Matthew 12 that the disciples are returned and back to Jesus Christ, --after going out to heal the sick and show the signs of the Kingdom-- With that in mind notice what is recorded in Matthew 11:

> [20]Then began he to upbraid the cities wherein most of his mighty works were done, because they repented not: (Matt. 11:20)

When Jesus Christ upbraids the cities the disciples are out healing the sick and cleansing the lepers. By this time Jesus has already done many mighty works throughout the cities of Galilee. In Mark 1 it reads:

> [39]And he preached in their synagogues throughout all Galilee, and cast out devils. (Mark 1:39)

The preaching in their synagogues would have been on the Sabbath days, and He preached throughout Galilee. With a minimum (though likely more) of sixteen cities in all of Galilee that had a synagogue, it would have taken at least four months to do that. They had to walk to each one, so it is likely six months has taken place just for preaching throughout Galilee.

You then add to that the forty days of temptation in the wilderness, and there is over seven months right there. So the number of events and time that passes until you reach Matthew 12 are easily a full year. If you will also check the dates in a Scofield Reference Bible or in a Ruckman Reference Bible, you will see it was at least a year that takes place before the sending out of the disciples in Matthew 10. And I do believe it is easily possible that a year and a half has transpired by the time you reach Matthew 12.

Brian Donovan takes many pages in his booklet to supposedly lock down the exact date of the baptism of Jesus Christ in order to claim that is the fulfillment of **"to anoint the most holy."** But now he allows for a minimum of a whole year to elapse, and then claims this is the confirmation of the covenant. It's at least a whole year off, and could be off by a year and a half. The ministry of Jesus Christ has already started, a year has taken place, yet Bro. Donovan claims the first three and a half years are the fulfillment of the first half of Daniel's 70th week.

Secondly, the signs and healing that take place when the disciples go out in Matthew 10 are to show Israel that Jesus Christ is their Messiah.

If Judas "is the antichrist" (pg 41), and the signs and wonders that he performed confirmed the covenant, then the eleven other apostles HELPED THE ANTICHRIST in his ministry. It would mean that when Jesus Christ sent out His disciples, they helped the Antichrist, which would mean they were helping the satanic trinity work against God.

Now that is a real mess!

> [24]Then came the Jews round about him, and said unto him, How long dost thou make us to doubt? If thou be the Christ, tell us plainly.

²⁵Jesus answered them, I told you, and ye believed not: **the works that I do in my Father's name, they bear witness of me.** (John 10:24-25)

John 10:24-25 takes place at the same time frame as the sending forth of the disciples in Matthew 10. The healing and working of signs gets the Jews attention, for according to 1 Corinthians 1:22 **"...the Jews require a sign."** So the Lord gives them many signs. These works and signs are to show them that Jesus is the Christ. That is what is taking place when the disciples are sent out in Matthew 10 a whole year after the start of our Lord's ministry.

Judas is not confirming anything with anybody, and nowhere in the verse can you find that if you searched a thousand years with a magnifying glass. Again, this is Bro. Donovan wresting the scriptures to make them teach what he needs them to say in order to prove his teaching. It doesn't work, and it is wrong.

The third problem with it is the fact that if Judas is the Antichrist, then he has to be resurrected and come up out of Hell, also known as **"his own place."** (Acts 1:25). This resurrection does not take place until the middle of the Tribulation. (Rev. 13:3). It does not take place at the beginning of Daniel's 70th week. So again, the timing is off. The first three and one half years of the Tribulation are headed up by a man who is not Judas, and not the spirit of Judas. He gets killed and the spirit of Judas resurrects and comes into him and then he becomes the Son of Perdition.

> ^{3}¶ Let no man deceive you by any means: for
> *that day* shall *not come*, except there come a
> falling away first, and **that Man of Sin be
> revealed, the son of perdition**; (2 Th. 2:3)

The revealing of the Son of Perdition takes place three and one half years into the 70th week. Donovan's times are off by at least 2,003 and a half years. He attempts to be exact with dates for our Lord's baptism, but is very inconsistent when he needs to skew the time a bit.

The covenant is confirmed for one week. Do you know what that means? It means that the covenant will be confirmed for one week. And it is confirmed at the beginning of the week, not a year into the week. In Matthew 10, Judas never confirmed anything with anybody for any length of time.

> ^{27}"...and **in the midst of the week he shall
> cause the sacrifice and the oblation to
> cease...**". (Daniel 9:27)

Again because of his wresting the scriptures, Bro. Donovan has Calvary taking place in the midst of the week. (Pg 41, *The Revelation of the Seventy Weeks*, Brian Donovan). This is again very wrong.

What is going to take place is the Antichrist confirming a covenant with the Jews for seven years. That covenant is to allow the Jews to worship their God in the temple, and to offer sacrifices and oblations according to the Jewish law. But the Antichrist does not realize what is going to be included with this agreement on the part of the Jews.

God is going to dwell in the temple as He did in the Old Testament when Israel was under the law. Along with this, there is going to be two very, very powerful prophets that will arrive by the names of Moses and Elijah. They will begin to torment the world as described in Revelation 11.

> ⁶These have power to shut heaven, that it **rain not in the days of their prophecy:** and have **power over waters to turn them to blood, and to smite the earth with all plagues, as often as they will.** (Rev. 11:6)

> ¹⁰And they that dwell upon the earth shall rejoice over them, and make merry, and shall send gifts one to another; because **these two prophets tormented them that dwelt on the earth.** (Rev. 11:10)

As their tormenting of the world continues, nations and peoples are furious and want them killed. After three and a half years the Beast comes out of the bottomless pit and makes war with Moses and Elijah and kills them.

The Antichrist will then walk into the temple, set up an image of himself, sit down in the holy place, and proclaim there that he is God. And all the world will go after the Beast and worship him, except for a remnant of people. When he goes into the temple, obviously the sacrifices and oblations cease.

This did not happen when Judas betrayed the Lord

for thirty pieces of silver. Judas did not cause the sacrifices and oblations to cease; he did not! He betrayed the Lord. But after Jesus' death on the cross, the sacrifices and oblations did not cease. Some may claim, "Well, they were no longer in effect. They ceased in the sense that they were no longer required under the law." But that is not WHAT IT SAYS! It says that the sacrifices will cease, which they did not.

> [20]And when they heard _it_, they glorified the Lord, and said unto him, Thou seest, brother, how many thousands of Jews there are which believe; and they are **all zealous of the law**:
> [21]And they are informed of thee, that thou teachest all the Jews which are among the Gentiles to forsake Moses, saying that they ought not to circumcise _their_ children, neither to walk after the customs.
> [22]What is it therefore? the multitude must needs come together: for they will hear that thou art come.
> [23]Do therefore this that we say to thee: **We have four men which have a vow on them;**
> [24]Them take, and purify thyself with them, and be at charges with them, that they may shave _their_ heads: and all may know that those things, whereof they were informed concerning thee, are nothing; but _that_ thou **thyself also walkest orderly, and keepest the law.** (Acts 21:20-24)

The dating for Acts 21 is A.D. 60. That is almost thirty years after Christ died on the cross. The sacrifices are still being observed and performed. Did God acknowledge the sacrifices? Absolutely not! But the point is they had not ceased, and Judas did not cause them to cease. They were still being made and observed.

> [27]"...and for the overspreading of abominations he shall make *it* desolate..." (Daniel 9:27)

So what is meant by the overspreading of abominations?

The subject of abominations will occur a number of times as we study the various scriptures that concern the 70th week. I will try not to repeat myself too much, but since this is the first time in this book that I am dealing with the subject, I will cover it thoroughly.

This subject is mentioned in:

> 1. [11]...**the abomination that maketh desolate**... (Daniel 12:11)
> 2. [15]When ye therefore shall see **the abomination of desolation**, spoken of by Daniel the prophet... (Matt. 24:15)
> 3. [14]¶ But when ye shall see **the abomination of desolation**, spoken of by Daniel the prophet... (Mark 13:14)

To start with the abomination is an idol, or graven image. This has to do with the second commandment.

> [4]Thou shalt not make unto thee any graven image, or any likeness *of any thing* that *is* in heaven above, or that *is* in the earth beneath, or that *is* in the water under the earth:
> [5]Thou shalt not bow down thyself to them, nor serve them: for I the LORD thy God *am* a jealous God, visiting the iniquity of the fathers upon the children unto the third and fourth *generation* **of them that hate me**; (Ex. 20:4-5)

Graven images are referred to as abominations in the word of God. They are evidence of a hatred of God.

> [25]The graven images of their gods shall ye burn with fire: thou shalt not desire the silver or gold *that is* on them, nor take *it* unto thee, lest thou be snared therein: for **it *is* an abomination to the LORD thy God.**
> [26]Neither shalt thou bring **an abomination** into thine house, **lest thou be a cursed thing like it**: *but* thou shalt utterly detest it, and thou shalt utterly abhor it; for it *is* a cursed thing. (Deut. 7:25-26)

(See also Deut. 13:14, 27:15; 2 Kings 23:13, Isa. 44:19)

When the Man of Sin, as part of the satanic trinity, enters the temple in the middle of the Tribulation, one of the first things he does is set up an idol of himself in the Temple of God. He then proclaims himself to be God.

What he is doing is purposefully breaking the first and second commandments. As part of the satanic trinity, he has no fear of God (Job 41:33). He seeks to provoke, jab and rebel against any and all authority from God Almighty. Associated with this rebellion is the desire to be God himself, and thus declares to the world that he is God. Worldwide they accept him and worship him.

God's presence was in the temple for the first half of the Tribulation, but when this takes place the presence of God leaves the temple, thus making it desolate. Now there is no doubt about this. Notice the correlation to what Jesus Christ says in Matthew 23:

> [37]O Jerusalem, Jerusalem, *thou* that killest the prophets, and stonest them which are sent unto thee, how often would I have gathered thy children together, even as a hen gathereth her chickens under *her* wings, and ye would not!
> [38]Behold, **your house is left unto you desolate.**
> [39]For I say unto you, Ye shall not see me henceforth, till ye shall say, Blessed *is* he that cometh in the name of the Lord. (Matt. 23:37-39)

Jesus Christ is weeping over Jerusalem and is leaving His temple, His house, and it breaks His heart. The term He uses when He leaves is that it is left desolate.

That is the term when God is absent from a place. That is not the only way the word desolate is used in the Bible. But in the context of the temple and what we are studying, it is a reference to the fact that God has deserted the place.

So the idol is an abomination to God, and the desolation is the fact that God departs when idols are set up and worshipped. The **"overspreading of abominations"** has to do with the worldwide command to make an image to the Beast.

> [14]And deceiveth them that dwell on the earth by *the means of* those miracles which he had power to do in the sight of the beast; saying **to them that dwell on the earth, that they should make an image to the beast,** which had the wound by a sword, and did live. (Rev. 13:14)

Worldwide images are made and set up, and wherever they are, God deserts the place thus making it spiritually desolate. The people damn their souls to Hell. This is the overspreading of abominations, which in turn makes it desolate.

> [9]And the third angel followed them, saying with a loud voice, If any man worship the beast and his image, and receive *his* mark in his forehead, or in his hand,
> [10]The same shall drink of the wine of the wrath of God, which is poured out without mixture into the cup of his indignation; and

he shall be tormented with fire and brimstone in the presence of the holy angels, and in the presence of the Lamb:
[11]And the smoke of their torment ascendeth up for ever and ever: and they have no rest day nor night, who worship the beast and his image, and whosoever receiveth the mark of his name. (Rev. 14:9-11)

[27]...even until the consummation, and that determined shall be poured upon the desolate. (Daniel 9:27)

The consummation is the end when this whole satanic kingdom is consumed by fire and slaughter from Jesus Christ Himself. His judgment is poured out upon the desolate which are worldwide: all who have set up images to the Beast and have received his mark.

We will be in the battle as well as at the Second Advent. The consummation takes place at the end of the 70th week, thus again fulfilling verse 24 by bringing it all to an end. From this point on for 1,000 years on this earth, Jesus Christ will be reigning over the world from Jerusalem, and David will be reigning as King over Israel in Jerusalem.

Daniel 8:9-14
The Prophecy of the 2300 days

The following scriptures bring out some more information concerning Israel, the Antichrist, and especially the temple. The prophecy here in Daniel 8 takes place during the seven-year Tribulation.

So even though we just finished in Daniel 9 with the end of the Tribulation, now back up in your mind to the beginning of the Tribulation. This is where this prophecy begins as well.

I originally had this in numerical order based upon the chapters, but the information here seemed a bit too deep and detailed to begin with. So now that you have the layout of the Tribulation set before you in Daniel 9, we will go into the following.

> ⁹And out of one of them came forth a little horn, which waxed exceeding great, toward the south, and toward the east, and toward the pleasant _land._
> ¹⁰**And it waxed great, _even_ to the host of heaven; and it cast down _some_ of the host and of the stars to the ground, and stamped upon them.** (Dan. 8:9-10)

The first part of the chapter covers Media-Persia, and how Alexander the Great came and busted up their kingdom. The goat with the notable horn is Alexander the Great. I am skipping this because I do not want to write a commentary on the chapter. I just want to deal with those verses that concern the Tribulation, and specifically how they apply to rightly dividing it.

You get a sense of the character of the little horn when it says **"to the host of heaven."** The verse is dealing in the spiritual realm now. To cast some of the host of heaven and stars to the ground and stamp upon them, it gives you a clear picture that you are dealing with a satanic being here.

¹¹Yea, he magnified *himself* even to the prince of the host, and by him the daily *sacrifice* was taken away, and **the place of his sanctuary was cast down.**

¹²And an host was given *him* **against the daily *sacrifice*** by reason of transgression, and it **cast down the truth to the ground**; and it practised, and prospered. (Dan. 8:11-12)

"**The prince of the host**" would be the host of heaven and therefore he is magnifying himself against God, the Lord Jesus Christ. This happens when the Man of Sin walks into the Temple of God and sits down as God. "…**so that he as God sitteth in the temple of God, shewing himself that he is God.**" (2 Thess. 2:4b) This is also when the daily sacrifice is taken away. This matches Daniel 9:27, "…**in the midst of the week he shall cause the sacrifice and the oblation to cease.**" This is also the same event as Matt. 24:15 when the abomination of desolation stands in the holy place. The image is set up in the temple. Daniel 8:11-12 is dealing with events in the middle of the Tribulation, and on out unto the end.

When the "**place of his sanctuary**" is cast down, this happens in the middle of the Tribulation. Here is what that is referring to. The "**place of his sanctuary**" is the holy place in the temple where the presence of God will dwell. The casting down is the defiling of the place of His sanctuary when the Man of Sin walks into it and proclaims himself to be God. The casting down is spiritually complete when he walks into it, but is physically finished as well by the end of the Tribulation. By the end of the Tribulation, Jerusalem is destroyed as well as the temple. Ah, yes! The temple is the key to understanding and rightly dividing the Tribulation.

> ¹³Then I heard one saint speaking, and another saint said unto that certain *saint* which spake, How long *shall be* the vision **concerning** the daily *sacrifice*, **and the transgression of desolation,** to give both the sanctuary and the host to be trodden under foot?
> ¹⁴And he said unto me, Unto **two thousand and three hundred days**; then shall the sanctuary be cleansed. (Dan. 8:13-14)

Now this is an interesting portion of scripture. How long shall the vision be concerning:
1. The daily sacrifice
2. The transgression of desolation
3. Specifically it is 2,300 days, then the sanctuary shall be cleansed.

Well, this is a very definite time frame.

If the cleansing of the sanctuary takes place after the 2,300 days, because it says, **"...then shall the sanctuary be cleansed..."** then the 2,300 days end with the second advent of Jesus Christ. The 2,300 days mark the end of the Tribulation.

The length of the 2,300 days is 6.4 years, depending on how many days you figure for each month. I have used 30 days since that is the length of a prophetic month in the Bible.

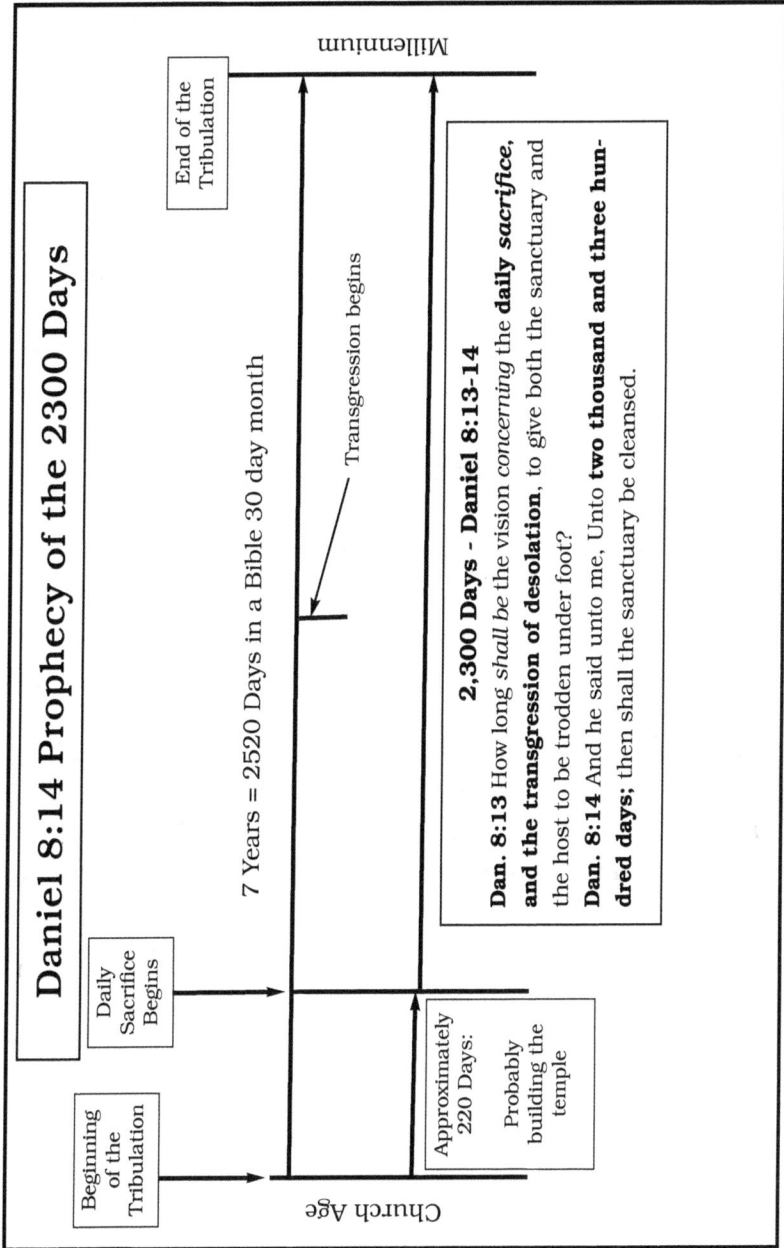

Daniel 8:14 Prophecy of the 2300 Days

Millennium

End of the Tribulation

Transgression begins

7 Years = 2520 Days in a Bible 30 day month

2,300 Days - Daniel 8:13-14

Dan. 8:13 How long *shall be* the vision *concerning* the **daily sacrifice, and the transgression of desolation**, to give both the sanctuary and the host to be trodden under foot?

Dan. 8:14 And he said unto me, Unto **two thousand and three hundred days**; then shall the sanctuary be cleansed.

Daily Sacrifice Begins

Beginning of the Tribulation

Approximately 220 Days:

Probably building the temple

Church Age

Seven Years

Seven years, with a 30 day month, comes out to be 2,520 days. That is the total length of the Tribulation. By starting at the end of the Tribulation and counting backwards, since we know the end, then you arrive at approximately 200 to 220 days after the seven year Tribulation has begun.

So once the covenant is confirmed, the daily sacrifice doesn't begin until about 200 days, or 6 to 7 months into the Tribulation. Why the delay, it doesn't say. I would guess that the temple is not ready those first 200 days. The temple is probably being constructed and sanctified during those first 200 days. The covenant opened up the way, and gives Israel liberty to build their temple.

Then in the midst of the week, three and a half years into the Tribulation, the Man of Sin enters the temple and declares himself to be God. For the rest of the Tribulation, the temple is slowly destroyed along with Jerusalem.

The total length of this prophecy is 2,300 days, like it says. So approximately for the first 1,080 days —three years— the daily sacrifice and oblation takes place. It ceases when the transgression of desolation begins and continues until the end of the Tribulation. That is when Jesus Christ returns and puts an end to the blasphemy.

Matthew

Ah, yes! Matthew 24, the chapter that so many Christians break their necks over. Matthew, Acts and Hebrews are the three books of the New Testament that are transitional books. If you don't know that, and if you don't rightly divide the Word of God, then you will end up applying doctrinally the three books into the Church age and end up in a mess.

One of the major mistakes that has been made over the centuries by applying these books to the Church age is the command to **"...endure unto the end."** Pentecostals, Methodists, Church of God, Amish, and others all claim that if you don't endure unto the end of your life—in other words, if you ever backslid— then you lose your salvation and go to Hell when you die. Unless you repent and get saved again, and endure unto the end, then you probably will go to Heaven. But even then they are not sure about that because of

Hebrews 6 where it says it is impossible to renew them unto repentance.

Terri and I had just left Seminole, Alabama, where we are based, and were heading northward on I-65. As we were passing through Montgomery, my diesel Ford truck had engine trouble. Though on an incline, I pulled over and got out to find diesel fluid running down the road. We called a tow truck and got towed into the local Ford dealer. The fuel pump had disintegrated and basically destroyed the motor. It was a real mess, to say the least.

The mechanic that worked on the truck was a good man. He was probably in his thirties, married and had children. We were stuck there for quite a few days, so I got to know him. He went to church. It was an old time Holiness Church, and they did not believe in eternal security.

As I witnessed to the man, from what he told me, he was born again. But he had absolutely no joy. After talking to him and finding out where he went to church, I realized that he did not know if he was saved. He had gotten away from the Lord, also known as being backslidden, some years earlier and did some drinking, partying and such. But because of the improper application of Tribulation verses upon how he had lived, he literally feared he was going to Hell.

As I showed him verse after verse on salvation and eternal security, he would read the verses but not allow himself to believe them. It was so sad! I am guessing he had heard as well that the doctrine of eternal security is a damnable doctrine. Thus he was unable

124

to allow himself to believe that the Lord will keep anyone in His love.

When we finally left the dealership, it was still sad to see him so beat down. He never laughed or even smiled. I believe he lived under a daily cloud of fear.

To believe that once you are saved, then you are secure and cannot lose your salvation is loudly decried and preached against in many churches. Their texts for preaching such doctrine are mainly found in Matthew, Acts and Hebrews. And yes, that is what the texts say. But they do not apply doctrinally to the Church age today.

Notice the following verses in the book of...who? Hebrews! Does that mean throw it out and ignore it? Absolutely not! All scripture is profitable. But when a verse or series of verses contradict what Paul wrote to the body of Christ, then you must place it in the proper context.   The whole Bible is not written just to Christians in the Church age. You do know that, don't you?

> ²⁵Not forsaking the assembling of ourselves together, as the manner of some *is*; but exhorting *one another:* and so much the more, as ye see the day approaching.
> ²⁶For if we sin wilfully after that we have received the knowledge of the truth, there remaineth no more sacrifice for sins,
> ²⁷But **a certain fearful looking for of judgment and fiery indignation, which shall devour the adversaries.**
> ²⁸He that despised Moses' law died without

mercy under two or three witnesses:

²⁹Of how much sorer punishment, suppose ye, shall he be thought worthy, who hath trodden under foot the Son of God, and hath counted the blood of the covenant, **wherewith he was sanctified**, an unholy thing, and hath done despite unto the Spirit of grace?

³⁰For we know him that hath said, **Vengeance *belongeth* unto me, I will recompense, saith the Lord. And again, The Lord shall judge his people.**

³¹*It is* **a fearful thing to fall into the hands of the living God.** (Heb. 10:25-31)

I have heard verse 25 preached to Christians, and it will work. Yes, you need to be in church, and you are not to forsake the assembling of yourself with other Christians. I know of Christians who at one time were in church, but because of trouble in the church, they no longer attend services. (Let me mention here that Jesus is worth the trouble!) They have forsaken the assembly and assembling together with other Christians, and consequently they are not getting under the preaching of the word of God. That is not right.

There is nothing wrong with using that verse on Christians. It does not contradict Paul, who was the apostle of the Gentiles and wrote to the body of Christ. But when a verse contradicts Paul's writings, then you have to rightly divide and realize that DOCTRINALLY it applies in another period of time, which is also known as a dispensation.

Now look at verses 26-27 and ask yourself, Have you sinned willfully after you got saved? Well then, according to verse 27 you are going to Hell. That is how it is preached, but that is not doctrinally right for a Christian.

Notice the word **"certain"** in verse 27. It is certain; it is going to happen. And notice that it is "fiery indignation." Do you know what the word fiery means? It means fire as in fiery. Indignation means God is angry with you. It is doctrinally wrong to apply this to a Christian.

Notice in verse 29 he **"was sanctified"** by the blood, but obviously he is not anymore.

Now look at verse 31 and see that it is a fearful thing to fall into the hands of the living God. But for a born again Christian it is NOT a fearful thing. Why?

> [35]**Who shall separate us from the love of Christ?** *shall* tribulation, or distress, or persecution, or famine, or nakedness, or peril, or sword?
>
> [36]As it is written, For thy sake we are killed all the day long; we are accounted as sheep for the slaughter.
>
> [37]Nay, in all these things we are more than conquerors through him that loved us.
>
> [38]**For I am persuaded, that neither death, nor life, nor angels, nor principalities, nor powers, nor things present, nor things to come,**
>
> [39]**Nor height, nor depth, nor any other**

creature, shall be able to separate us from
the love of God, which is in Christ Jesus our
Lord. (Rom. 8:35-39)

Do you see the difference? If you are born again, then
nothing, did you get that, nothing is going to separate
you from the love of God, which is in Christ Jesus our
Lord. If is not a fearful thing to fall into the hands of
the living God during the Church age, but it is in the
Tribulation.

If someone in the Tribulation receives the truth and
refuses to take the Mark of the Beast, then they are
going to get really hungry and hunted like an animal.
If they give in and take the mark, it's all over for them.
There is a certain fearful looking for of judgment and
fiery indignation. They go to Hell, or at the second
coming they face the fires of Jesus Christ as He returns
and destroys people with the brightness of His coming.
People are hiding in the caves of the earth saying, *"Hide
us from the face of the Lamb."* Why? Because to see His
face, you will get melted as you stand on your feet.

The book of Romans is written to Christians under
grace during the Church age, and the book of Hebrews
is written to Hebrews during the Tribulation. And when
someone tells you that they know that Paul wrote the
book of Hebrews, they are lying. No one alive today
KNOWS who wrote the book of Hebrews. There are
those who guess and claim to know, but they do not
have absolute scriptures to prove it. There are
scriptures used with conjecture, but it is not absolute.

Every one of the Pauline epistles starts with the name

of Paul. Obviously the book of Hebrews does not begin that way.

Alright, on to the next. The Gospel of Matthew is written with the theme of Jesus as King of the Jews. It is not written, or aimed at the Church age. Again, and I don't mean to keep repeating myself, but as soon as you say that about the gospel of Matthew, the brethren go nuts. I didn't say "throw it out and don't use it," like the hyper-dispensationalists do. But you have to rightly divide it, and that is what we are going to do as we go through chapter 24. This book is about rightly dividing the 70th week, and in order to do that you must rightly divide the scriptures as well.

Matthew 24

> ¹¶ And Jesus went out, and departed from the temple: and his disciples came to *him* for to shew him the buildings of the temple.
> ²And Jesus said unto them, See ye not all these things? verily I say unto you, There shall not be left here one stone upon another, that shall not be thrown down. (Matt. 24:1-2)

The disciples are obviously impressed with the temple and sought to show it to Jesus. They didn't realize that the One they are talking to is the God of that temple. He then tells them that it is going to be destroyed, which sparked a genuine desire to understand what He was talking about and when it was going to happen. Upon reaching the mount of Olives, they privately ask Him.

In Matthew 24 verse 3, the disciples privately ask Jesus Christ three questions, and this is where our study begins for this chapter.

> ³And as he sat upon the mount of Olives, the disciples came unto him privately, saying, Tell us, **when shall these things be? and what *shall be* the sign of thy coming, and of the end of the world?** (Matt. 24:3)

It is very important to remember that all three questions have NOTHING to do with the Church age. Did you get that? You have got to get that! We are not talking about the Church age in this study now. The chapter of Matthew 24 DOCTRINALLY is not dealing with anything that takes place during the Church age, which is before the Rapture of the Church. Matthew 24 is covering the time frame after the Rapture of the Church, the body of Christ. Thus, in this chapter when you read about enduring unto the end, you are reading about conditions taking place during the Tribulation, not during the Church age.

If you limit verse 2 to the destruction of the Temple in A.D. 70, then you have just placed the chapter into the Church age, which will not work. Yes, the temple was destroyed in A.D. 70 under the Roman general Titus but that was merely the physical destruction of the temple. What do I mean by this?

By A.D. 70 God had already turned to the Gentiles and the Church age had begun. (Rom. 11). Doctrinally, and thus spiritually, nothing happened when the temple was destroyed in A.D. 70 other than the temple was destroyed. Granted, I'm sure it was a big blow to the Jews; unfortunately they were about 35 years behind God. Too late, and even still, when the temple was destroyed in A.D. 70 they still did not realize that Jesus Christ was their Messiah.

When you get into the rest of the chapter, it obviously is a reference to the Tribulation, so doctrinally it will apply to the upcoming temple that will again be destroyed by the end of the Tribulation.

The subject matter of their questions concerned:

1. **"When will these things be?"** A.D. 70 but could also be Daniel 9:27 **"...shall destroy the city and the sanctuary..."** Doctrinally Daniel 9:27 fits with the verse, especially when the other two questions are answered.

2. **"What shall be the sign of thy coming?"** This is obviously a reference to His second coming to this earth, which takes place at the end of the Tribulation, not long after they destroy the sanctuary. If the sanctuary is destroyed, then the temple is destroyed as well.

3. **"And of the end of the world?"** The end of the world is the end of the Tribulation. When the Millennium begins it will be a new world. It will not be a new earth, but a new world. There is a difference.

The end of the world is not the same as the dissolving away and the melting of the elements that's mentioned in 2 Peter.

> [10]But the day of the Lord will come as a thief in the night; in the which the heavens shall pass away with a great noise, and **the**

elements shall melt with fervent heat, the
earth also and the works that are therein
shall be burned up. (2 Pet. 3:10)

This world, as in the system of governance, not in
reference to the material earth, is going to change at the
end of the Tribulation and become a new world in the
Millennium.

So all three questions concern the events that take
place AT THE END of the Tribulation, and will be
fulfilled at that time. They have no application and
bearing upon anything during the Church age, which
is what we are in at this present time. So nothing in
the chapter applies doctrinally to you and me, if you are
born again.

If you are lost and reading this, then it will apply to
you beginning immediately after the Rapture. The
Rapture is when the born-again people leave this world
to rise and meet the Lord in the air. This event can
happen at any time: today. Are you ready to go? There
will be no warning before the Rapture takes place.

Now let me run a little rabbit trail here just to warn
you of another strange teaching that is going around.
The dead in Christ are NOT going to be walking around
for 40 days and nights before the Rapture. They're not
going to be walking around one day before the Rapture.
And if they were, they would be invisible anyway
because they would not have their new bodies, for the
dead in Christ and those who are alive at the time of
the Rapture, are changed "AT" the same time.

132

⁵¹¶ Behold, I shew you a mystery; We shall
not all sleep, but **we shall all be changed,**
⁵²In a moment, in the twinkling of an eye, **at
the last trump:** for the trumpet shall sound,
and the dead shall be raised incorruptible,
and we shall be changed. (1 Cor. 15:51-52)

We shall all be changed "**at the last trump.**" The "all"
is a reference to those living and those who have
already died. It does not read "by" the last trump. It
is likely the Rapture occurs within seconds; we are
changed in the twinkling of an eye, but the Rapture will
take place in seconds.

Now notice the wording. The trumpet sounds and the
dead are raised. (1 Cor. 15:52, 1 Thess. 4:16) That is
the first trump. Then "**at the last trump**" we are all
changed. So there are only two trumps sounded. Do
you see that? And at the last trump is when we put on
incorruption. (1 Cor. 15:53) Then both dead in Christ
and those alive at the Rapture (ie. His coming,) both
rise together to meet the Lord in the clouds.

Immediately after the Rapture, the world is placed
back under the law of the Old Testament, along with
the need for faith in Jesus Christ.

¹⁷And the dragon was wroth with the woman,
and went to make war with the remnant of
her seed, which **keep the commandments of
God, and have the testimony of Jesus
Christ.** (Rev. 12:17)

133

^{12}Here is the patience of the saints: here *are* **they that keep the commandments of God, and the faith of Jesus.** (Rev. 14:12)

It's both a faith and works setup in the Tribulation in order to be saved. Now you are either going to believe the verses you just read, or you are not. That is up to you, but the word of God says what it means and means what it says, and it said they had the faith of Jesus Christ AND keep the commandments of God. That is what it says, whether you believe it or not. They are doing the commandments which is something the Christians have not done and do not need to do in the Church age. For example, a Christian has NEVER had to keep the Sabbath in order to be, or to stay saved..

^{4}¶And Jesus answered and said unto them, **Take heed that no man deceive you.** (Matt. 24:4)

Alright now, it's going to get deep. Get in your mind that the Rapture has happened, so all of the born again believers have vanished from the earth.

This is the start of the Tribulation. The amount of chaos on the earth will probably by great. Millions of people will just disappear. Keep in mind that salvation is a free gift right now, and there are relatively a lot of people that are saved on the earth. No way is it a majority, and I doubt that it is even one third of the earths population, but there are quite a bunch of people that profess to be saved.

The professing born-again population of the United

States of America is at least a third of the country. To be a little more on the safe side, let's say a quarter of the country is born again. That is almost 100 million people gone in a moment. Do you realize what that will do to the nation? Many of the Christians will be in the workforce, and generally, though not always, it's the Christians that are the dependable workers at their jobs. With that many workers that vanish, it will severely cripple the nation. Even to the point of not being able to recover.

Worldwide there's no way it's a fourth, but it will be a noticeable portion that abruptly goes missing. Can you imagine those who go looking for their loved ones and will not find them?

> [5]By faith Enoch was translated that he should not see death; and **was not found**, because God had translated him: for before his translation he had this testimony, that he pleased God. (Heb. 11:5)

Enoch is the only man in the Bible who will never die, besides the Christians who are alive at the time of the Rapture. As such, he is one of, if not, the greatest type of a Christian alive on the earth at the time of the Rapture. Notice that the Bible states that he **"was not found."** Somebody went looking for him and couldn't find him. There are going to be people out looking for loved ones and they are not going to find them because they are gone.

It will be a time of great sorrow. It will also be a time of great confusion, and with that confusion will come a great deception. The first thing the Lord tells His disciples is, **"Take heed that no man deceive you."**

> [3]**Let no man deceive you** by any means:
> (2 Th. 2:3)

> [11]And many false prophets shall rise, and **shall deceive many.** (Matt. 24:11)

> [6]For many shall come in my name, saying, I am *Christ*; and **shall deceive many.**
> (Mark 13:6)

> [8]And he said, **Take heed that ye be not deceived:** for many shall come in my name, saying, I am *Christ*; and the time draweth near: go ye not therefore after them. (Luke 21:8)

> [5]For many shall come in my name, saying, I am Christ; and **shall deceive many.**
> (Matt. 24:5)

This happened before the first coming of Jesus Christ as well, and it is going to happen before the second coming of Christ.

> [36]**For before these days rose up Theudas, boasting himself to be somebody; to whom a number of men, about four hundred, joined themselves:** who was slain; and all, as

3

many as obeyed him, were scattered, and brought to nought.

³⁷**After this man rose up Judas of Galilee in the days of the taxing, and drew away much people after him:** he also perished; and all, *even* as many as obeyed him, were dispersed. (Acts 5:36-37)

Except after the Rapture it will be many.

⁶And ye shall hear of wars and rumours of wars: see that ye be not troubled: for all *these things* must come to pass, but **the end** is not yet.
⁷For nation shall rise against nation, and kingdom against kingdom: and there shall be famines, and pestilences, and earthquakes, in divers places. (Matt. 24:6-7)

"**The end**" of verse 6 is the same as "**the end**" of Daniel's 70th week, also known as the Tribulation.

So many have applied verses 6-7 to the Church age, and I have done it as well. There is no doubt that wars and rumors of wars are taking place in the time in which we live, but the amount of wars and rumors of wars will rise greatly after the Rapture. NO, the first part of the Tribulation is NOT a time of peace.

I couldn't believe what I was hearing!
Terri and I were parked in an RV park out in the desert of south Arizona. An older single lady pulled up into the space next to us. After a couple of days we

began to talk and she was from northern Minnesota. As we talked the subject of politics, the world condition and other topics came up as Terri and I tried to witness to her. She evaded our attempts, and in so doing at one point she said something that caught me so off guard I was at a loss for words.

She, with all seriousness and with a matter-of-factness said, *"War is obsolete. It's just obsolete and we don't need to worry about war any more."* I literally was stunned! I had never heard such a statement before. It was so wrong and contrary to what the word of God says that I was caught completely flat footed, so to speak. I couldn't believe she was that deceived, blind, and living in a dream world. All I can say is such is the liberal mindset. But it is completely opposite to what the word of God states is coming. And we are watching the beginning, or the prelude to it all.

During the first half of the Tribulation, there are two prophets, or two witnesses, who will be preaching and sending plagues, disasters, and torments worldwide. These two witnesses are likely to be Moses and Elijah. They will be working from Jerusalem; at least that is where the temple will be, and that is where they are killed in the middle of the Tribulation. I will cover this in greater detail when I comment upon Revelation chapter 11.

When the world realizes that these two Jews are responsible for the torments that are coming on the earth, people worldwide become furious towards the Jews.

⁸All these *are* the beginning of sorrows.

⁹**Then shall they deliver you up to be afflicted, and shall kill you: and ye shall be hated of all nations for my name's sake.**

¹⁰**And then shall many be offended, and shall betray one another, and shall hate one another.** (Matt. 24:8-10)

The world today tolerates Israel. But during the Tribulation, that will all change. When the pressure comes, the true characteristics of people are brought to the surface. With the plagues, droughts, pestilence, and other torments, people will turn against one another, as well as turn against the Jews.

¹¹And **many false prophets shall rise, and shall deceive many.** (Matt. 24:11)

Many false prophets to confuse and to deceive people from the two true prophets, who are smiting the world with all of these torments.

It is similar to what happened when Moses and Aaron stood before Pharaoh and performed the miracles, plagues, and such. For a while the magicians of Egypt matched the works that Moses was doing. But only for so long, and then they couldn't "keep up."

There has been a teaching over the years that the first three and a half years of the Tribulation are years of peace, but this is not true. There is a political agreement, or a covenant with the Jews, but worldwide, and in a "side effect" from the agreement, the two witnesses are tormenting the world. I use the word "torment" because of the following verse:

> [10]And they that dwell upon the earth shall rejoice over them, and make merry, and shall send gifts one to another; because **these two prophets tormented them that dwelt on the earth.** (Rev. 11:10)

This takes place during the first half of the Tribulation, and we will see that when I comment on Revelation 11.

It will be a very hard time to live, but much, much harder for those who are not deceived and thus try to do right. When the Bible says **"endure,"** that is exactly what it will be. There will be no events of pleasure, or happy times, or restful times of peace and tranquility for those who are doing right. It will be an endurance—plain and simple. Every day and every night is a time of enduring betrayal, disasters, plagues, and more.

Along with this **"enduring unto the end"** is the constant temptation to take the mark so you can eat and be safe. This is where the **"If we sin willfully after that we have received the knowledge of the truth"** comes in. And there will be many who "fall." There is no question where someone goes who takes the Mark of the Beast. They go to Hell.

> [9]And the third angel followed them, saying with a loud voice, **If any man worship the beast and his image, and receive _his_ mark in his forehead, or in his hand,**

¹⁰The same shall drink of the wine of the wrath of God, which is poured out without mixture into the cup of his indignation; and he shall be tormented with fire and brimstone in the presence of the holy angels, and in the presence of the Lamb: ¹¹And the smoke of their torment ascendeth up for ever and ever: and they have no rest day nor night, **who worship the beast and his image, and whosoever receiveth the mark of his name.** (Rev. 14:9-11)

Those who endure unto the end, who also will be those who are not deceived, will have survived for one reason. They loved and believed the truth. That truth they were able to hold in their hands and read. If they are a Jew, they will have been open enough to read the New Testament, also known as the Christian Bible to the Jews.

Now notice that **"the end"** is not a reference to the end of someone's life:

⁶And ye shall hear of wars and rumours of wars: see that ye be not troubled: for all *these things* must come to pass, but **the end is not yet.** (Matt. 24:6)

¹³But he that shall **endure unto the end,** the same shall be saved. (Matt. 24:13)

According to verse 6 "the end" is a period of time on this earth, not the end of someone's life. Many have taken verse 13 and claimed it is referring to the end of a Christian's life, and if you backslide then you will go to Hell. This is not true.

> [14]And this gospel of the kingdom shall be preached in all the world for a witness unto all nations; and **then shall the end come.** (Matt. 24:14)

"This gospel of the kingdom" is not the Gospel of the grace of God that Paul preached. It is not the same thing. More and more you are hearing Christians talk about bringing in the kingdom. There is no telling how many millions of people have been killed in wars that were started with the goal of bringing in God's kingdom. The kingdom will not come until the King, Jesus Christ comes back and sets up the kingdom. Until that time, it is going to be wars and rumors of wars, especially during the 70th week.

Middle Point of the Tribulation

Whether it is Sir Robert Anderson, Clarence Larkin, Brian Donovan or others, they all have attempted to date the beginning of Daniel's 70th week. But at some point all of them have to use their own conjecture to make the study complete.

There is no absolute date for the commandment of when it was actually given. There no absolute calendar that is used in order to date the time. And in Daniel 9:25 it reads, **"Unto Messiah the Prince."** Was that his birth? In Isaiah 9:6 his birth is referenced, and

he is called the **"Prince of Peace."** Or maybe **"unto Messiah the Prince"** refers to the start of His ministry, His baptism, or maybe it is a reference to Calvary. It is not clear in the scriptures. Perhaps because there is a 2,000 year insertion into the time frame? All I am saying is that when the beginning of the 70th week will take place is not absolutely clear in the word of God.

Dispensationally it makes sense that the 70th week would begin immediately after the Rapture.

There are two other events, or times in the Tribulation which are distinctly clear. Events concerning the middle of the Tribulation are absolutely clear, and events concerning the end of the Tribulation are absolutely clear.

There is no doubt to the fact that the following event occurs in the middle of the Tribulation.

> [15]When ye therefore shall see **the abomination of desolation,** spoken of by Daniel the prophet, **stand in the holy place,** (whoso readeth, let him understand:) (Matt. 24:15)

This is plainly the middle of the Tribulation, and I'll show you why. I may end up repeating myself quite a bit in this book on this point, and if so, please forgive me, but it is very important that you understand this midpoint in the Tribulation. It is essential to understand so that you rightly divide the Tribulation. I have already mentioned the dilemma some have because the book of Revelation does not ever record the Tribulation as being seven years in length.

When the Man of Sin enters into the temple and sets

up the abomination, he makes the temple desolate. It is such a profound break in the Tribulation that God records the Tribulation as two three-and-a-half-year segments. Did you get that? *This is very important! God divides the Tribulation into two three-and-one-half-year segments.*

The first half has God dwelling in the Jewish temple. The second half has Satan, the Man of Sin, dwelling in the temple. *This is why in the book of Revelation the time frame is never given as one week, or seven years.* It has to do with the temple. If you understand what takes place in the Jewish, or the Lord's, temple, during the 70th week, then you will understand and rightly divide the 70th week.

The first half has God in His temple, and the second half has Satan, the Man of Sin, in the temple. *They are so opposite to each other that God does not want the time frame to be given with God and Satan both included in the same time frame.*

So what is meant by the abomination of desolation?

The Abomination of Desolation

> [27]And he shall confirm the covenant with many for one week: and in the midst of the week he shall cause the sacrifice and the oblation to cease, and for **the overspreading of abominations he shall make** *it* **desolate, even until the consummation, and that determined shall be poured upon the desolate.** (Dan. 9:27)

³¶ Let no man deceive you by any means: for *that day shall not come,* except there come a falling away first, and that man of sin be revealed, the son of perdition;

⁴Who opposeth and exalteth himself above all that is called God, or that is worshipped; **so that he as God sitteth in the temple of God, shewing himself that he is God.**

(2 Thes. 2:3-4)

The Temple of God is going to be rebuilt sometime between now and immediately after the Rapture. There is no doubt about that. Even as I write this, I am told by many sources that the Temple Mount Jews have all of the materials ready: the furniture, the red heifers, the stones etc. for the building of their new temple. It is all ready to go. All they are waiting for is the green light to begin.

Wouldn't it be comical if Hezbollah, Hamas or another enemy of Israel fired a rocket and it veered off course and destroyed the Al-Aqsa mosque?

Jews begin building Third Temple on Israel Independence Day

While most Israelis were celebrating Independence Day by having family barbecues, a small group gathered in the Old City of Jerusalem and began chipping away at stones, preparing them to be used to build the prophesied Third Temple.

The event was organized by Rabbi Aryeh Lipo ... Rabbi Lipo realized that it was possible to begin to actually perform this mitzvah by preparing the stones that will be used to build the Third Temple.

(A mitzvah is a Torah Commandment)

In order to perform the mitzvah properly, Rabbi Lipo had to consult with several rabbis who were expert in issues concerning the Temple. Because of its politically sensitive nature, an aspect some rabbis consider when ruling about the Temple Mount and Third Temple, there are normally vastly divergent views regarding such issues.

"All of the rabbis we consulted agreed that we should begin preparing the stones," Lipo said

"The unifying identity of the Jewish people is expressed in the Temple in Jerusalem," Rabbi Lipo explained. "On this day, 74 years ago, Israel became a state but the essence of the nation is the Temple in Jerusalem."

Most quarries in Israel are operated by Arabs and they preferred not to use stones from those locations. They collected 23 sizable stones from a field near the community of Eish Kodesh (holy fire) in Samaria. A contractor from Judea transported the stones to an area near the Hurva Synagogue in the Old City. Lipo's mother, who was born with the State of Israel 74 years ago, took part, enthusiastically helping to chip away at the stones.

Lipo plans on holding more events of this type to prepare more stones for the Third Temple. *(Berkowitz Adam Eliyahu, Jews begin building Third Temple on Israel Independence Day, https://israel365news.com/352915/jews-begin-building-third-temple-on-israel-independence-day/, May 6, 2022, viewed 5/10/24)*

If you were going to look for anything that would signal the Rapture to be imminent it would be the building of the Jewish temple. Just the fact that they are ready to build it is evidence of how close we are. When, not IF, it gets built, do you realize how great a piece of prophetical evidence that the Bible is the inerrant words of God that will be? The fulfillment of prophecy would be amazing, though I am sure the world, under the realm of the god of this world, would look at it with little to no interest. But for those of us who are saved, and if the building of the temple begins before the Rapture takes place, it will be a massive prophetic event that will signal the beginning of the end of the Church age. Of course, the construction of the temple may begin after the Rapture.

This is what I mean about the beginning of the Tribulation. There are so many variables at play that nothing is absolutely certain as to the specific time of the beginning. The middle is certain, as well as the end. But the beginning is not plain. God made it that way on purpose so you have to live by faith and not by sight.

The temple does not have to be built before the

Rapture. But if the 70th week begins immediately after the Rapture, it is quite possible that it will at least be under construction. I am told that the Jews already have an operational altar for the sacrificing of animals. With the help of God, the new temple could be built quite rapidly. It appears though, for at least the first 220 days of the Tribulation period, there is no daily sacrifice according to Dan. 8:14.

As for an absolute, we know that the Temple of God is going to be built, and it is important to realize that it is the Temple of God. Right now in the Church age, the body of the born-again believer is the Temple of God. But after we leave, the Jewish temple in Jerusalem will once again be the physical place where the presence of God will reside. He will reside in His temple until the middle point of the Tribulation. The temple will obviously be located in Jerusalem, and the presence of God will be there. I mention that again because that is very, very important. Why?

Because of what the Bible says:

> [4]These are the two olive trees, and the two candlesticks **standing before the God of the earth.** (Rev. 11:4)

When Moses and Elijah prophesy for three and a half years, they are said to be standing before the God of the earth. With the presence of God in His temple, this is where and how they are standing before the God of the earth. They are communicating directly with the Lord, and He directly to them. Same as the prophets did in the Old Testament. (Lev. 9:5, Deut. 18:7, 29:10, 1 Kings 17:1)

148

This takes place for three and a half years, and at this point Moses and Elijah get killed. Their bodies lie in the street of Jerusalem for three and a half days. Then they stand upon their feet and ascend up to Heaven right in front of their enemies eyes. The sight terrifies the enemies of the Lord.

At this point the Man of Sin, whose coming is after the working of Satan, goes into the temple and erects a statue of himself. He then has a throne placed in the temple, sits down and proclaims that he is God, and all are to worship Him.

When the statue is set up in the temple, God vacates the temple, as well as the Jews who worshipped inside the temple. Now as to the abomination of desolation.

Notice what God says about idols in the word of God.

¹¶ And God spake all these words, saying,

²I *am* the LORD thy God, which have brought thee out of the land of Egypt, out of the house of bondage.

³Thou shalt have no other gods before me.

⁴Thou shalt not make unto thee any graven image, or any likeness *of any thing* that *is* in heaven above, or that *is* in the earth beneath, or that *is* in the water under the earth:

⁵Thou shalt not bow down thyself to them, nor serve them: for I the LORD thy God *am* a jealous God, visiting the iniquity of the fathers upon the children unto the third and fourth *generation* of them that hate me; (Ex. 20:1-5)

The first commandment is "no other gods."

The second commandment is "no graven image."

Satan being the rebel that he is, the first thing he does is break the first two commandments by setting up a graven image in the temple and proclaiming that he is God. God calls the image that is set up in the temple the abomination of desolation. So what does that mean? Why is it called that? Notice what it says in Matthew 24:

> [15]When ye therefore shall see **the abomination of desolation,** spoken of by Daniel the prophet, stand in the holy place, (whoso readeth, let him understand:) (Matt. 24:15)

For many years after Bible school, I did not know nor understand what the Abomination of Desolation was or is. But by the grace of God I do know now, and by the end of this study you will know what it is, too. At least that is my desire and goal. So notice what God says about graven images, statues and idols:

> [15]Cursed *be* the man that maketh *any* graven or molten image, **an abomination unto the LORD,** the work of the hands of the craftsman, and putteth *it* in a secret *place.* And all the people shall answer and say, Amen. (Deut. 27:15)

> [19]And none considereth in his heart, neither *is there* knowledge nor understanding to say, I

have burned part of it in the fire; yea, also I
have baked bread upon the coals thereof; I have
roasted flesh, and eaten *it*: and **shall I make the
residue thereof an abomination?** shall I fall
down to the stock of a tree? (Is. 44:19)

I have already gone over this in the commentary on
Daniel 9, but just as a reminder, an idol is an
abomination to the Lord.

Knowing that the Man of Sin erects an image in the
temple of the Lord explains what the abomination is
and when it takes place. But then it says the
abomination of desolation. Why does it say desolation?

³¹And arms shall stand on his part, and they
shall pollute the sanctuary of strength, and
shall take away the daily *sacrifice*, and **they
shall place the abomination that maketh
desolate.** (Dan. 11:31)

The abomination is the graven image that is set up in
the temple. It is said that it "maketh desolate." When
the image is set up in the temple OF GOD, then God
leaves the temple. And when God is absent it is
desolate.

It is very important to realize that God goes where He
is wanted. The reason you got saved is because for
whatever reason, and they are all good, you came to a
point where you wanted Jesus Christ. You prayed and
asked Him to save you. He had been waiting patiently
and wanting to save you all along, but He does not force
Himself upon anyone. Even in the Tribulation, He is

using His prophets to send torment upon the world, but this is mercy in the sense that He is trying to cause people to repent and turn to Him.

So the abomination of desolation is the graven image that is set up in the temple. God leaves the temple, and even though the Man of Sin is present in the temple, it is desolate. When God leaves anything it becomes desolate. That is the condition of the lost. They are desolate. They have absolutely no spiritual life.

I remember like it was yesterday, yet it was over forty-seven years ago as of the writing of this book. It had been about a week or two after I had asked Jesus Christ to save me. I remember being on my knees praying when I saw so clearly how empty I was before I got saved. The word "empty" is the right word for it, for when I got saved Jesus Christ came to dwell within me. Amen! The word God uses for the lost condition, or for the place where God is not, is the word "desolate."

> [27]And he shall confirm the covenant with many for one week: and in the midst of the week he shall cause the sacrifice and the oblation to cease, and for **the overspreading of abominations he shall make** *it* **desolate,** even until the consummation, and that determined **shall be poured upon the desolate.** (Dan. 9:27)

Here you have the **"overspreading of abominations."** Now knowing what an abomination is, you have a great clue as to what is going on. Notice the following verse.

[14]And deceiveth them that dwell on the earth by *the means of* those miracles which he had power to do in the sight of the beast; **saying to them that dwell on the earth, that they should make an image to the beast,** which had the wound by a sword, and did live. (Rev. 13:14)

So there is given a worldwide command to build an image unto the Beast. People then all over the world obey and build an image to the beast. This causes an overspreading of abominations, thus making those who do this desolate as well. They have sealed their future in Hell by doing so.

This would explain the following verse.

[25]And **through his policy also he shall cause craft to prosper** in his hand; and he shall magnify *himself* in his heart, and by peace shall destroy many: he shall also stand up against the Prince of princes; but he shall be broken without hand. (Dan. 8:25)

Oh yes, craft is going to prosper. There is going to be a worldwide demand for images (ie., abominations.) Very similar to statues of Mary that you see all over the place in a grove in the yard of houses. But this will be an image of the Beast. Whether in a house or in the front yard, or both, it will be obvious whose side you are on.

^{14}...saying to them that dwell on the earth, that they should make an image to the beast, which had the wound by a sword, and did live.

^{15}And **he had power to give life unto the image of the beast, that the image of the beast should both speak,** and cause that as many as would not worship the image of the beast should be killed. (Rev. 13:14-15)

The image of the Beast is singular; so this might be a stretch, but I wonder if there will be a sort of communication system worldwide through the image? We already have live images worldwide through the internet and computers. Just a thought.

^{16}Then let **them which be in Judaea flee into the mountains:**

^{17}Let him which is **on the housetop not come down to take any thing out of his house:**

^{18}**Neither let him which is in the field return back to take his clothes.**

^{19}And woe unto them that are with child, and to them that give suck in those days!

^{20}But pray ye that your flight be not in the winter, neither on the sabbath day:

^{21}For then shall be great tribulation, such as was not since the beginning of the world to this time, no, nor ever shall be. (Matt. 24:16-21)

In order to survive that, as soon as Jews see the image set up in the temple, they must flee without stopping at their house to get anything. The implication being that those who stop for something will not make it.

It is common for Jews to love money. And they are good at making money. They love nice things as well. But in the middle of the Tribulation, only those Jews who are ready to leave it all at the drop of a hat, are the ones who will escape the wrath of the Man of Sin.

The Jews who are ready to flee will be those who have read and believed the scriptures in Matthew 24. Those scriptures are just as much the word of God as the scriptures in the Old Testament. Though the Jews do not recognize the New Testament, or as it is termed "the Christian Bible," by the middle of the Tribulation there will be some who will have at least read it with a certain belief that these things just might truly happen. When I read Matthew 24 and how fast they have to be ready to flee, it sure looks like some will have had a warning ahead of time, and know what they need to do.

> [19]And woe unto them that are **with child, and to them that give suck** in those days! (Matt. 24:19)

Why? Because that baby is going to slow her down. It shows that they are literally running for their lives.

> [20]But pray ye that your flight be not in the winter, **neither on the sabbath day:** (Matt. 24:20)

155

This also implies that there will be a certain amount of transportation used to get outside of Jerusalem, as well as Judaea, if the idol is not set up on the Sabbath. On the Sabbath day in Israel, airports and all other public transportation is closed.

> Israel has never had official public transportation on Shabbat due to opposition from religious lawmakers. *(Staff TOI, The Times of Israel, In extraordinary move, trains to keep running on Shabbat amid war, 13, October 2023, https://www.timesofisrael.com/in-extraordinary-move-trains-to-keep-running-on-shabbat-amid-war/#:~:text=Israel%20has%20never%20had%20official,to%20opposition%20from%20religious%20lawmakers., Viewed 5/10/2024)*

> [21]**For then shall be great tribulation, such as was not since the beginning of the world to this time, no, nor ever shall be.** (Matt. 24:21)

> [20]¶ **Come, my people, enter thou into thy chambers, and shut thy doors about thee: hide thyself as it were for a little moment, until the indignation be overpast.** (Is. 26:20)

For the first half of the Tribulation, God deals with the world through Moses and Elijah. But once they are dead and the remnant of the Jews flee to the wilderness, then it is said to be the indignation of the Lord. During this time of the last half of the

156

Tribulation, God deals directly with the inhabitants of the earth. His dealings are punishing and harsh, which is born from wrathful indignation.

God has been patient and forgiving for 6,000 years. The objects of His patience, mercy, and forgiveness have been guilty, sinful, unworthy, and unjust: sinners who rightfully deserve to be in Hell. Yet over and over, God has been gracious because the Lord delights in being gracious as well as showing mercy. But at this point, His graciousness and mercy are just about over. I say "just about," because even as He deals harshly with the inhabitants of the earth, yet He still has a desire for them to repent. He desires them to get right so they can spend eternity with Him. His grace is not fully over, but it is very close.

Notice the following verses to illustrate this.

> [8]¶ And the fourth angel poured out his vial upon the sun; and **power was given unto him to scorch men with fire.**
> [9]And men were scorched with great heat, and **blasphemed the name of God,** which hath power over these plagues: and **they repented not to give him glory.** (Rev. 16:8-9)

God is sending these plagues by heavenly angels and is no longer using men. He is desiring for the people to repent of their sins and get right with Him, yet they blaspheme His name. Puny little sinners shaking their fists into the face of God Almighty. He who has the power to snuff their lives out in a twinkle, yet He still waits with the desire for them to repent. Those who do repent find Jehovah ready to forgive. He will make them fit for eternity with Him, instead of eternity with Satan in Hell, and then afterwards the lake of fire.

> ²²And **except those days should be shortened,** there should no flesh be saved: but for the elect's sake **those days shall be shortened.** (Matt. 24:22)

> ⁶And the woman fled into the wilderness, where she hath a place prepared of God, that they should feed her there **a thousand two hundred *and* threescore days.** (Rev. 12:6)

So the number of days has been set. It looks like the days are literally shortened.

Notice again the three and a half year reference. For the first three and a half years, Israel is in the land with the temple in operation in Jerusalem. For the last half of the Tribulation, Israel is in the wilderness communing and in fellowship with God the Father. You must rightly divide the 70th week.

To claim Israel was in fellowship with God the Father during the ministry of Christ does not work.

> ¹²And the fourth angel sounded, and the third part of the sun was smitten, and the third part of the moon, and the third part of the stars; so as the third part of them was darkened, and **the day shone not for a third part of it, and the night likewise.** (Rev. 8:12)

I am not teaching this doctrinally because I am not sure of this. With the shortening of the night and the day by a third you end up with a day that is eight hours less. So a day would be sixteen hours long. It does say the days will be shortened. Whether this is what it is talking about or not, I am not sure.

There is no doubt that the heavens and the earth go through a great change at the end of the Tribulation and the beginning of the Millennium. During the Millennium the sun and the moon are seven times brighter than they are right now.

> [26]Moreover **the light of the moon shall be as the light of the sun, and the light of the sun shall be sevenfold,** as the light of seven days, in the day that the LORD bindeth up the breach of his people, and healeth the stroke of their wound. (Is. 30:26)

> [5]And ye shall flee *to* the valley of the mountains; for the valley of the mountains shall reach unto Azal: yea, ye shall flee, like as ye fled from before the earthquake in the days of Uzziah king of Judah: and the LORD my God shall come, *and* all the saints with thee.
> [6]And **it shall come to pass in that day,** *that* **the light shall not be clear,** *nor* **dark:**
> [7]**But it shall be one day which shall be known to the LORD, not day, nor night:** but it shall come to pass, *that* **at evening time it shall be light.** (Zech. 14:5-7)

Seven Years

At the second coming of the Lord Jesus Christ, all His saints come with Him. They are His born-again people. And at this time there is a change in the heavens and earth. The big change is the curse is removed from the natural world. The animals return to being vegetarians, yet man will still have his Adamic sinful nature.

Back to our text now. The days are going to be shortened. Absolutely what that is describing, I am not sure. One way or another the days are going to be shortened...for the elect's sake.

The Jews who are being slaughtered, as well as the Jews who are hiding out at Petra, it is for their sake that the days are shortened.

> ²³**Then** if any man shall say unto you, Lo, here
> *is* Christ, or there; believe *it* not. (Matt. 24:23)

Notice the word "then" in these verses in Matthew 24.
vs. 9 - Then shall they deliver you up...
vs. 10 - Then shall many be offended...
vs. 15 - **Middle of the Tribulation**
vs. 16 - Then let them which be in Judea flee...
vs. 21 - Then shall be great Tribulation...
vs. 30 Then shall appear the sign of the Son of man...

The chapter lays out in order events that will take place in the Tribulation. The abomination of desolation shows exactly when the middle of it all takes place.

> ²⁴For there shall arise **false Christs, and false prophets**, and shall shew great signs and wonders; insomuch that, if *it were*

160

possible, they shall deceive the very elect.
(Matt. 24:24)

^{9}*Even him*, whose coming is after the working
of Satan with all power and **signs and lying
wonders,**
^{10}And with all deceivableness of
unrighteousness in them that perish;
because they received not the love of the
truth, that they might be saved.
^{11}And for this cause God shall send them
strong delusion, that they should believe a
lie:
^{12}That they all might be damned who
believed not the truth, but had pleasure in
unrighteousness. (2 Thess. 2:9-12)

When the disciples first asked the Lord about these
things, in verse 4 He tells them first of all **"Take heed
that no man deceive you."** Now here in verse 24, the
Lord tells them of false Christs and false prophets who
are performing great signs and wonders. And yes, they
will be performing them in front of everyone's eyes. But
it is to deceive.

God will allow the Antichrist to have great power to
deceive and to perform "lying wonders." During the last
half of the Tribulation, it will be a time of great
deception and counterfeits of the real; there will be the
true prophets of the Lamb traveling around the world
and preaching the Gospel of the kingdom. There will
be 144,000 male virgin Jews who will have all of the

apostolic signs. They will be able to work wonders and will be going worldwide with the truth. Here are the signs that they will have.

> ^{17}And these **signs shall follow them that believe**; In my name shall they **cast out devils; they shall speak with new tongues;** ^{18}They shall **take up serpents; and if they drink any deadly thing, it shall not hurt them; they shall lay hands on the sick, and they shall recover.** (Mark 16:17-18)

The proliferation of fake signs and wonders is taking place right now in these last days before the Rapture. Now and then I will monitor some of the latest leaders in "Christianity," and it gets worse and worse. Visions and prophesying are supposedly being received from Heaven to guide and minister to the people of God. Don't believe it! It is all fake and false. The only thing you can trust is the King James 1611 Bible.

Every now and then someone will take up a poisonous snake in a church service, get bit, and die. They then blame the person for not having enough faith. Or someone will drink some bleach, or poisonous liquid, and end up dead. Then they will blame them for not having enough faith. Sad, so sad!

The Tampa Tribune of April 10, 1973 carried a news story about two preachers of a "Holiness" sect in Newport, Tennessee, who drank strychnine at a religious service "to test their faith." They died. *(Himmel Irvin, "And If They Drink Any Deadly Thing, It Shall Not Hurt Them", TRUTH*

MAGAZINE XVII: 44, pp. 2-3, September 13, 1973, Quoted from:
https://www.truthmagazine.com/archives/volume17/TM017691.ht
ml, Guardian of Truth Foundation, viewed 5/8/2024)

Feb. 17, 2014; The "snake handling" pastor of a small Pentecostal church in Kentucky died after being bitten by a rattlesnake during a weekend church service. *(ABC News, Snake-Handling Pentecostal Pastor Dies From Snake Bite, February 17, 2014&#151, abcnews.go.com/US/snake-handling-pentecostal-pastor-dies-snake-bite/story?id=22551754#:~:t ext=Pastor%20Jamie%20Coots%20died%20after,during%20a%20wee kend%20church%20service., viewed 5/10/2024)*

To not rightly divide the word of God can be deadly! The fake signs and wonders in the Tribulation are to spread confusion so people will not know what is right or wrong. The only way they will be able to know is if they get into the word of God and read it, believe it, and obey it. Very similar to today, except in the Tribulation it is much more deadly to not believe the word of God. It is very likely those who do not read and believe the word of God in the Tribulation will take the Mark of the Beast and end up in Hell.

In this Church Age, which is the Age of Grace, if a person is born again then they are kept by the power of God. They are eternally secure and going to Heaven when they die. If in their saved life time they get deceived or messed up spiritually, they are still going to Heaven. But that is not the case in the Tribulation. If someone is keeping the commandments of God and has the faith of Jesus Christ, but they fall away and take the Mark of the Beast, then they will go to Hell when they die.

If you are saved, you should stop and think about that. You and I have been greatly blessed to live in and be saved in this age of grace!

> [25]Behold, I have told you before.
> [26]Wherefore **if they shall say unto you, Behold, he is in the desert; go not forth: behold, *he is* in the secret chambers; believe *it* not.**
> [27]For as the lightning cometh out of the east, and shineth even unto the west; so shall also the coming of the Son of man be. (Matt. 24:25-27)

> [8]**And then shall that Wicked be revealed, whom the Lord shall consume with the spirit of his mouth, and shall destroy with the brightness of his coming:** (2 Thess. 2:8)

> [12]And this shall be the plague wherewith the LORD will smite all the people that have fought against Jerusalem; **Their flesh shall consume away while they stand upon their feet, and their eyes shall consume away in their holes, and their tongue shall consume away in their mouth.** (Zech. 14:12)

> [8]For *it is* **the day of the LORD'S vengeance,** *and* the year of recompences for the controversy of Zion.
> [9]¶ And the streams thereof shall be turned into pitch, and the dust thereof into

164

Matthew

brimstone, and the land thereof shall become
burning pitch. (Is. 34:8-9)

As I have said many times, I am glad that when the
Lord comes back with vengeance and wrath that I am
behind Him!!

If you are saved, then let me remind you that you are
on the winning side. You already have the victory in
Christ. Nations are going to fall, and the world is going
to fail and fall as well. But the saved of the Lord are
going to Heaven. We are getting new bodies. And we
are going to be married to our Lord Jesus Christ. What
you are reading is not depressing, nor should you be
discouraged by it all. What you are reading about is
our Lord Jesus Christ taking over the world. He will
bring in 1,000 years of righteous, world-wide rule, along
with 1,000 years of "peace on earth, good will to men."
Your attitude ought to be, "Amen, even so, come Lord
Jesus!"

> ²⁹Immediately after the tribulation of those
> days shall **the sun be darkened, and the
> moon shall not give her light, and the stars
> shall fall from heaven, and the powers of the
> heavens shall be shaken:** (Matt. 24:29)

In this portion of scripture, it is referring to the end
of the 70th week. Again, you will notice there seems to
be a change in the atmosphere, along with the sun,
moon and the stars.

As to the stars falling from Heaven, notice "**...and the
powers of the heavens shall be shaken...**" Stars in the

165

Bible are not only a reference to the lights in the night sky. They are also a reference, or can be a reference to angels.

> [20]The mystery of **the seven stars** which thou sawest in my right hand, and the seven golden candlesticks. **The seven stars are the angels** of the seven churches: and the seven candlesticks which thou sawest are the seven churches. (Rev. 1:20)

> [20]They fought from heaven; **the stars in their courses fought** against Sisera. (Judg. 5:20)

> [7]When **the morning stars sang together,** and all the sons of God shouted for joy? (Job 38:7)

> [13]Raging waves of the sea, foaming out their own shame; **wandering stars, to whom** is reserved the blackness of darkness for ever. (Jude 13)

Now if that sounds strange to you, it shouldn't. Haven't you heard of a place called Hollywood where there are stars? You know, the movie stars. When you wish upon a star, it makes no difference who you are. Why do they say that someone starred in a movie instead of someone who acted in a movie? Strange, isn't it?

> [30]And then shall appear **the sign of the Son**

> of man in heaven: and then shall all the
> tribes of the earth mourn, and **they shall see
> the Son of man coming** in the clouds of
> heaven with power and great glory.
> ³¹And **he shall send his angels** with a great
> sound of a trumpet, and **they shall gather
> together his elect** from the four winds, from
> one end of heaven to the other. (Matt. 24:30-31)

This is NOT, I repeat, THIS IS NOT A REFERENCE TO
THE RAPTURE OF THE BRIDE OF CHRIST!!! No matter
how many scholars, Bible commentators, pastors and
whoever else says it is, they are wrong!

The context here has nothing to do with the Church
age. The context has to do with the second coming of
Jesus Christ and according to Revelation 19, we are
coming back with Him.

In the above passage the angels gather His elect.
When the Lord comes for the Church (1 Thes. 4:16), the
Lord Himself will descend with a shout and with the
voice of the archangel. One angel, not many, and the
Lord Himself comes. (As one preacher so aptly stated,
"Things different are not the same!) Here in Matthew
24:31, it's plural angels and they gather His elect from
one end of Heaven to the other. They are not gathering
them from the earth. This is a Jewish gathering.

> ⁴For Jacob my servant's sake, and **Israel
> mine elect**, I have even called thee by thy
> name: I have surnamed thee, though thou
> hast not known me. (Is. 45:4)

Did you see it? **"And then shall appear..."** which takes place after Matt. 24:29. Immediately after the tribulation of those days. That defines when verse 31 takes place. It is after the Tribulation of those days which is not during the Church age at any time. It is after the Tribulation which follows the Church age. You must rightly divide the word of truth or you will end up in a mess.

I wonder how many people in the Tribulation will be told that they are eternally secure and can't lose their salvation? There are many now days in the Church age that claim you can lose your salvation. I believe there will be plenty in the Tribulation who will proclaim eternal security when there is none during the Tribulation.

Wouldn't it be something to have deceived religious people telling others that it will be alright if they take the mark. They would easily find plenty of scriptures to prove you can't lose your salvation. For example, they could preach, *"...the Bible says that nothing is going to separate you from the love of God which is in Christ Jesus our Lord. It says so right here in the Romans 8."*

Those who "trust' their beguiled leaders will have a false security and end up taking the Mark of the Beast, thus damning their souls.

To not rightly divide the word of God can be very deadly!

2 Thessalonians

The Thessalonians were more spiritual than most of the other people that Paul wrote to. They seem to be one of, if not the most mature group of Christians that Paul writes to. In light of this though, I find it interesting that there is quite a bit in these two Thessalonian epistles that have to do with the second coming of Jesus Christ.

In 1 Thessalonians 4, Paul mentions that, **"...I would not have you to be ignorant, brethren concerning them which are asleep..."** (1 Thess. 4:13) And then he explains what is going to happen at the Rapture. But in chapter five, he goes into information about the second coming of Christ. He reminds them that they are children of light and children of the day; then he contrasts that by telling them they are not children of the night or darkness.

The coming of the Lord that he references in chapter

five is the second coming of the Lord to this earth. He then reminds them that God hath not appointed us to wrath, but to obtain salvation by our Lord Jesus Christ. The wrath in the passage is a reference to the wrath of God at the second advent; the salvation is the fact that born-again Christians will not go through that wrath for God has not appointed us to that. It seems the Thessalonians had trouble with believing they will not miss the Rapture.

Sometime between 1 Thessalonians and 2 Thessalonians, these Thessalonians received some letters and some "news" as if it had come from Paul. The subject of the news was that they had missed the Rapture. Someone was not rightly dividing the word of truth, and they were so convinced, as well as convincing, that it was affecting the Thessalonians in a bad way. There is also something like it in 2 Timothy:

> [15]Study to shew thyself approved unto God, a workman that needeth not to be ashamed, **rightly dividing the word of truth.**
>
> [16]But shun profane *and* vain babblings: for they will increase unto more ungodliness.
>
> [17]And their word will eat as doth a canker: of whom is Hymenaeus and Philetus;
>
> [18]Who concerning the truth have erred, **saying that the resurrection is past already;** and overthrow the faith of some. (2 Tim. 2:15-18)

The Rapture is part of the first resurrection. The resurrection can be likened to a harvest so you have first fruits:

170

⁵⁰¶ Jesus, when he had cried again with a loud voice, yielded up the ghost.

⁵¹And, behold, the veil of the temple was rent in twain from the top to the bottom; and the earth did quake, and the rocks rent;

⁵²And the graves were opened; and **many bodies of the saints which slept arose,**

⁵³**And came out of the graves after his resurrection,** and went into the holy city, and appeared unto many. (Matt. 27:50-53)

After the first fruits, then next you have the main harvest, which is the Rapture of the Church age saints. The Rapture is the next resurrecting of dead people after the first fruits.

After the harvest comes the next resurrecting of saints. Agriculterally this is known as the gleanings. Biblically this consists of the Tribulation saints.

⁴And I saw thrones, and they sat upon them, and judgment was given unto them: and *I saw* the souls of them that **were beheaded for the witness of Jesus, and for the word of God, and which had not worshipped the beast, neither his image, neither had received** *his* **mark upon their foreheads, or in their hands;** and they lived and reigned with Christ a thousand years.

⁵But the rest of the dead lived not again until the thousand years were finished. This *is* the first resurrection. (Rev. 20:4-5)

The first resurrecting of dead people, which is known as the first resurrection, is made up of three different resurrections. If you have part in one of the three, then you are "good to go." If you do not have part in one of the three, then you will die the second death, which is eternal death in the lake of fire.

To claim that the resurrection is past is to be a-millennial. In other words you believe that there is no Millennium. There is just one grand judgment at the end of time. There are many such religions that believe this very thing. But Paul commands us to shun profane and vain babblings.

These Thessalonians were troubled by such unbiblical teachings when they were deceived into thinking that Paul was teaching this. It shook their faith to the point that they thought they had missed the Rapture and were going to be under the wrath of God. I must admit that if I got deceived into thinking that I was going through the Tribulation and end up under the wrath of God, that would shake me up and trouble me quite a bit.

That is the very thing that more and more Christians are believing. More and more are believing that they are going to go through the Tribulation or at least half way through the Tribulation with a mid-Tribulation Rapture. Both of these positions are unscriptural and troubling if truly believed.

This is why so many people are building secret places and storing preserved foods. They think that they are going into the Tribulation. So they are prepping for it. But they don't realize something. If they are lost and go into the Tribulation, once it is found out that they have food, the hungry will simply torture them until they tell them where it is.

Something along the lines of either a mid-Tribulation Rapture, or going all the way through the Tribulation, is what the Thessalonians had been deceived into believing. So Paul deals with it directly in this second chapter of his epistles to the Thessalonians. This will be very applicable for many in this age in which we now find ourselves living.

> ¶ Now we beseech you, brethren, by the coming of our Lord Jesus Christ, and *by* our gathering together unto him,
> **²That ye be not soon shaken in mind, or be troubled, neither by spirit, nor by word, nor by letter as from us, as that the Day of Christ is at hand.**
> ³¶ **Let no man deceive you by any means:** for *that day shall not come*, except there come a falling away first, and that man of sin be revealed, the son of perdition;
> ⁴Who opposeth and exalteth himself above all that is called God, or that is worshipped; so that he as God sitteth in the temple of God, shewing himself that he is God.
> (2 Thess. 2:1-4)

You may remember the story in the gospels that took place just after the Lord, Peter, and John came down from the mount after the Lord was transfigured. When they arrived at the bottom of the mount, a man comes to him in earnest in order to have the Lord heal his son who has a devil. Often it had thrown the boy into the fire and into the water to kill him. The father of the boy cries out:

> [38]...Master, I beseech thee, **look upon my son: for he is mine only child.** (Luke 9:38)

This father is imploring the Lord to help him when Jesus responds:

> [23]Jesus said unto him, **If thou canst believe, all things _are_ possible to him that believeth.** [24]And straightway the father of the child cried out, and said with tears, **Lord, I believe; help thou mine unbelief.** (Mark 9:23-24)

Such a great response! But it illustrates by way of example of what it means to beseech someone.

Paul starts off with, and includes Silvanus and Timothy in his writing, when he says, **"...we beseech you."** He is telling them to please, please listen to what I am going to write to you. He is trying to get their attention so they will truly hear what he is writing to them. It is like they are so troubled that they are distracted from the truth and sound doctrine.

I am told that one of the ways a wolf will get to a sheep is that it will follow the flock from within the distant tree line. The sheep know the wolf is there, and the shepherd knows it is there as well. The shepherd knows the flock is safe, though he is ever vigilant.

The wolf, however, will seek to spook the sheep. It will try to get them scared, and when a sheep is scared, they can bolt without even thinking. They will dart away from the safety of the flock and the shepherd. Once away the wolf catches and kills the sheep.

Paul is seeking to get these Thessalonians' attention so that they will listen to what he is saying.

He already covered this subject in 1 Thessalonians, and is now having to go over it again. In the last part of 1 Thessalonians, he covers the Rapture. Then in chapter five, he covers the second advent. In 2 Thessalonians chapter one he covers the second advent again, and here in chapter two he is going into great details concerning the Tribulation and the second advent.

It's as if he is telling them, *"I already went over this once with you. Would you please listen to what I am saying?"*

Along with his beseeching them is his comforting mention of the coming of the Lord and our gathering together unto Him. This is a direct reference to the Rapture.

You will notice though, that the phrase "coming of the Lord" can apply to two different events. It can refer to the Rapture:

> [15]For this we say unto you by the word of the Lord, that we which are alive *and* remain unto **the coming of the Lord** shall not prevent them which are asleep.
> (1 Thess. 4:15)

And it can also refer to the second coming of Jesus Christ back to this earth:

> ⁷Be patient therefore, brethren, unto the **coming of the Lord.** Behold, the husbandman waiteth for the precious fruit of the earth, and hath long patience for it, until he receive **the early and latter rain.**
> ⁸Be ye also patient; stablish your hearts: for **the coming of the Lord draweth nigh.** (James 5:7-8)

These references here in James are referring to the second advent, when our Lord comes back to this earth after the Tribulation, and we come back with Him. If there is any doubt about this, notice the following verse:

> ¹⁷**Elias** was a man subject to like passions as we are, and he **prayed earnestly that it might not rain:** and it rained not on the earth by the space of **three years and six months.** (James 5:17)

This is a direct Tribulation reference to the prophet Elijah, (Elias is the Greek equivalent.) as well as the reference to no rain which matches Revelation 11.

Here in 2 Thessalonians 2 though it is a reference to the Rapture. Paul knows that the Thessalonians are troubled and shaken in mind. So thus as he wrote in 1 Thessalonians, the truth of the Rapture is to be a comfort to one another. (1 Thess. 4:18) Being that it seems they were troubled with the belief that they had missed the Rapture, this would get their attention no doubt. But what was troubling to them was the thought that the Day of Christ was at hand.

> ²**That ye be not soon shaken in mind**, or be **troubled**, neither by spirit, nor by word, nor by letter as from us, as **that the Day of Christ is at hand.** (2 Thess. 2:2)

Some men have written and preached that the Day of Christ is a reference to the Rapture, but if this is so then why would the Thessalonians be troubled that the Rapture was at hand? As I have already mentioned, the Rapture is to be a comfort, and what's more it is our blessed hope that we are to be looking for.

We are not to be looking for the Antichrist, nor are we to be looking for the dead in Christ up walking around for 40 days and nights before the Rapture. (If you have never heard that, then count your blessings!)

> ¹⁷Then we which are alive *and* remain shall be caught up together with them in the clouds, to meet the Lord in the air: and so shall we ever be with the Lord.
> ¹⁸**Wherefore comfort one another with these words.** (1 Thess. 4:17-18)

> ¹¹¶ For the grace of God that bringeth salvation hath appeared to all men,
> ¹²Teaching us that, denying ungodliness and worldly lusts, we should live soberly, righteously, and godly, in this present world;

177

¹³Looking for that blessed hope, and the glorious appearing of the great God and our Saviour Jesus Christ; (Titus 2:11-13)

We are to be looking for our bessed hope. We are not to be afraid of it. Thus the Day of Christ that is being referred to in the text is not a reference to the Rapture.

What the Day of Christ is a reference to is an amazing study that we will get into now.

The Day of Christ actually has three events associated with it. The first event is the Judgment Seat of Christ. When it is finished the second event begins which is the beginning of the second advent of Jesus Christ, and His Heavenly armies of which the body of Christ is one, returning to the earth to take over with Jesus Christ reigning for 1,000 years.

The third event is the Judgment of nations, which takes place on the earth after Jesus Christ returns.

If the thought of three events that make up the Day of Christ seems odd, consider the following example of such.

The first resurrection has three events associated with it. The first fruits in Matthew 27:

⁵²And the graves were opened; and many bodies of the saints which slept arose... (Matt. 27:52)

The first fruits would include all of the Old Testament saints. How do I know this? Because in the Old Testament, the saints went to Paradise until the perfect sacrifice was made by Jesus Christ upon Calvary. But

Paradise is now said to be in Heaven.

> ¹¶ It is not expedient for me doubtless to glory. I will come to visions and revelations of the Lord.
>
> ²I knew a man in Christ above fourteen years ago, (whether in the body, I cannot tell; or whether out of the body, I cannot tell: God knoweth;) such an one caught **up to the third heaven.**
>
> ³And I knew such a man, (whether in the body, or out of the body, I cannot tell: God knoweth;)
>
> ⁴How that he was **caught up into paradise,** and heard unspeakable words, which it is not lawful for a man to utter. (2 Cor. 12:1-4)

So the Old Testament saints are in Heaven now waiting to come back with Jesus Christ and His Bride, the Church, at the Second Advent. This is why the Scriptures mention the "armies" in Heaven. The Old Testament saints make up one army, and the Church makes up another army.

We, the Church, gather together unto Jesus Christ (2 Thess. 2:1) after the Judgment seat of Christ, along with the saints from the Old Testament. Along with this gathering is the gathering of His elect:

> ³¹And he shall send his angels with a great sound of a trumpet, and **they shall gather together his elect** from the four winds, from one end of heaven to the other. (Matt. 24:31)

179

> [14]And the armies *which were* in heaven
> followed him upon white horses, clothed in
> fine linen, white and clean. (Rev. 19:14)

The second event of the first resurrection is the harvest, which is the Rapture of the born-again saints.

> [35]Say not ye, There are yet four months, and
> *then* cometh harvest? behold, I say unto you,
> Lift up your eyes, and look on the fields; **for
> they are white already to harvest.** (John 4:35)

> [30]Let both grow together until the harvest:
> and in the time of harvest I will say to the
> reapers, Gather ye together first the tares,
> and bind them in bundles to burn them: but
> **gather the wheat into my barn.** (Matt. 13:30)

The saved are likened unto wheat. In the old times the wheat was taken by pitchfork and thrown up into the loft of the barn. Even in this age the wheat is lifted up into the silo. That lifting of the wheat is a type of a Rapture.

The harvest is always when the most fruit is "harvested." Today is the day of salvation. These last 2,000 years have been a harvest of souls. Isn't it good to be in on it?

As I have already briefly mentioned, the third event that takes place in the first resurrection is the gleanings: those souls that are saved during the Tribulation, of whom there will be many.

> ⁴And I saw thrones, and they sat upon them, and judgment was given unto them: and *I saw* the souls of them that were **beheaded for the witness of Jesus, and for the word of God, and which had not worshipped the beast, neither his image, neither had received *his* mark upon their foreheads, or in their hands**; and they lived and reigned with Christ a thousand years.
>
> ⁵But the rest of the dead lived not again until the thousand years were finished. **This *is* the first resurrection.** (Rev. 20:4-5)

There are three deaths in the Bible. The age of accountability in Romans 7:9, then there is physical death, and then spiritual death i.e. the second death.

Did you know that the coming of the Lord has three parts? Jesus came at His birth. Then there is the Rapture (1 Thess. 4:15), and after that there is the day of the Lord when Jesus returns and puts His feet upon the earth.

Thus three events make up the Day of Christ. As to the first event of the Day of Christ, which is the Judgment Seat of Christ, you will notice that it is a sobering time and event:

> ¹⁰For we must all appear before the judgment seat of Christ; that every one may receive the things *done* in *his* body, according to that he hath done, whether *it be* good or bad.
>
> ¹¹**Knowing therefore the terror of the Lord, we persuade men**; but we are made manifest

181

unto God; and I trust also are made manifest
in your consciences. (2 Cor. 5:10-11)

The Judgment Seat of Christ ought to be a sobering
truth for the saints. There is terror associated with it,
but let me run a small rabbit trail here. First of all,
keep your sins confessed. If you will judge your sins
now and confess them to Jesus Christ, you will not
meet them later at the Judgment Seat of Christ.

³¹For **if we would judge ourselves, we should
not be judged.** (1 Cor. 11:31)

Also look at the following:

²¹And you, that were sometime alienated and
enemies in *your* mind by wicked works, yet
now hath he reconciled
²²In the body of his flesh through death, **to
present you holy and unblameable and
unreproveable in his sight:**
²³**If ye continue in the faith grounded and
settled, and *be* not moved away from the
hope of the gospel**, which ye have heard, *and*
which was preached to every creature which
is under heaven; whereof I Paul am made a
minister; (Col. 1:21-23)

If you will keep your sins confessed, continue in the
faith grounded and settled, and keep your blessed hope,
then you can appear before your Saviour holy,

182

unblameable and unreproveable in His sight. It can be done. Don't quit! Stay grounded in your doctrine! Keep looking for your blessed hope and the glorious appearing of Jesus Christ! You need not fear going to Heaven, and you ought not fear going to Heaven! Lately I have met some saints who are afraid of going to Heaven, and that is not right.

Now, as to the Day of Christ, all of the references in the word of God concerning **"the Day of Christ"** are found in the Pauline epistles. Therefore it is a real likelihood that the Day of Christ does concern the body of Christ. There are only four verses that mention the Day of Christ.

> [6]Being confident of this very thing, that he which hath begun a good work in you will perform *it* until **the day of Jesus Christ:** (Phil. 1:6)

While not exactly the "Day of Christ," it is close enough to pass. Your Lord Jesus Christ began a good work in you the moment you were born again. And He is going to continue that good work until the day of Jesus Christ. Does that work end at the Rapture? No! We have our new bodies at the Rapture, but there are still some things that need to be taken care of before the work in you ceases.

In a way it is like finals in school. You may have finished the course, but you must take the final exam. The teaching is over, but the teacher is not finished for they must hand out the grades. Maybe the modern method of taking and scoring a final test doesn't involve the teacher, but most of the time it does.

Not only that, but there is going to be a time, either before the Judgment Seat of Christ, or during the Judgment Seat of Christ, when the saints get reconciled with one another. The wrongs that have been inflicted upon each other must be dealt with. To let them pass with no accountability is not like the Lord. So during the seven years we are up in Heaven, there is going to be a time for the saints to apologize to one another and be properly reconciled.

> ¹⁵¶ Moreover if thy brother shall trespass against thee, go and tell him his fault between thee and him alone: if he shall hear thee, thou hast gained thy brother.
> ¹⁶But if he will not hear *thee, then* take with thee one or two more, that in the mouth of two or three witnesses every word may be established.
> ¹⁷And if he shall neglect to hear them, tell *it* unto the Church: but if he neglect to hear the Church, let him be unto thee as an heathen man and a publican.
> ¹⁸Verily I say unto you, **Whatsoever ye shall bind on earth shall be bound in heaven: and whatsoever ye shall loose on earth shall be loosed in heaven.** (Matt. 18:15-18)

The context here is wrongs between the brethren, and the binding of those wrongs in Heaven if they are not taken care of on earth. This in no way contradicts any of Paul's epistles to the body of Christ. "Brother" is mentioned in the passage which can easily refer to a brother in the Lord.

If there is a time for the reconciling of the saints, there is no doubt that Jesus Christ will be overseeing it all. But this may take place at the Judgement Seat of Christ, and there will not be a separate time for the reconciliation to take place. Either way the element that will make this time a joy and blessing is the fact that we will no longer have our old sinful man. Pride will be gone, and it will be a time where we will voluntarily seek those with whom we need to apologize to. All sinful emotions— pride, jealousy, envy and such— will be absent. Nevertheless, it will be a time that must take place.

After the Judgment Seat of Christ, you will be personally perfected. You will have your new perfect sinless body which you received at the Rapture, and you will have everything right between you and Jesus Christ. There is still the matter of the Millennial reign, and if you want to study that I would suggest my book titled, *The Sons of Zadok, What Will You Do for One Thousand Years?* The work that Jesus Christ started "in" you will be finished at the Judgment Seat of Christ, also known as the Day of Christ.

> ^{10}That ye may approve things that are excellent; that ye may be sincere and without offence till **the Day of Christ**; (Phil. 1:10)

> ^{16}Holding forth the word of life; that I may rejoice in **the Day of Christ**, that I have not run in vain, neither laboured in vain. (Phil. 2:16)

Again, both of these references can refer to the Judgement Seat of Christ. Both of these verses have elements of results that could be present in a judgment: that being offence and laboring in vain. Neither of these are subject matters that will we will be readily concerned with at the moment we meet our Lord and Saviour in the air. And lest you should still be quite dubious about the application of these verses to the Judgment Seat of Christ, let's look and see what the word of God says about the Judgment Seat of Christ.

> [11]¶ For other foundation can no man lay than that is laid, which is Jesus Christ.
> [12]Now if any man build upon this foundation gold, silver, precious stones, wood, hay, stubble;
> [13]Every man's work shall be made manifest: for **the day shall declare it**, because it shall be revealed by fire; and the fire shall try every man's **work of what sort it is.**
> [14]If any man's **work abide** which he hath built thereupon, he shall receive a reward.
> [15]If any man's **work shall be burned**, he shall suffer loss: but **he himself shall be saved**; yet so as by fire. (1 Cor. 3:11-15)

This is a major portion of Scripture that concerns the Judgment Seat of Christ. Look at verse 13, for it is said to be a day. **"The day shall declare it..."** Therefore it is safe to claim that the Judgment Seat of Christ is also referred to as the Day of Christ. And on that day, there is going to be a declaration made of what sort of work you wrought during your saved life upon the earth.

Now, let's see if it will work in 2 Thessalonians 2:2.

> ¹¶ Now we beseech you, brethren, by the coming of our Lord Jesus Christ, and *by* our gathering together unto him,
> ²That ye be not soon shaken in mind, or be troubled, neither by spirit, nor by word, nor by letter as from us, as that **the Day of Christ** is at hand.
> ³¶ Let no man deceive you by any means: for *that day shall not come*, **except there come a falling away first, and that man of sin be revealed, the son of perdition;**
> ⁴Who opposeth and exalteth himself above all that is called God, or that is worshipped; so that he as God **sitteth in the temple of God, shewing himself that he is God.**
> (2 Thess. 2:1-4)

There is no problem with the first verse being the Rapture as Paul is seeking to comfort them. If they have been deceived into thinking that they had missed the Rapture, then Paul is letting them know that they haven't missed it.

Verse two is where things change from what we have already gone over. There is no doubt that all other references to the Day of Christ have referred to the Judgment Seat of Christ. But when you try to apply it here it doesn't work.

187

If the Day of Christ only refers to the Judgment Seat of Christ, then it would be impossible for these Thessalonians to appear at it if they have missed the Rapture, which they hadn't. They would be on earth, while the Judgment Seat of Christ was taking place in Heaven, so that interpretation will not work here.

Not only that, but if they have been deceived into thinking they had missed the Rapture, and if the Day of Christ only refers to the Judgment Seat of Christ, then it would be impossible for the Day of Christ to be at hand. It would not be imminent, and they would not be troubled, or they would not need to be troubled. Perhaps if they were deceived and had things mixed up in their minds, then they might be troubled. Either way though, here in 2 Thessalonians for the Day of Christ to be the Judgment Seat of Christ just does not fit. So the Day of Christ here must refer to another time or event.

Just as the coming of the Lord can either refer to the Rapture or the Second Advent, so too there must be at least two applications, or definitions, for the Day of Christ.

Verse three is the key to understanding the application of the Day of Christ here in 2 Thessalonians. In verse three you plainly have events that take place in the middle of the Tribulation, which we will cover here shortly. But that being so, and then you have the statement **"that day,"** which is obviously a reference to the Day of Christ. Now notice the verse:

> ³¶ Let no man deceive you by any means: for *that day shall not come*, except there come a

falling away first, and **that man of sin be revealed, the son of perdition;**...
(2 Thess. 2:3)

The Day of Christ comes AFTER the Man of Sin is revealed. There is no doubt about when that takes place, for it takes place smack dab right in the middle of the seven-year Tribulation. For the first half of the Tribulation, the Man of Sin is leading the world by confirming the covenant with the Jews, but it is not revealed to the world who he truly is. In the middle of the Tribulation it is revealed when he walks into the Temple of God and proclaims that he is God. This is when the abomination of desolation takes place with him setting up the image of the Beast in the temple. The middle of the Tribulation is very plain to see and understand.

So the Day of Christ will not come before this event. Considering that it is "the Day of Christ," then there is only one possibility left which is the Second Advent of Jesus Christ. This would explain why the Thessalonians were troubled. If they believed that they had missed the Rapture and were headed for the wrath of God at the Second Advent then, yes, that would be very troubling.

Many books and explanations have been given over the years. They have taught that the **"falling away"** is a reference to the last days of the Church Age, that there is going to be a falling away in the Church. But this teaching has some major problems.

First of all is the fact that the Church cannot fall away. It is impossible for the Church, which includes all born-again people in it, to fall away. Why? Because:

³⁵Who shall separate us from the love of Christ? *shall* tribulation, or distress, or persecution, or famine, or nakedness, or peril, or sword?

³⁶As it is written, For thy sake we are killed all the day long; we are accounted as sheep for the slaughter.

³⁷Nay, in all these things we are more than conquerors through him that loved us.

³⁸For I am persuaded, that neither death, nor life, nor angels, nor principalities, nor powers, nor things present, nor things to come,

³⁹Nor height, nor depth, **nor any other creature, shall be able to separate us from the love of God, which is in Christ Jesus our Lord.** (Rom. 8:35-39)

⁴To an inheritance incorruptible, and undefiled, and that fadeth not away, reserved in heaven for you,

⁵**Who are kept by the power of God** through faith unto salvation ready to be revealed in the last time. (1 Pet. 1:4-5)

Christians are safe in Jesus Christ. For there is nothing that is going to separate them from the love of God which is in Christ Jesus, as well as the fact that they are kept by the power of God. It is impossible for the Church, which is made up of all born again people, to fall away.

Another reason the Church can not fall away is because when a person is born again, they are baptized into the body of Christ. This baptism is a literal baptism and is not to be taken figuratively at all. Notice what the word of God says:

> [13]For by one **Spirit are we all baptized into one body**, whether *we be* Jews or Gentiles, whether *we be* bond or free; and have been all made to drink into one Spirit.
> (1 Cor. 12:13)

> [30]**For we are members of his body, of his flesh, and of his bones.**
> [31]For this cause shall a man leave his father and mother, and shall be joined unto his wife, and they two shall be one flesh.
> [32]This is a great mystery: but **I speak concerning Christ and the church.**
> (Eph. 5:30-32)

Before you were born again, you were in Adam. But when you were born again, you were baptized into Jesus Christ. You were baptized into Jesus Christ by the Spirit of God, and there is no water anywhere around that verse. Water had nothing to do with it, other than your physical birth according to John 3.

To show this even more, notice that when you were baptized into one body you were also made to drink into one Spirit. The moment you were saved you drank of the Spirit of God. It was not when you joined a church, and it was not when you were immersed in water to be baptized. You drank of the Spirit of God the moment you were saved.

At that moment you were immersed into the body of Jesus Christ by the Holy Spirit, and the Holy Spirit entered your body. So now "**...ye are the body of Christ, and members in particular.**" (1 Cor. 12:27) And when it says body of Christ, it means the body of Christ.

Perhaps you say, _"But I don't understand that. How can that be?"_

You have to remember that it said, **"This is a great mystery."** There is an element to it that you will not understand, so what you have to do is believe the word of God for what it says.

Baptist Briders seek to take the spiritual away and thus make it understandable, and they end up in a mess. It is a spiritual truth that we will not fully understand until we reach Heaven. (For a detailed study on Baptist Briderism see my book _Here Comes the Bride_, Every Word Publishing. It is available online or can be ordered from stores.)

There are many such truths that I know are real and true, but I do not understand them. For instance: the virgin birth. I do not understand how that can be, but I believe it and I know it is true. I believe in the Trinity, but I do not understand it.

So the born-again people make up the Church, which is His body. You are said to be bone of His bone and flesh of His flesh. It is impossible for you to fall away, and thus it is impossible for the Church to fall away.

Therefore the "falling away" mentioned in verse 3 is not a reference to anyone any time in the Church Age.

The Church in these last days of the Church Age is lukewarm, which is the word for neutral. It is not hot nor cold. The Church as a whole can be said to be

192

apostate. But it is still the Church and the bride of Jesus Christ. The believers, no matter how apostate or lukewarm they are, are still spiritually one with Jesus Christ. There is no way that they cannot ever be one with Jesus Christ after they are born again. The standing of the believer in Christ never changes, regardless of how ungodly their physical daily life is. So falling away is not a reference to the Church.

So the falling away is a reference to the people in the Tribulation who fall away to the Man of Sin and worship him as God, especially if they are Jews. And there will be plenty of Jews who will fall away to the Man of Sin, also known as the Beast. With the first part of the verse giving the warning to not be deceived, that is a really good clue that we are dealing with a Tribulation passage.

Just a reminder, 1 Thessalonians 5 dealt with the Tribulation and the Second Coming. 2 Thessalonians 1 deals with the Second Advent as well. The next part of the verse is very plain:

> [3b]...and **that man of sin be revealed, the son of perdition**... (2 Thess. 2:3b)

There is absolutely no doubt that this is a Tribulation reference to the event that takes place smack dab in the middle of the Tribulation. The revealing of the Man of Sin takes place right after Moses and Elijah get killed by him. It is a reference to the halfway point, 42 months into the seven-year Tribulation.

Now notice that verse 3 says, "**...falling away, and...**" The falling away is tied to the event of the Man of Sin being revealed. It has nothing to do with anyone in the Church Age, and has everything to do with the middle of the Tribulation. There is no doubt that in the middle of the Tribulation, the world turns to the Beast and worships him as God. Yes, there are some who will not do this, but the vast majority of the world will accept Satan manifest in the flesh as their true God. And it is likely he comes in the name of Judas.

> [43]I am come in my Father's name, and ye receive me not: if another shall come **in his own name,** him ye will receive. (John 5:43)

The reason I mention Judas coming in his own name is because Judas is referred to as the Son of Perdition by Jesus Christ in the Gospel of John.

> [12]While I was with them in the world, I kept them in thy name: those that thou gavest me I have kept, and none of them is lost, but **the son of perdition;** that the scripture might be fulfilled. (John 17:12)

There is no doubt about whom the Lord is referring to here. It is Judas Iscariot. This gets into the satanic trinity and the rise of the Beast out of the bottomless pit in Revelation 11:7. It is at this point in the Tribulation that the falling away is fulfilled. As the Beast comes up out of the pit and kills Moses and Elijah the world rejoices and accepts the Beast as God. Amongst the deceived worldwide are many Jews who fall away to the Beast.

2 Thessalonians 2:3 is a Tribulation verse. The fear of God and worship of the one true God that there was before the revealing of the Man of Sin, that fear and worship vanishes worldwide. The world "falls" for the Beast.

And it becomes even clearer when you read verse four that it is talking about the Tribulation and events that will be taking place then.

Paul admonishes them, to cause them to settle down and be established in the faith. He is effectively telling them: if the Day of Christ is at hand, these things would have to take place before the Day of Christ; since you are not seeing these things happen, you have nothing to worry about.

It seems like the Thessalonians were concerned or troubled that they were going to go through the Tribulation. In 1 Thessalonians 5, Paul told them that God hath not appointed us to wrath, but to obtain salvation by our Lord Jesus Christ. The salvation there is not saved from going to Hell when you die, but saved from going into the Tribulation and being under the wrath of God. Here in chapter 2 he has a similar admonition for them as well.

This application of the Day of Christ being the Second Advent will not change the falling away at all. The falling away takes place in the Tribulation and not in the Church Age.

So what Paul tells them is because you have not seen the falling away, and the Man of Sin has not been revealed, then you are troubled about nothing. And then he gives them a gentle rebuke and a reminder.

Seven Years

> ⁵Remember ye not, that, when I was yet with you, **I told you these things?** (2 Thess. 2:5)

And then Paul gives them a review of what he had already taught them and reminds them of it all.

> ⁶And now **ye know** what withholdeth that he might be revealed in his time.
> ⁷For **the mystery of iniquity doth already work**: only he who now letteth *will let*, until he be taken out of the way. (2 Thess. 2:6-7)

The mystery of iniquity is one of the seven mysteries given to the apostle of the Gentiles, the apostle Paul. These are truths that were not revealed in the Old Testament. And isn't it strange that some of the most detailed information in the word of God about the Man of Sin and the Tribulation is given to the Church? The information in this passage does not affect nor is it related to the Church Age, yet God gives this revelation to Paul and has it written to the body of Christ. Yet the Thessalonians, who were more mature than say, the Corinthians, if they were afraid that they had missed the Rapture, or that they were going through the Tribulation then that would explain why the Lord is having Paul write this to the body of Christ. It is to reaffirm to Christians that we are not going into nor through any part of the tribulation.

In these last moments before the Rapture of the Church, it is amazing to watch and see how common it is for born-again saints to believe that they are going into the Tribulation. Most of them are Christians who

196

do not know where the inerrant words of God are. Yet more and more Bible-believing Christians who do know where the inerrant words of God are have succumbed to this delusion too. This being the case, then what is written here is of great importance for the day and age in which we now live.

I have heard where "**he who now letteth**" is a reference to Gabriel or Michael. Then there is the old standard fundamental Baptist teaching that "**he who now letteth**" is a reference to the Holy Spirit, and once the Church is removed from the earth then there will be no longer any restraint against the Devil to work. But both of these teachings ignore the antecedent of "he." The antecedent of he is the Son of Perdition, the Man of Sin.

> [8]And then shall **that Wicked** be revealed, **whom** the Lord shall consume with the spirit of his mouth, and shall destroy with the brightness of his coming: (2 Thess. 2:8)

He is referred to here as "that Wicked." There is no doubt then that it is a reference to the god of this world which is also the satanic trinity. Satan is holding things back until the right time for him to reveal himself, which he does in the middle of the Tribulation.

In this age that we now live in, satanic activities are usually done in the dark. Men love darkness rather than light because their deeds are evil. Witches meet at night in the dark and secret places. The satanic councils that run the world under the direction of Satan meet in secretive dark places. The avowed followers of Satan meet and do their works in the dark.

197

Judges, movie stars, rock and roll singers, politicians, military commanders as well as the billionaires meet and follow Satan in secret. (No, I do not believe all such people are satanic.) But those who are following Satan do so in secret in this age. But in the midst of the Tribulation, all cover is removed and the world openly pledges their allegiance to the Beast, and the Dragon in Revelation 13. That is when the Man of Sin is revealed, and that is when the mystery of iniquity is taken out of the way.

> [9]*Even him,* whose coming is **after the working of Satan** with all power and signs and **lying wonders,**
> [10]And with **all deceivableness** of unrighteousness in them that perish; because they received not the love of the truth, that they might be saved.
> (2 Thess. 2:9-10)

Paul is reminding these Thessalonians of what is going to happen before the Day of Christ, if the Day of Christ is a reference to the Second Advent. If the Thessalonians believed that they had missed the Rapture or that they were going to go through the Tribulation, then I can understand why they would be troubled. But Paul is reminding them of what is going to happen before that day, and because they are not seeing these things, then the Day of Christ is not at hand. Thus they have not missed the Rapture, and they are not going to miss the Rapture.

Now notice the one whose coming is after the working

of Satan. Satan is the one who is working it out for this man to come on the scene. He has been leading the world for three and a half years but he is not revealed during that time. The Man of Sin is revealed in the midst of the Tribulation. It is at this time that the Beast comes out of the bottomless pit and goes into the Man of Sin, just as Satan entered the Son of Perdition, Judas Iscariot.

> ²⁵He then lying on Jesus' breast saith unto him, **Lord, who is it?**
> ²⁶Jesus answered, He it is, to whom I shall give a sop, when I have dipped *it.* And when he had dipped the sop, he gave *it* to Judas Iscariot, *the son* of Simon.
> ²⁷And **after the sop Satan entered into him.** Then said Jesus unto him, That thou doest, do quickly. (John 13:25-27)

This man is said to have "all power." That is not the same as what our Lord Jesus Christ has. Jesus Christ has all power in Heaven and earth. The Man of Sin does not have that much power. But he does have enough power to kill Moses and Elijah, whom many had tried to kill and ended up dead attempting to do it. But the Man of Sin is given the power and succeeds in killing the two witnesses. This causes the world to proclaim, "Who is like the beast? Who can make war with him?" This is when the world accepts him as their He is able to give miraculous signs.

> ²⁴For there shall arise **false Christs, and**

> false prophets, and shall shew great signs
> and wonders; insomuch that, if *it were*
> possible, they shall deceive the very elect.
> (Matt. 24:24)

While many false Christs and prophets come at this time so that there is tremendous deception that takes place, yet the Man of Sin exceeds them all in the signs that he brings. At this time life is given to an image of the Beast. No one up to this point had done something like that.

This Man of Sin is able and has all power to bring forth lying wonders. These are real wonders, but they are a lie? Yes! They are miraculous displays of power, but they point to Satan and the satanic trinity as the one to worship and follow. It is a time of great deception.

> [10]And with all deceivableness of
> unrighteousness in them that perish;
> because they received not the love of the
> truth, that they might be saved.
> [11]And for this cause God shall send them
> strong delusion, that they should believe a lie:
> [12]That they all might be damned who
> believed not the truth, but had pleasure in
> unrighteousness. (2 Thess. 2:10-12)

Do you get the sense that God is fed up with man and his idolatry? He is fed up with man's love of self, instead of loving His Creator who died on the Cross and paid for all of his sins! Yes, by the time the Tribulation arrives --and especially by the middle of the Tribulation when 95% of the world population deserts all acknowledgment of the true God and readily submits to the Dragon and the Beast by taking the mark --God is fed up with man. This is the time of His indignation.

In a sense He says to mankind, the same way parents who get fed up with their children say, "Fine, you want it, go ahead. I have warned you but you won't listen, so go ahead and kill yourself for all I care!" And so the teenager gets on the motorcycle and has a bad accident, or does whatever their loving parents have told them no to.

God gets to the end of His patience. He sends a strong delusion to the world. God sends it! Did you get that? And the reason He sends it is so that they will believe a lie in order to damn their souls to Hell. They didn't love the truth so God is going to give them a lie.

Now I know some of you will have a very hard time with the thought of God wanting to damn souls to Hell, but that is what the word of God says right here. Some of you have heard all your life that God is a loving God, and He is. You've heard that God wants everybody to be saved, and He does; that God loved you so much He died on the Cross and paid for your sins, and He did. But so many have heard that for so long that you think God would never deceive anyone in order to damn their souls so they end up in Hell, but that is what the word of God says.

During the time of the Tribulation, is there any hope for anyone to be saved? Who could possibly survive the deception that is sent by God? Who could come out recognizing it as lies, thus believing the truth and escaping eternal damnation in Hell? Who could make it through that? Those who love the truth MORE than they love pleasure, that's who!

I remember hearing the story of an army soldier who had been carrying a New Testament on his person while on the battlefield. In the midst of an artillery barrage he had jumped into another foxhole, and when he did he left his Bible behind in the last foxhole he had been hunkered down in. He said the Lord spoke to him to go back and get the Bible. Though this was dangerous and would expose him to enemy fire, yet he went back to get his Bible. Upon running and diving into the foxhole, he heard an explosion. The foxhole he had just left got a direct hit. His love for God, and the word of God saved his life.

The ones who survive this tremendous time of deception are the ones who love the truth. They are the ones who go by and believe every word of God. It is their love for the truth, the word of God, that preserves their lives during this time. And there are many, many who love the truth who get their heads cut off as well, but they do not go to an eternal Hell. They end up in glory for ever and ever.

It is a mighty short season when the pleasure of sin is enjoyed. Especially when compared to eternity in torments of flames in Hell.

> [25]Choosing rather to suffer affliction with the people of God, **than to enjoy the pleasures of sin for a season;** (Heb. 11:25)

The few Jews who leave Judaea as the armies surround Jerusalem, are the ones who have recognized the New Testament as the word of God as well as their Old Testament Scriptures. Because of this, they see what is happening and based upon the word of God they leave their homes, their jobs, their food, and head into the wilderness. They thus escape the clutches of Satan and what is getting ready to transpire in Israel.

The Jews who are ready to flee when the abomination of desolation is set up in the Temple are those who have read and believe what Matthew wrote in chapter 24. Thus they are ready to run, even as the abominable idol is being transported towards the Temple. I'm sure those who love the truth and are sober see what is getting ready to take place, they thus flee even before the idol is set up. This enables them to make it into the wilderness.

But those who do not love the truth, those who do not recognize the words of God as written in the New Testament as well as their Old Testament, they do not make it. Too late! They didn't love the truth. They had pleasure in unrighteousness.

Then there are the Gentiles who had been witnessed to, or had been around the truth during the Church Age, merely four years or so earlier. Yet they rejected the truth and didn't get saved, God sends them the strongest delusions in order to damn their souls. For those Gentiles who had the truth and did nothing with it, God sends them --yes, aimed straight at the -- strong delusion so they will believe a lie that they might be damned. As it has been said, *"Light rejected, becomes lightening."*

Rev. Jonathan Edwards painted that picture with words in his sermon *Sinners in the Hands of an Angry God.* The Bible declares that God holds the breath of every living thing, and He can withhold that breath anytime He wants to. It is as if God holds the sinner by the nape of the neck and has them dangling over the flames of Hell. He can drop them into Hell any time He wants to. The only thing preventing Him from letting go, and thus dropping them into the flames of Hell, is His longsuffering and desire to see them saved. But there comes a time when His longsuffering and love run out. They are replaced with justice and judgment. In an instant they pass away and are dropped into the flames of Hell.

> ²For all those *things* hath mine hand made, and all those *things* have been, saith the LORD: but **to this *man* will I look,** *even* to *him that is* **poor and of a contrite spirit, and trembleth at my word.** (Is. 66:2)

In the Tribulation the world does not tremble at the word of God. The world does not want the word of God. In the Tribulation the world wants to have fun and pleasure. It's party time! So God sends them a strong delusion that they should believe a lie, which they all believe. Did you notice the word "all"? That they all might be damned, not all of the world population, but all of the world population that **"believed not the truth, but had pleasure in unrighteousness."** And at that time, I am guessing about 95% of the world goes after the Beast and takes the mark. That is a bunch of people! Well over 7 billion. That's something to think about! Over 7 billion people cast into Hell at the Judgment of Nations.

Alright, so let's get back to the context of the passage.

Paul is saying to the Thessalonians that they are not seeing all of this taking place, therefore they do not need to be troubled because the Day of Christ could not possibly be at hand. Therefore, you Thessalonians, you have not missed the Rapture. All is good.

Then Paul admonishes them and comforts them as well with the following verses.

> ¹³¶ But **we are bound to give thanks alway to God for you, brethren beloved of the Lord,** because God hath from the beginning chosen you to salvation **through sanctification of the Spirit and belief of the truth:**
> ¹⁴Whereunto he called you by our gospel, **to the obtaining of the glory of our Lord Jesus Christ.**
> ¹⁵**Therefore, brethren, stand fast, and hold the traditions which ye have been taught, whether by word, or our epistle.** (2 Thess. 2:13-15)

The salvation of verse 13 is not salvation in the sense of being born again, because he calls them **"brethren."** The salvation is them being saved from going into the Tribulation and suffering under the wrath of God just as he had already told them.

> ⁹For **God hath not appointed us to wrath, but to obtain salvation by our Lord Jesus Christ...** (1 Thess. 5:9)

If the Day of Christ applies to the second coming in this passage, then it would seem to fit better with what Paul is telling them. The problem is that it does not fit the usage in the other places where the term is used. But just like the term, "The coming of the Lord" can refer to the Rapture or the Second Coming, then perhaps, "The Day of Christ" is used in two different ways as well. It can refer to the Judgement Seat of Christ and the Second Advent.

Again though, either way it is used, it does not change the meaning of the falling away. The falling away is not applicable to the Church, it is applicable to the Tribulation period.

So the term, "the Day of Christ," can refer to either the Judgment Seat of Christ, or it can refer to the Second Advent of Jesus Christ. Therefore the Day of Christ has at least two events that are associated with it.

Now here are some things to think about.

The Judgment Seat of Christ ends just before the Second Advent of Jesus Christ begins. In both of these events, Jesus Christ is judging. He is judging the body of Christ, and He is judging those who fight against Him at His return. And from what I can tell, there are three battles that take place when He returns.

There is the battle around Bozrah in Edom in Isaiah 63. Then there is the battle of Jerusalem which is described in Joel 2. And finally there is the battle in the valley of Megiddo which is known as Armageddon in Revelation 16.

In this second coming of Jesus Christ He is said to "judge."

¹¹¶ And I saw heaven opened, and behold a white horse; and he that sat upon him *was* called Faithful and True, and in righteousness **he doth judge** and make war. (Rev. 19:11)

Not only does He judge at both of these events, but both of these events are called a "day." The Judgment Seat of Christ is said to be a day:

¹³Every man's work shall be made manifest: for **the day shall declare it,** because it shall be revealed by fire; and the fire shall try every man's work of what sort it is. (1 Cor. 3:13)

The Second Coming of Jesus Christ is also said to be a "day."

¹¶ Blow ye the trumpet in Zion, and sound an alarm in my holy mountain: let all the inhabitants of the land tremble: for **the day of the LORD cometh,** for *it is* nigh at hand; ²**A day** of darkness and of gloominess, **a day** of clouds and of thick darkness, as the morning spread upon the mountains: **a great people and a strong; there hath not been ever the like,** neither shall be any more after it, *even* to the years of many generations. (Joel 2:1-2)

There is one more event that takes place immediately

after Jesus Christ arrives on this earth which is the Judgment of Nations.

At the judgement of nations Jesus Christ is the Judge who is doing the judging, just like the other two previous events. And the Judgment of Nations is said to be a day:

> ^{12}Let the heathen be wakened, and come up to the valley of Jehoshaphat: for **there will I sit to judge all the heathen round about.** ^{13}Put ye in the sickle, for the harvest is ripe: come, get you down; for the press is full, the fats overflow; for their wickedness *is* great. ^{14}Multitudes, multitudes in the valley of decision: for **the day of the LORD** *is* near in the valley of decision. (Joel 3:12-14)

Another curious thing about these three events is that in all three events those being judged will have never died.

A Christian is said to never die for they have eternal life. There are many verses on this but I will merely give these two to prove my point:

> ^{26}And whosoever liveth and believeth in me **shall never die.** Believest thou this? (John 11:26)

> ^{24}Verily, verily, I say unto you, He that heareth my word, and believeth on him that sent me, hath everlasting life, and shall not come into condemnation; but **is passed from death unto life.** (John 5:24)

Then at the Second Advent, the people that are fighting have not died yet.

Then those at the Judgment of Nations have not died yet as well.

With the Judgment Seat of Christ finishing right before the Second Advent, and then the Judgment of Nations taking place right after the Second Advent it looks like these three events make up the Day of Christ. There is no doubt about the first two being the Day of Christ.

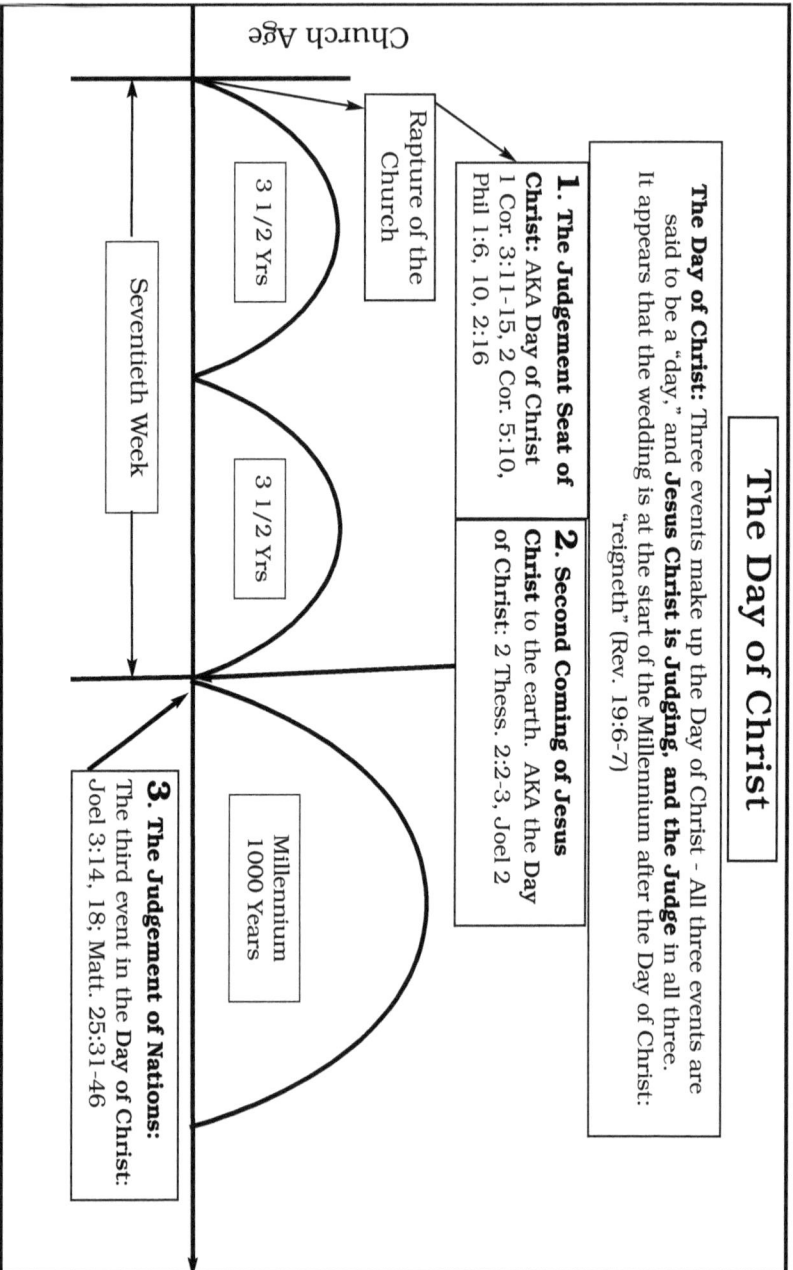

The Day of Christ

The Day of Christ: Three events make up the Day of Christ - All three events are said to be a "day," and **Jesus Christ is Judging, and Jesus Christ is the Judge** in all three. It appears that the wedding is at the start of the Millennium after the Day of Christ: "reigneth" (Rev. 19:6-7)

Church Age

Rapture of the Church

3 1/2 Yrs

3 1/2 Yrs

Seventieth Week

Millennium 1000 Years

1. The Judgement Seat of Christ: AKA Day of Christ 1 Cor. 3:11-15, 2 Cor. 5:10, Phil 1:6, 10, 2:16

2. Second Coming of Jesus Christ to the earth. AKA the Day of Christ: 2 Thess. 2:2-3, Joel 2

3. The Judgement of Nations: The third event in the Day of Christ: Joel 3:14, 18; Matt. 25:31-46

Revelation 11

Of the three chapters covered, Revelation 11 is the one that stands out from the others. This chapter sheds much light upon rightly dividing the seven-year Tribulation. It is also key to understanding much of the prophecy throughout the word of God. The events that take place in this eleventh chapter explain many obscure passages in the word of God. Thus much confusion is removed, and understanding takes its place. Much like clouds of a storm clearing and leaving the clean fresh landscape to be illuminated by the bright, shining sun.

For many years I was not really comfortable in my knowledge of the book of Revelation. Even today am I not quick to know and answer many things concerning the events that take place during Daniel's 70th week. As always, we are studying the word of God, our final authority for all things. The Authorized Version of 1611 is inerrant, infinite, and we will never master it in our earthly lives. In spite of that though, I find this portion of our study to be very fascinating. My prayer is that you, dear reader, will be helped and encouraged in your walk and service for our Lord and Saviour, Jesus Christ.

It's obvious that we are starting in the middle of the book of Revelation. This study is not a Bible commentary on the book of Revelation. It is a study on rightly dividing the seven-year Tribulation. The eleventh chapter of Revelation is essential in understanding and rightly dividing the book of Revelation. But we must back up into Revelation 10 a little in order to get the context and to get our bearings on where we are at.

The book of Revelation gives an overview of the Tribulation more than once. Just as the gospels give four accounts of the life and death of Jesus Christ; so too, the book of Revelation gives four accounts of the seven-week period of the Tribulation.

As I have covered already, some have questioned why people still believe that the book of Revelation covers a seven-year period when it never states seven years. Over and over in the Book of Revelation, it states three and a half years, and never seven. This chapter will answer that "dilemma." But before we get into chapter 11, we need to back up and get some context from chapter 10.

> [5]And the angel which I saw stand upon the sea and upon the earth lifted up his hand to heaven,

⁶And sware by him that liveth for ever and
ever, who created heaven, and the things that
therein are, and the earth, and the things
that therein are, and the sea, and the things
which are therein, **that there should be time
no longer:**
⁷But in the days of the voice of the seventh
angel, when he shall begin to sound, **the
mystery of God should be finished**, as he
hath declared to his servants the prophets.
(Rev. 10:5-7)

At the point "in time" when there is time no longer,
that is a point way beyond the White Throne Judgment
of Revelation 20. The mystery of God is obviously
finished when there is time no more; the Great White
Throne Judgment is over, all sin and sinful souls are
cast into the lake of fire, and the new heavens and earth
are created. Think about it. One day you will
understand it all. No more faith. No more confusion,
doubt, nor fear. The mystery of God, and all things will
be finished. But I bring this out to show that there is a
break in the narrative. Chapter 10 is an "intermission"
so to speak, and then in Revelation chapter 11 begins
another account of the Tribulation. In Revelation 11:1
you are at the beginning of the Tribulation with seven
years to go.

Not only is chapter 10 a break in the narrative
concerning the seven-year Tribulation, the chapter also
ends with the prophesy that John is not finished with
his earthly ministry. He is told that he is going to
continue in his ministering and preaching.

[11]And he said unto me, Thou must prophesy again before many peoples, and nations, and tongues, and kings. (Rev. 10:11)

The following is one such story about the apostle John and his ministering as an old man. I find this story very interesting:

Quoted from A History of Christianity, by John Abbott, 1872:

> Such a man was Nerva. He immediately recalled all the Christians who had been banished from Rome by the Emperor Domitian. He issued a decree forbidding that any one should be molested for cherishing the faith either of the Jews or of the Christians. The dungeons, which were filled with the victims of tyranny, he opened, and liberated the captives. The venerable apostle John was released from his exile at Patmos, and returned to Ephesus, where it is said that he remained for the rest of his life.
>
> It is often difficult to discriminate between what should be regarded as true and what as fable in the annals of those early days. But the following incident, given by the Abbé Fleury, is alike interesting and instructive, as showing the reputation which the venerable apostle enjoyed. It is said that St. John one day attended a meeting of the disciples in a

small village a few miles from Ephesus. A young man of remarkable personal beauty was also present, who was so frank and genial in his manners as at once to win the tender regard of the affectionate disciple whom Jesus loved. Addressing himself to the pastor of the church after the young man had left, the apostle said, "In the presence of this church, and of our Lord and Saviour Jesus Christ, I commend to your especial care this young man." As he left to return to Ephesus, he very emphatically repeated the solemn charge.

The bishop or pastor of the church sought the young man, won his confidence, taught him the religion of Jesus, and finally by baptism received him to the church. The young man having partaken of the sacrament of the Lord's supper, the bishop deemed him safe, and relaxed his vigilance. But he, being exposed anew to temptation, fell into bad company, was lured to midnight festivals, gradually abandoned all religious restraints, and plunged into the most reckless course of dissipation. His last state became so much worse than the first, that he at length became captain of a gang of robbers, whose rendezvous was among the mountains, and who were the terror of the community.

Some time after this, the apostle again visited this rural church. With deep interest he inquired for the young man. The bishop, with tears filling his eyes, replied:

"--He is dead--dead to God. He has become a bad man and a robber. Instead of frequenting the church, he has established himself in the fastnesses of the mountains."

The venerable apostle was overwhelmed with grief. After a moment's reflection, he said, "Bring me immediately a horse and a guide." Without any preparation, in the clothes he then wore, he advanced towards the region infested by the robbers. Scarcely had he entered their rocky haunts ere some of the gang who were on the lookout arrested the defenceless, penniless, humbly-clad old man. "Conduct me to your chief," said the apostle: "I have come expressly to see him."

The captain soon made his appearance, armed from head to foot. The moment he recognized the apostle, overwhelmed with shame, he turned, and endeavored to escape by flight. John, notwithstanding the infirmity of years, pursued him with almost supernatural speed, and cried,--

"My son, why will you fly from your father, an old man without arms? Have pity upon me, my son: do not fear. There is still hope that you may be saved. I will plead for you with Jesus Christ. If it be necessary, I will willingly give my life for yours, as he has given his for us. Believe me that Jesus Christ

216

has sent me to you."

At these words the young man arrested his steps, but could not raise his eyes from the ground. He threw aside his arms, and then, trembling, burst into tears, weeping bitterly. When the apostle had reached him, the young man threw his arms around the neck of the aged Christian, and with sobbings, either of remorse or penitence, embraced him tenderly. The apostle endeavored to console the guilty wanderer from the fold of Christ. He assured him that Jesus was ready to forgive all. He led him back to the church, engaged all the disciples to pray for him, and kept him constantly by his side as a companion and a friend. Under these influences, it is said that the prodigal became a true penitent, re-entered the church, and ever after continued one of its brightest ornaments. *(Abbott John S. C., The History of Christianity, Chapter 10, Boston: Published by B.B. Russell, 55 Cornhill, Philadelphia, Quaker-city Publishing-House, San Francisco: A.L.Bancroft & Co., Detroit, Michigan., R.D.S. Tyler, 1872, downloaded from https://www.gutenberg.org/ebooks/59400)*

With the break in the narrative established we shall now begin our study of Revelation 11. Keep in mind that we are at the beginning of the seven years, not half way through the seven years. It will be obvious as we look at the verses.

> ¹¶ And there was given me a reed like unto a rod: and the angel stood, saying, Rise, and measure **the temple of God**, and the altar, and them **that worship therein.** (Rev. 11:1)

The first thing to see is the Temple of God. Notice that it is the temple... of God. God is present in the temple, thus it is not desolate.

After the Rapture, which is also known as the *"calling out of the body of Christ,"* (I regret having to explain the Rapture like that, but sure as anything, someone is going to read this and then shout, "RAPTURE IS NOT FOUND ANY WHERE IN THE BIBLE!! No it's not, but the EVENT IS!!) the world immediately is back under the Jewish law. It is no longer under grace, in the sense of salvation by grace through faith.   I know that's counted as heresy, but it's what the word of God says.

> ¹⁷And the dragon was wroth with the woman, and went to make war with the remnant of her seed, which **keep the commandments of God, and have the testimony of Jesus Christ.** (Rev. 12:17)

> ¹²Here is the patience of the saints: here *are* they that **keep the commandments of God, and the faith of Jesus.** (Rev. 14:12)

As a born-again Christian under grace, you and I do not keep, nor do we attempt to keep the commandments of God. You do not attempt to keep the

218

Jewish Sabbath, and neither do the Seventh Day Adventists. You are not under law, you are under grace in this present Church Age. One day soon though the church is leaving and the Church Age is ending. Then the world will be back under the law, though there will be one major change from before the Cross. The saints in the Tribulation will also have the faith of Jesus Christ.

Did you read it? I put the verses in so you could read them. It says they kept the commandments of God, and the faith of Jesus Christ. That is what it says. Either you believe it or you don't. The Jewish law is brought back into effect in the Tribulation.

> [20]But pray ye that your flight be not in the winter, neither **on the sabbath day:** (Matt. 24:20)

Why is this mentioned? Because they are limited to how far they can travel on the Sabbath, as well as the airports and travel are shut down on the Sabbath in Israel.

You and I do not have to be concerned about sinning against God if we travel too far on a certain day of the week, do we? No, we don't! Not only that, but on the Sabbath in Israel, transportation services are closed. We'll cover this more when we come to the woman fleeing into the wilderness.

So one of the first things to notice in Revelation 11 is that the Temple of God is present, meaning the temple is going to be rebuilt.

³¶ Let no man deceive you by any means: for *that day shall not come*, except there come a falling away first, and that man of sin be revealed, the son of perdition;

⁴Who opposeth and exalteth himself above all that is called God, or that is worshipped; so that he as God **sitteth in the temple of God,** shewing himself that he is God.

(2 Thess. 2:3-4)

Before that Man of Sin sits in the Temple of God, which takes place three and one-half years into the seven years, there are Orthodox, Sabbath-observing, law-keeping Jews who worship God in that temple. And they worship God in that temple for the first three and a half years of the Tribulation. That is very important to understand. It shows that Revelation 11:1 is taking place at the beginning of the seven years.

During these last few days of the Church Age, there are some strange heresies springing up amongst Bible-believing Christians. It is to be expected strange heresies would spring up among those who do not know where the words of God are, but now there are strange things springing up amongst those who profess to believe what has been termed "the old time religion." One of them is being covered in this book concerning the seven-year Tribulation and it not being split, so that the first half took place during the ministry of Jesus Christ.

The other heresy is being taught by a well-known Bible believing evangelist. He believes that the dead in

Christ are going to be up walking around on the earth for up to forty days and nights before the Rapture. Thus, according to him, we will know exactly when the Lord is coming, because we will see the dead in Christ walking around on this earth.

(According to 1 Corinthians 15:52, both the dead in Christ and those alive at His appearing are changed AT the last trump—in other words, at the same time—so if the dead in Christ were up walking around for forty days and nights they would be **INVISIBLE**. You don't see the soul of your loved one depart at death.)

The problem I have with both of these heresies, aside from their being scripturally wrong, is the effect each teaching can have on a saint. The Bible says:

> [8]Henceforth there is laid up for me **a crown of righteousness**, which the Lord, the righteous judge, **shall give** me at that day: and not to me only, but **unto all them also that love his appearing.** (2 Tim. 4:8)

> [11]Behold, I come quickly: **hold that fast which thou hast, that no man take thy crown.** (Rev. 3:11)

Both of these heresies can have the effect of not looking for and being ready for the imminent coming of Jesus Christ. He might come right this minute as you are reading this book. Are you ready to go? Would you love to see Him? Or are you looking for the Antichrist? Or are you looking for the dead in Christ to be walking around? Both of these are detrimental to the saints. You and I are to be looking for the coming of our Saviour.

> [11]¶ For the grace of God that bringeth salvation hath appeared to all men,
> [12]Teaching us that, denying ungodliness and worldly lusts, we should live soberly, righteously, and godly, in this present world;
> **[13]Looking for that blessed hope, and the glorious appearing of the great God and our Saviour Jesus Christ;** (Titus 2:11-13)

The born-again saint of the Lord is to be looking for the coming of their Saviour, Jesus Christ. That is a command of the Lord that you just read.

If there is something a saint should be aware of, and in a sense looking for, it is the building of the Jewish temple. It does not have to be built by the Rapture, and if it is not built by the time of the Rapture, then it will be built immediately after the Rapture. As I have already covered in Matthew 24 under the Abomination of Desolation, if there is anything to be looking for today, it is the rebuilding of the Jewish Temple. That will be a very major development prophetically, should it happen before the Rapture occurs.

Concerning the Jewish Temple in the Tribulation, you need to remember that for the first half of the Tribulation, three and one-half years, GOD IS IN HIS TEMPLE. And there are Jews worshipping God in His Temple.

I need to qualify what I just wrote. Do you remember

222

Daniel 8:14 and the 2,300 days? The daily sacrifices don't begin until approximately 220 days into the seven years. That is a little over seven months. It looks like those first seven months are for the building of the Temple, and the sanctifying of it as well, but this is merely a guess. I do not have Scripture on this.

So for simplicity and clarity, since the days are approximate anyway, I am going to use three years as the time frame of the operating of the Jewish Temple. In the first half of the seven-year Tribulation, the Temple is operating with sacrifices for three years.

Those first six months will be very similar to when Haggai and Zechariah prophesied while the elders of the Jews built the Temple in Ezra 6:14.

> [14]And the elders of the Jews builded, and they prospered through the prophesying of Haggai the prophet and Zechariah the son of Iddo. And they builded, and finished *it*, according to the commandment of the God of Israel, and according to the commandment of Cyrus, and Darius, and Artaxerxes king of Persia. (Ezra 6:14)

The two prophets who will be prophesying during the building of the Temple of God in the first six months of the Tribulation will be Moses and Elijah. And if there is any opposition, or attempt to thwart the construction of the Temple, then Moses and Elijah may bring judgment upon whoever it is that is trying to hinder the construction. As we will see, they will have the power to send fire out of their mouths to destroy their enemies.

If this happens, and it is conjecture on my part, it would begin the grumbling of people who hate the Jews and didn't want the covenant confirmed.

> [1]¶ And there was given me a reed like unto a rod: and the angel stood, saying, Rise, and **measure the temple of God, and the altar,** and them that worship therein. (Rev. 11:1)

John is commanded to measure the Temple of God and the altar. The Temple is present and inside the Temple is the altar, and the Jews are performing the sacrifices according to the Jewish law upon the altar that is in the inner court. And the performing of the Jewish law is accepted by God at this time.

> [36]And he built **the inner court** with three rows of hewed stone, and a row of cedar beams. (1 Kings 6:36)

> [12]And **the great court** round about *was* with three rows of hewed stones, and a row of cedar beams, both for **the inner court** of the house of the LORD, and for the porch of the house. (1 Kings 7:12)

So there is an inner court, and an outer court. The outer court, according to Rev. 11:2, is given to the Gentiles to tread under their feet.

> [27]¶ And when the seven days were almost ended, the Jews which were of Asia, when

they saw him in the temple, stirred up all the people, and laid hands on him,

^{28}Crying out, Men of Israel, help: This is the man, that teacheth all *men* every where against the people, and the law, and this place: and further brought Greeks also into the temple, and **hath polluted this holy place**. (Acts 21:27-28)

This is how you know that the worshippers of verse 1 are Jews. There is a distinction made between the two courts, and who is allowed in the outer court. But the inner court will have the altar for sacrifices to be made according to the law of Moses. Can you just imagine the uproar that will be made by organizations like PETA when they hear that the Jews are killing animals in order to worship God?

I remember hearing Pastor Buddy Cargill, an ex-gang member and rough steel worker from Maryland who had gotten saved. Our Lord called him to preach and he was pastoring a church in Maryland. He was a special speaker at a preachers' meeting and said in one of his sermons concerning the Old Testament burnt sacrifices being offered to God, *"Well, a roadside barbecue smells good to me too."* I had never looked at the sacrifices like that before. He did have a point though, roadside barbecues do smell really good.

Realize now, these sacrifices are being performed during the first three and a half years of the Tribulation. Right here in Revelation 11 you have the Jewish Temple, the Jewish altar, and you have Jews who are worshipping Jehovah according to the Jewish law.

They obviously are not worshipping the Beast, for he has not been revealed yet. Let me say that again because it is very important to understand. These Jews are not worshipping the beast, for he has not been revealed yet. They are worshipping Jehovah. Notice what the word of God says about the Jews and how they worship the Lord.

> [1]¶ For the law having a shadow of good things to come, *and* not the very image of the things, can never with those sacrifices which they offered year by year continually make the comers thereunto perfect.
> [2]For then would they not have ceased to be offered? because that **the worshippers** once purged should have had no more conscience of sins. (Heb. 10:1-2)

The worshippers worship the Lord by doing the law. By performing the sacrifices and ordinances of the law, they are worshipping the Lord. Therefore this has to be in the first half of the Tribulation. As we proceed, the evidence for this gets overwhelming.

For now we KNOW:

1. The Jewish Temple of God is present.

2. The altar is being used and sacrifices are being performed.

3. Jews are worshipping Jehovah in this Temple of God.

4. This is the Temple of God that the Antichrist enters in the middle of the Tribulation. But he is not in the Temple at this point, therefore it is during the first

226

three and one half years of the Tribulation.

These four obvious points show that the first half of the Tribulation did not take place during the earthly ministry of Jesus Christ.

These four points also show that it is impossible for these works to be performed during the time of the reign of the Beast, which takes place in the second half of the Tribulation.

Understanding the Temple is absolutely essential to understanding how to rightly divide Daniel's 70th week.

> ²But the court which is without **the temple** leave out, and measure it not; for **it is given unto the Gentiles: and the holy city shall they tread under foot forty** *and* **two months.** (Rev. 11:2)

There is no doubt about the time frame being the first half of the Tribulation. Why? Because during the second-half, the inner court and the Temple itself is trodden down by the Gentiles and eventually destroyed by the end of the Tribulation.

The agreement (i.e. the covenant,) made with the Jews allowed them to worship Jehovah according to their law in their Temple, but that's it. The Jews had no jurisdiction over anything outside of the Temple, thus the outer court and beyond is open for Gentiles to occupy. The Gentiles tread this underfoot for 42 months. In other words they walk over it, all while the Jews are worshipping God inside the Temple. But in the end, in the second half, they destroy it.

Seven Years

> ^{26}And after threescore and two weeks shall Messiah be cut off, but not for himself: and the people of the prince that shall come shall **destroy the city and the sanctuary**; and the end thereof *shall be* with a flood, and unto the end of the war desolations are determined. (Dan. 9:26)

Notice the reference also to "the end." By the end of the seven years, the temple and city are destroyed. Because of this, it is impossible to correctly apply verse 2 any other way. If verse 2, the forty-two months, referred to the second half of the Tribulation, then by the end the inner court and the Temple would be destroyed, which it is not in verse 2. You cannot place the time frame of Revelation 11:1-2 on top of (in other words, occurring at the same time,) as the time frame given in Revelation 13. It will not work.

> ^{4}And **they worshipped the dragon which gave power unto the beast: and they worshipped the beast**, saying, Who *is* like unto the beast? who is able to make war with him?
> ^{5}And there was given unto him a mouth speaking great things and blasphemies; and power was given unto him to **continue forty *and* two months.** (Rev. 13:4-5)

That is different worship. They are worshipping the Beast worldwide. And the people are not Jews, they are Gentiles. The forty and two months of Rev. 13:4-5 take place in the second half of the Tribulation. Thus the events of Revelation 11:1-2 do not fit into the time frame of Revelation 13:4-5. Nor can they properly be placed simultaneously occurring—it will not work. Therefore what you have is two, three and one-half year time frames that take place to make up the seven year Tribulation.

With these truths established, we shall proceed to the following verse.

> ³¶ And I will give *power* unto my two witnesses, and they shall prophesy a thousand two hundred *and* threescore days, clothed in sackcloth. (Rev. 11:3)

Have you noticed that God keeps mentioning each time frame in different ways. Whether days, months or years, it all adds up to three and one-half years, which doubled makes seven years. And the reason He divides the seven years into two, three and one-half segments is because the two segments are so opposite to each other. At the very heart of the two halves is the Temple. The first half God is in it, and the second half, Satan is in it. This is also very important for you to understand.

For the first half of the Tribulation, God is in His Temple which is why it is referred to as the Temple of God. For the second half of the Tribulation, Satan is in the Temple with an idol (an abomination to God) erected in it, thus making the Temple desolate.

Based upon what we have now understood from the Scriptures, we are going to see a "revolutionary" truth that has probably been seen by some, but not very many. I am not so foolish to think that I have found something nobody else has found. Besides, it was my Pastor Wesley Givens, that showed me these things to begin with.

We will see that these two witnesses are Moses and Elijah, which is not revolutionary for others have seen that as well. But it is obvious now that these two witnesses prophesy during the first half of the Tribulation. They do not, I repeat, they do not minister during the second half of the Tribulation. First of all, let's locate these two prophets.

> ⁴These are the two olive trees, and the two candlesticks standing before the God of the earth. (Rev. 11:4)

So, who are these two witnesses?

These two witnesses that prophesy for three and a half years, they stand before the God of the whole earth. We know that they are in Jerusalem because when they get killed they lie in the street of Jerusalem according to Revelation 11:8. So they are doing the work of the Lord in Jerusalem. They obviously are Jewish, and thus are among those worshipping in the Temple of God. God's presence is in the Temple, and thus they are standing before the God of the whole earth as they minister from the Temple in Jerusalem. It is likely they are communing with the Lord Jehovah about the plagues and torments that they are sending throughout the world.

As to who they are there is no doubt. Moses and Elijah appear beside the Lord on the Mount of Transfiguration.

¹¶ And after six days Jesus taketh Peter, James, and John his brother, and bringeth them up into an high mountain apart,

²And was transfigured before them: and his face did shine as the sun, and his raiment was white as the light.

³And, behold, there appeared unto them **Moses and Elias talking with him.** (Matt. 17:1-3)

Both Moses and Elijah are anointed prophets and both of them stand before the Lord in their earthly ministry.

¹¹¶ Then answered I, and said unto him, What *are* these two olive trees upon the right *side* of the candlestick and upon the left *side* thereof?

¹²And I answered again, and said unto him, What *be these* two olive branches which through the two golden pipes empty the golden *oil* out of themselves?

¹³And he answered me and said, Knowest thou not what these *be*? And I said, No, my lord.

¹⁴**Then said he, These *are* the two anointed ones, that stand by the Lord of the whole earth.** (Zech. 4:11-14)

These are two men who have been anointed and stand by the Lord of the whole earth. What's more is that they have power to:

> [6]These have power to shut heaven, that it rain not in the days of their prophecy: and have power over waters to turn them to blood, and to smite the earth with all plagues, as often as they will. (Rev. 11:6)

You must admit, that is quite a lot of power! To be able to smite the earth at their own will.

> [17]**Elias** was a man subject to like passions as we are, and he prayed earnestly that it might not rain: and **it rained not on the earth by the space of three years and six months.** (James 5:17)

> [1]¶ And Elijah the Tishbite, _who was_ of the inhabitants of Gilead, said unto Ahab, **As the LORD God of Israel liveth, before whom I stand, there shall not be dew nor rain these years, but according to my word.** (1 Kings 17:1)

Did you notice in 1 Kings 17:1, "...but according to my word..."? This fits right in with Rev. 11:6, "...as often as they will."

That locates one of the two right there. Elijah [Elias] is one of the two witnesses.

> [20]And Moses and Aaron did so, as the LORD commanded; and he lifted up the rod, and smote the waters that _were_ in the river, in the sight of Pharaoh, and in the sight of his

servants; and **all the waters that *were* in the river were turned to blood.** (Ex. 7:20)

That locates the other one, and it is no doubt Moses. There is no other prophet in the word of God that turns water into blood. Moses is the only one who does that.

The two witnesses are Moses and Elijah. And yes, they prophesy for the first three and one-half years of the Tribulation.

> [5]And if any man will hurt them, fire proceedeth out of their mouth, and devoureth their enemies: and if any man will hurt them, he must in this manner be killed. [6]These have power to shut heaven, that it rain not in the days of their prophecy: and have power over waters to turn them to blood, and to smite the earth with all plagues, as often as they will. (Rev. 11:5-6)

I will come back to verse 5, but I must comment on verse 6 first. For three and a half years Moses and Elijah are sending plagues and smiting "...the earth... " verse 6. They have a worldwide effect as they prophesy from Jerusalem. They are smiting the world with droughts, turning water to blood, and sending plagues all around the world. This brings up something that needs to be addressed.

For many years commentators have taught that the first three and a half years of the Tribulation will be years of peace. That is not true. There will be three and a half years of agreement with the Jews that they may have their Temple and worship in it, but there is not three and a half years of peace.

The first three and a half years are years of:

> [5]For many shall come in my name, saying, I am Christ; and shall deceive many.
> [6]And ye shall hear of **wars and rumours of wars**: see that ye be not troubled: for all *these things* must come to pass, but the end is not yet.
> [7]For nation shall rise against nation, and kingdom against kingdom: and there shall be **famines, and pestilences, and earthquakes**, in divers places. (Matt. 24:5-7)

Notice what is recorded in Revelation:

> [10]And they that dwell upon the earth shall rejoice over them, and make merry, and shall send gifts one to another; because **these two prophets tormented them that dwelt on the earth.** (Rev. 11:10)

The people in the world are being tormented by Moses and Elijah. It is worldwide! They have a worldwide ministry, and they are hated worldwide. No doubt about it! Look at Revelation 11:5:

> [5]And **if any man will hurt them, fire proceedeth out of their mouth, and devoureth their enemies:** and if any man will hurt them, he must in this manner be killed. (Rev. 11:5)

What you are going to have described before you is very similar to the MCU, which is also known as the Marvel Comic Universe. There is nothing new under the sun. I have only seen short clips of the Avengers with Thor, Iron Man, Hulk, Superman and the gang. But in the clips there are super heroes and villains fighting with beams of fiery energy coming out of their mouths, eyes, or their weapons. Godzilla has this as well, but cinematically-speaking, he is not human.

The MCU is all fiction and thus it is not true, yet there are blasphemies and truths that are portrayed throughout all of the stories. It all started many years ago with comic books such as Superman. These superhero movies are modern comic books so to speak. They are full of witchcraft as in Dr. Strange and Scarlet Witch being directly occultic. There is no doubt about Batman and his sidekick Robin. Robin is the name spoken by the Devil's followers when they want to have a meeting with the man in black. (See the book titled: <i>Saducismus Triumphatus</i>, by Joseph Glanville, 1700)

During the first half of the Tribulation, Moses and Elijah are tormenting the world with supernatural plagues and disasters. It is not a secret that they are the ones taking responsibility for doing it all because along with the plagues they are preaching repentance. The world needs to repent and get right with God. Elijah preaches and many of the Jewish families, though the message is not limited to Jews, get right and healed.

⁵**Behold, I will send you Elijah the prophet before the coming of the great and dreadful**

> day of the LORD:
> [6]And he shall turn the heart of the fathers
> to the children, and the heart of the children
> to their fathers, lest I come and smite the
> earth with a curse. (Mal. 4:5-6)

Notice "he shall turn..." It's not a maybe so, but there will be a uniting of fathers to sons as well as daughters. Notice it's to the fathers.

During my lifetime, I was born in 1958, I have seen the position of the father destroyed in the world. It happens whenever the electronic entertainment comes in. It began with the television and has now spread through computers as well as the television. Strong fathers are almost against the law in this age.

I know of a good Christian man who loves and cares for his family. He told me that some years earlier, when his daughters were young, that one day his mother-in-law was visiting and something happened that caused him to make a stern decision. Nobody was in trouble, there was no spanking or anything like that, (though I am not against proper spanking) he merely took control of his home and told them in a firm voice what they were going to do.

Unbeknownst to him, his mother-in-law recoiled inwardly to what he had just done, but he, nor his family, knew that. She had been abused by a strong male years earlier, and thus she had a hatred for strong men.

She reported him to Child Protective Services, and they were coming to take the kids out of the home. The day before CPS was to arrive, somehow they found out what was happening. They packed up what they could and immediately left the state.

Some fifteen years later, the mother-in-law confessed why she did it, and realized that she was wrong. But oh, how strong male figures, especially if they are Christian, are reviled by the ungodly in this day and age. Strong Christian males are the biggest hindrance to the one world takeover.

Elijah will turn the hearts of the fathers to their children and the children to their fathers, for the first half of the Tribulation.

So while Elijah is ministering to families and fathers, he is also, along with Moses, sending plagues worldwide. Because of this the world is furious at these two men. Now notice verse 5.

> ⁵And **if any man will hurt them, fire proceedeth out of their mouth, and devoureth their enemies:** and if any man will hurt them, he must in this manner be killed. (Rev. 11:5)

Fire proceeds out of the mouths of Moses and Elijah, and kills whoever is trying to hurt them. "Crispy critters" end up on the ground around the Temple in Jerusalem. Oh, I'm sure they get cleaned up, but it becomes a common sight where someone gets flame-broiled alive out in front of the Temple in Jerusalem. Month after month this happens. Sometimes one person, and other times mobs of people are burned on the spot. Now you must admit, that is quite a sight!

No, it is not 42 months of peace. It is 42 months of

plagues, pestilence, furious anger, fighting and killing of people. It is the first half of the Tribulation.

> [8]And they answered him, *He was* an hairy man, and girt with a girdle of leather about his loins. And he said, It *is* Elijah the Tishbite.
>
> [9]¶ Then the king sent unto him a captain of fifty with his fifty. And he went up to him: and, behold, he sat on the top of an hill. And he spake unto him, Thou man of God, the king hath said, Come down.
>
> [10]And Elijah answered and said to the captain of fifty, If I *be* a man of God, then let fire come down from heaven, and consume thee and thy fifty. And there came down fire from heaven, and consumed him and his fifty.
>
> [11]Again also he sent unto him another captain of fifty with his fifty. And he answered and said unto him, O man of God, thus hath the king said, Come down quickly.
>
> [12]And Elijah answered and said unto them, If I *be* a man of God, let fire come down from heaven, and consume thee and thy fifty. And the fire of God came down from heaven, and consumed him and his fifty.
>
> [13]And he sent again a captain of the third fifty with his fifty. And the third captain of fifty went up, and came and fell on his knees before Elijah, and besought him, and said

unto him, O man of God, I pray thee, let my life, and the life of these fifty thy servants, be precious in thy sight.

[14]Behold, there came fire down from heaven, and burnt up the two captains of the former fifties with their fifties: therefore let my life now be precious in thy sight.

[15]And the angel of the LORD said unto Elijah, Go down with him: be not afraid of him. And he arose, and went down with him unto the king. (2 Kings 1:8-15)

When Elijah lived and ministered, he called down fire from Heaven, and so it came down and killed the soldiers. But in Revelation 11, it doesn't say that the fire comes down from Heaven. It says that the "...fire proceedeth out of their mouth." Notice also that both Moses and Elijah are fire-breathing prophets, not merely Elijah. Those who go up against Moses and Elijah must be killed in this manner. Moses and Elijah are untouchable for the first half of the Tribulation. God is in the Temple, and they are coming out front preaching and burning those up who seek to kill them. No, it is not a time of peace!

[6]**These have power to shut heaven, that it rain not in the days of their prophecy: and have power over waters to turn them to blood, and to smite the earth with all plagues, as often as they will. (Rev. 11:6)**

Seven Years

My earlier comments on Revelation 6 concerned the subject of the first half of the Tribulation not being a time of peace, and it is not. But I didn't mention much about the plagues that Moses and Elijah are smiting and tormenting the world with. I find it very interesting how the Lord uses the word "tormented" for the judgements that Moses and Elijah send worldwide. People are in pain from it all.

First of all, they have power to shut Heaven, which is what Elijah did during the days of King Ahab. He will do this again during the first half of the Tribulation thus showing that when you read the Old Testament you are reading about future events. You are reading prophetical scriptures.

Notice the result of the drought brought about by Elijah. It is a famine. This is prophetic.

> [1]¶ And it came to pass *after* many days, that the word of the LORD came to Elijah in the third year, saying, Go, shew thyself unto Ahab; and I will send rain upon the earth. [2]And Elijah went to shew himself unto Ahab. And **there was a sore famine in Samaria.** (1Kings 18:1-2)

> [7]For nation shall rise against nation, and kingdom against kingdom: and there shall be **famines, and pestilences, and earthquakes, in divers places.** (Matt. 24:7)

> [6]¶ And I also have given you **cleanness of**

teeth in all your cities, and **want of bread** in all your places: yet have ye not returned unto me, saith the LORD.

[7]And also I have withholden the rain from you, when *there were* yet three months to the harvest: and I caused it to rain upon one city, and caused it not to rain upon another city: one piece was rained upon, and the piece whereupon it rained not withered.

[8]So two *or* three cities wandered unto one city, to drink water; but they were not satisfied: yet have ye not returned unto me, saith the LORD.

[9]I have smitten you with blasting and mildew: when your gardens and your vineyards and your fig trees and your olive trees increased, the palmerworm devoured *them*: yet have ye not returned unto me, saith the LORD. (Amos 4:6-9)

These are all glimpses of what is getting ready to take place in the near future upon this earth. Notice that the Lord, in spite of the rebellion in the vast majority of the people of the world, is still looking for those who will repent and return unto Him. He is still looking for that one who will turn from their sin and trust Him as Saviour, though during the Tribulation it will likely cost you your life by getting your head cut off.

Not only is the rain from Heaven shut off, but then the Lord gives them blood to drink. Have you ever been really thirsty? When you're really thirsty, you want water, not soda. You might take an electrolyte drink like Gatorade, but for the most part you want water. Can you imagine being extremely thirsty and then be given blood?

I know that witches and warlocks drink blood in their ceremonies. Roman Catholics and Greek Orthodox believe they drink the literal blood, and eat the literal body of Jesus Christ in their masses. So here is the attitude in Heaven towards all of this drinking of blood. Revelation 16 takes place during the second half of the Tribulation. The world is getting blood to drink during the Tribulation.

> [4]And the third angel **poured out his vial upon the rivers and fountains of waters; and they became blood.**
> [5]And I heard the angel of the waters say, Thou art righteous, O Lord, which art, and wast, and shalt be, because thou hast judged thus.
> [6]For **they have shed the blood of saints and prophets, and thou hast given them blood to drink; for they are worthy.** (Rev. 16:4-6)

You can easily imagine the amount of anger that is going to be directed towards Moses and Elijah worldwide. Anger is a characteristic of those who are not right, and those who believe in lies. They are agitated and easily angered, especially towards those who are doing right. It goes all the way back to Cain and Abel in Genesis 4 when Cain slew Abel.

Abel's offering was accepted by God and Cain's was not. Cain didn't like that, and ended up committing the first murder in the word of God.

¹²Not as Cain, *who* was of that wicked one, and slew his brother. And wherefore slew he him? **Because his own works were evil, and his brother's righteous.** (1 John 3:12)

You can see it in politics. Those who are seeking and trying to promote liberty, justice and freedom have much more grace than those who are trying to convince and promote sodomy, lawlessness and debauchery out of a greed for power and money. The wicked are always intolerant of the upstanding law-abiding people. During the Tribulation the wicked are in control and those who are trying to obey God are running for their lives. This attitude is beginning to manifest itself more and more in these last days of the Church Age.

Some of the brethren preach and promote the possibility of a worldwide revival or a national revival, saying that God is able. Well, yes, He is able, but the world doesn't want a revival.

Nineveh wanted revival once they heard the message, right? And didn't Nineveh repent after they heard the message? Yes, they did! Well, America has been hearing the message for 200 years, and in the last 100 years America has not repented nor desired to get right with God. In this age now, street preachers are getting shot on the streets in America.

Just this past November, 2023, I was preaching a meeting in Glendale Arizona. While there, a street preacher was standing on the corner of a street he had preached at many times before. A car drove by, and someone from inside the car aimed a gun out the window and shot him. He survived, praise the Lord, but it shows the intolerance of hearing the gospel in this age.

America, as well as the world doesn't want a holy God. So they are getting ready to get a god they can like. He is the Antichrist, and he is wicked just like they are. He makes them feel good about theirselves. Gives them a high self-esteem making them much more "balanced." Yes, worldwide they will like him very much.

But the true God is not going to let them enjoy their time with him. There are going to be droughts, no water to drink. Most of the available water is going be turned into blood. And on top of that, Moses and Elijah are going to be smiting the world with plagues as often as they want to. All the while, the world is getting more and more furious at Moses and Elijah, as well as at the Lord God Almighty.

The best thing you can ever do, and one that you should make a practice of, is to repent quickly when you are wrong. Be swift to condemn yourself, esteem others better than yourself, and be quick to justify God. It is a fool who won't admit they are wrong, especially before God. And if you are a soldier, you have been trained to never give up, don't back down and quit. You are to fight on and not accept defeat. That is right and good for a soldier in battle, but that is how you lose with the Lord Jesus Christ. The way to win spiritually with Jesus Christ is to surrender. The enemy of surrender is pride, which the Bible says, **"...goeth before destruction..."** (Prov. 16:18)

244

⁷And when they shall have finished their testimony, **the beast** that ascendeth out of the bottomless pit shall make war against them, and **shall overcome them, and kill them.** (Rev. 11:7)

This is Moses and Elijah. According to verse 3, their testimony lasts 1260 days, which equals three and a half years. It can't be the same time as the time the Beast reigns because the Beast ascends out of the bottomless pit and kills Moses and Elijah after they have finished their testimony. He was in the bottomless pit the whole time Moses and Elijah were smiting and tormenting the world. Not only that, but the first half of the Tribulation, the presence of God is residing in His Temple, and the second half the Son of Perdition is residing in the Temple. When this takes place, the Temple is said to be desolate. (Dan. 9:27)

How did the Beast get out of the bottomless pit? Did he finally escape God's prison? Not at all. God let Him out, knowing he will do exactly what God wants him to do.

Knowing that the Beast has a free will and knowing that he wants to defeat the true God, then one way to beat God is to not do what God has said he —the Beast— is going to do. That would break the word of God and destroy the whole thing. But there is such power in the word of God, and the word of God cannot be broken. God knows the devil well, and so the Beast does exactly what God says he —the Beast— is going to do.

¶ Canst thou draw out leviathan with an hook?

^{5}Wilt thou play with him as *with* a bird?

(Job 41:1a,5a)

Our Lord has it all under control. Everything is going to take place exactly the way He says it will happen as recorded in the inerrant words of God. He allows all who will to read about it so that there is no surprise when things begin to happen. Aren't you glad that even though the world is falling apart, you can rest easy, if you are born again, knowing that the God who lives inside your body, is the One who is running all of Creation. You are safe with Jesus in you, and you in Jesus Christ.

In Revelation 11:7 it says that the beast shall make war with Moses and Elijah.

For forty-two months Moses and Elijah have been killing all who come against them. Individuals, or mobs, or armies, have all lost and have all been devoured by fire that has come out of the mouths of Moses and Elijah. I say armies because in the middle of the Tribulation, armies travel the globe and assemble outside of Jerusalem. (Luke 21) I am guessing they are there to destroy the two prophets who have been tormenting the world with plagues, blood and drought. The attempts at killing the two witnesses increase each day with larger scale battles happening as well, yet to no avail.

There is no doubt that if God the Father wanted to protect the two witnesses and defend them continually, He most certainly could. But by the end of their forty-two month ministry, the world has shown its great hatred for God, His people, and the truth. During that time the world has progressively moved more and more away from whatever fear of God they may have had, and gravitated to outright rebellion against their Creator. It is worldwide rebellion against the truth.

> [9]*Even him*, whose coming is after the working of Satan with all power and signs and lying wonders,
> [10]And with all deceivableness of unrighteousness in them that perish; because they received not the love of the truth, that they might be saved.
> [11]And for this cause God shall send them strong delusion, that they should believe a lie:
> [12]That they all might be damned who believed not the truth, but had pleasure in unrighteousness. (2 Thess. 2:9-12)

They had pleasure in unrighteousness so God allows the king of unrighteousness to come out of the bottomless pit. The pit that was created for the Devil and his angels. The pit where it is said that:

> [41]Then shall he say also unto them on the left hand, Depart from me, ye cursed, into everlasting fire, prepared for the devil and his angels: (Matt. 25:41)

> [25]That he may take part of this ministry and apostleship, from which Judas by

transgression fell, **that he might go to his own place.** (Acts 1:25)

¹²While I was with them in the world, I kept them in thy name: those that thou gavest me I have kept, and none of them is lost, but **the son of perdition;** that the scripture might be fulfilled. (John 17:12)

³¶ Let no man deceive you by any means: for *that day shall not come*, except there come a falling away first, and **that man of sin be revealed, the son of perdition;** (2 Thess. 2:3)

So you have a thing here where Hell, also known as the bottomless pit, was prepared for the devil and his angels. But Judas, who is also known as the Son of Perdition, is said to have gone "to his own place." So even though Judas had an earthly father, for he was the son of Simon (John 6:71), yet he is called the Son of Perdition, thus making him part of the satanic trinity. Satan seeks to counterfeit the true Trinity.

Whether the Beast arises out of the bottomless pit in the spirit of Judas, I am not sure. What I know is that it is the Beast. It is part of the satanic trinity.

¹³And I saw three unclean spirits like frogs *come* out of the mouth of the dragon, and out of the mouth of the beast, and out of the mouth of the false prophet. (Rev. 16:13)

(After reading Revelation 16:13, I have never thought

of nor looked at a frog the same.)

What it looks like is that Moses and Elijah have been tormenting the world for the first half, (forty-two months), of the Tribulation. People all over the world are furious and want them dead. It has gotten to the point that armies are gathering around Jerusalem to do battle with these two prophets. It is also likely that these armies have arrived from various nations around the world. Moses and Elijah have a worldwide ministry, and worldwide there is a hatred for these two prophets.

> ²⁰¶ And when ye shall see Jerusalem compassed with armies, then know that the desolation thereof is nigh.
> ²¹Then let them which are in Judaea flee to the mountains; and let them which are in the midst of it depart out; and let not them that are in the countries enter thereinto.
> ²²For these be the days of vengeance, that all things which are written may be fulfilled. (Luke 21:20-22)

By this time in our study, we are at the middle of the Tribulation. The middle of the Tribulation is one of the most clearly-defined events in all of the word of God. The Beast is now let out of "prison" and ascends up to the surface of the earth at the location of Jerusalem. (Rev. 13:11) The scene (which I will go into more detail in book two on the overview), is one of fiery warfare. People over and over are trying to kill Moses and Elijah, but without success. Fire is streaming out of the

249

mouths of Moses and Elijah, and it says that the enemies must in that manner be killed. (Rev. 11:5) The people are not killed with swords, or bullets, tanks, bombs or missiles. They are killed by the fire that comes out of the mouths of the two witnesses.

As I have already mentioned, it really seems to be something like a Hollywood superhero battle. The god of this world is now getting the people ready for such a battle. Except the people will be cheering for the wrong side.

Over and over the enemies of the two witness end up burned to death, devoured by the fire that streams out of the mouths of the two witnesses. Now comes a new force. A new enemy who is called the Beast. He has arrived straight out of the bottomless pit, and joins in the battle to kill Moses and Elijah.

I was thinking about this one day. Moses and Elijah know the Bible very well. They are going to know these Scriptures better than you and I do. It's only a guess on my part, but I would think they will know the outcome of this battle. They know they are going to die in this battle. I find this interesting to think about.

Well, the Beast engages the two witnesses in battle. With a cataclysmic crescendo of fighting, the two witnesses end up dead in the street; along with them the Beast ends up dead as well. All three lie there in the street motionless.

Perhaps, and this is only a guess for I do not have Scripture for this, the Beast, is picked up and prepared for burial. The world at this time is thrilled and rejoices that Moses and Elijah are dead, and they let their dead bodies lie on the streets of Jerusalem. Then on the third day, for it has been three days and nights, the Man of Sin, the Beast, wakes up and steps out of his coffin. To this the world is ecstatic with glee.

His right eye is blind and one of his arms, probably his right, but it doesn't say which, is paralyzed, or "clean dried up."

> [17]Woe to the **idol shepherd** that leaveth the flock! **the sword** *shall be* **upon his arm, and upon his right eye: his arm shall be clean dried up, and his right eye shall be utterly darkened.** (Zech. 11:17)

It says sword, but it still could be a flaming sword.

> [24]So he drove out the man; and he placed at the east of the garden of Eden Cherubims, and **a flaming sword which turned every way,** to keep the way of the tree of life. (Gen. 3:24)

> [15]And **out of his mouth goeth a sharp sword,** that with it he should smite the nations: and he shall rule them with a rod of iron: and he treadeth the winepress of the fierceness and wrath of Almighty God. (Rev. 19:15)

> [21]And the remnant were slain with the sword of him that sat upon the horse, **which** *sword* **proceeded out of his mouth:** and all the fowls were filled with their flesh. (Rev. 19:21)

Moses and Elijah continue to lie dead in the street in front of the Temple in Jerusalem. No doubt the world will cheer, and along with their cheering they will have a new hero. It will be the Beast, who has just arrived from the bottomless pit.

Welcome to the middle of the Tribulation. The first half is over. You are now up to one of the most prophesied events in all of the word of God.

> [8]And their dead bodies *shall lie* in the street of the great city, which **spiritually is called Sodom and Egypt, where also our Lord was crucified.**
>
> [9]And they of the people and kindreds and tongues and nations shall see their dead bodies three days and an half, and **shall not suffer their dead bodies to be put in graves.**
>
> [10]And they that dwell upon the earth shall rejoice over them, and make merry, and shall send gifts one to another; **because these two prophets tormented them that dwelt on the earth.** (Rev. 11:8-10)

Verse 8, there is no doubt where it is, for it is where our Lord was crucified, which is Jerusalem.

In verse 9 do you see the attitude towards them from the people? It says the world will see their dead bodies and not permit their dead bodies to be put into graves. Somebody, probably those who are worshipping in the Temple, will want to bury the bodies of Moses and Elijah. But the world steps in and says to them, "No way! You leave those bodies right where they are. We want to see them rot and get eaten by dogs, birds and whatever else. This has been one of the greatest events we have ever seen." So their bodies are left to lie in the street for 42 hours. During this time there is a worldwide party and celebration.

The world sends gifts one to another in celebration. They are thinking their torments are now over. These two men, along with their God are now defeated. We can now live our lives the way we want to live them. There will be no more negativity, and suffering. Finally the world will be a better place because they are dead and gone. At least that is what they will be thinking, or something like that.

At this point in the Tribulation there are many many things that take place.

Once the Beast comes, he is accepted as a god. As a matter of fact, they accept him as God. It is at this point the world goes through a falling away, along with many of the Jews. No, the world was never "with God," but there was an acknowledgment of God in a general sense. But now, the world will readily accept Satan as their god.

> ³¶ Let no man deceive you by any means: for *that day shall not come*, except there come a falling away first, and **that man of sin be revealed, the son of perdition;**
> ⁴**Who opposeth and exalteth himself above all that is called God, or that is worshipped; so that he as God sitteth in the temple of God, shewing himself that he is God.** (2 Thess. 2:3-4)

The first thing to realize is that the church cannot fall away. It is impossible for the church to fall away. Why? Because we are bone of His bone and flesh of His flesh. The Church, the Bride of Jesus Christ, is one with Jesus Christ.

> [17]But he that is **joined unto the Lord is one spirit.** (1 Cor. 6:17)

It did not say one in spirit. It said one spirit. You are in Christ if you are saved.

> [20]¶ Neither pray I for these alone, but **for them also which shall believe on me through their word;**
> [21]**That they all may be one; as thou, Father, art in me, and I in thee, that they also may be one in us:** that the world may believe that thou hast sent me.
> [22]And the glory which thou gavest me I have given them; **that they may be one, even as we are one:**
> [23]**I in them, and thou in me, that they may be made perfect in one;** and that the world may know that thou hast sent me, and hast loved them, as thou hast loved me. (John 17:20-23)
> [13]For **by one Spirit are we all baptized into one body**, whether *we be* Jews or Gentiles, whether *we be* bond or free; and have been all made to drink into one Spirit. (1 Cor. 12:13)

There is no water anywhere in the passage. The moment you were born again, the Spirit of God immersed you into the body of Jesus Christ. Not when you were baptized by someone in water. And to make it even more clear, notice it says, **"...and have been made to drink into one Spirit."** The moment a sinner trusts Jesus Christ as their personal Saviour, they drink of the Spirit of God. He comes into their body. This does not take place when a person joins a local Baptist church. But that is what Baptist Briders believe and teach. They are just plain wrong.

> ²⁷¶ Now **ye are the body of Christ,** and members in particular. (1 Cor. 12:27)

> ³⁰For **we are members of his body, of his flesh, and of his bones.** (Eph. 5:30)

There is no way a Christian nor the Church can fall away. In this age the Church is lukewarm (Rev. 3:14-20), and the Church is becoming more and more apostate in its beliefs. Yet, spiritually, --you have to get this-- spiritually the Church is without spot and blemish. Spiritually the Church is perfect because it is in Christ. So the great falling away does not apply to the Church.

> ³¶ Let no man deceive you by any means: for *that day shall not come*, except there come a falling away first, and that man of sin be revealed, the son of perdition; (2Thes. 2:3)

Now notice some things about 2 Thessalonians 2:3:

When does the following take place? "**...that man of sin be revealed, the son of perdition...**" The revealing of the Man of Sin takes place beginning with the death of Moses and Elijah. Up to this point he has been a political world leader, but his demonic spiritual side has not been manifested until this half way point in the Tribulation. How do we know that?

Because right after Moses and Elijah are killed, the Man of Sin, who is also the Son of Perdition, walks into the Temple of God and declares himself to be God.

> [4b]...**so that he as God sitteth in the temple of God, shewing himself that he is God.** (2 Thess. 2:4b)

There is a possession by an unclean spirit (i.e. the Beast), that takes place in the Man of Sin at this time, same as happened to Judas Iscariot. The Man of Sin becomes the Son of Perdition which is the same name given to Judas.

> [26]Jesus answered, He it is, to whom I shall give a sop, when I have dipped *it*. And when he had dipped the sop, he gave *it* to Judas Iscariot, *the son* of Simon.
> [27]And after the sop **Satan entered into him.** Then said Jesus unto him, That thou doest, do quickly. (John 13:26-27)

> [12]While I was with them in the world, I kept them in thy name: those that thou gavest me

I have kept, and none of them is lost, but **the son of perdition;** that the scripture might be fulfilled. (John 17:12)

(A study of Judas, the Beast, the Man of Sin, and the Son of Perdition is a deep study. But as it is not essential to understanding the proper division of the 70th week, I will not get into that study here and now.)

So back to the Man of Sin walking into the Temple, sitting down and proclaiming to the world that he is God.

It is at this point that the Abomination of Desolation is set up in the Temple. So in that verse, (2 Thess. 2:4) as well as the next verse, the timeframe is the middle of the Tribulation. The setting up of the Abomination of Desolation is one of the most specifically-pivotal events in all of the Bible, and especially in the Tribulation. It is the time when there is a worldwide transition to the worshipping of the Beast. All religions, including many of the Jews fall away and profess allegiance to and worship the Beast. The "falling away" is a reference to either the world, or to all of the Jews who are not in the remnant, or both. There will be no middle ground. You are either for the Beast, or you are not.

And so ends the first half of the Tribulation.

[11]And **after three days and an half the Spirit of life from God entered into them, and they stood upon their feet;** and great fear fell upon them which saw them.
[12]And they heard a great voice from heaven saying unto them, Come up hither. And **they ascended up to heaven in a cloud; and their**

enemies beheld them.
¹³And the same hour was there a great earthquake, and the tenth part of the city fell, and in the earthquake were slain of men seven thousand: and the remnant were affrighted, and gave glory to the God of heaven. (Rev. 11:11-13)

Possibly the Beast was dead three days and nights. If so, then twelve hours later as the world rejoices, Moses and Elijah stand up. If their heads have been cut off, their heads reattach to their bodies in the sight of all, and they ascend upward and disappear through the clouds and beyond.

¹⁴¶ The second woe is past; *and*, behold, the third woe cometh quickly.
¹⁵And the seventh angel sounded; and there were great voices in heaven, saying, **The kingdoms of this world are become *the kingdoms* of our Lord, and of his Christ; and he shall reign for ever and ever.** (Rev. 11:14-15)

⁷But in the days of the voice of the seventh angel, when he shall begin to sound, **the mystery of God should be finished**, as he hath declared to his servants the prophets. (Rev. 10:7)

Revelation 11:15 is now a glimpse of goings on in Heaven which take place after the Tribulation is over,

258

so you have now jumped over the last half of the Tribulation. How do you know that? Because the third woe is not described here. It is described in Chapter 12.

The Lord separates the two halves of the Tribulation so that they are not confused with one another. (But that is not being done by some of the brethren today.) The Lord describes the Tribulation as two separate, three-and-a-half-year periods of time. There is a great indignation in our Lord towards the second half of the Tribulation. It is referred to as the time of the Lord's indignation.

> ¹⁶And the four and twenty elders, which sat before God on their seats, fell upon their faces, and worshipped God,
> ¹⁷Saying, We give thee thanks, O Lord God Almighty, which art, and wast, and art to come; because **thou hast taken to thee thy great power, and hast reigned.** (Rev. 11:16-17)

These two verses then take you up to the end of the Millennium. The reigning of the Lord is said to have taken place in the past, "...hast reigned."

> ¹⁸And the nations were angry, and thy wrath is come, and the time of the dead, **that they should be judged, and that thou shouldest give reward unto thy servants the prophets, and to the saints, and them that fear thy name, small and great;** and shouldest destroy them which destroy the earth. (Rev. 11:18)

The time of the dead that they should be judged is plainly the Great White Throne Judgment of Revelation 20. This would put the Millennial Reign in the past, which is why it is in the past in the previous verse.

The time of the dead can not refer to the Judgment of Nations because at that judgment the people are still alive when they are judged. They have never died.

> [19]And the temple of God was opened in heaven, and **there was seen in his temple the ark of his testament:** and there were lightnings, and voices, and thunderings, and an earthquake, and great hail. (Rev. 11:19)

Somewhere between the time that Moses and Elijah get killed, and when the Man of Sin enters into the Temple, the presence of God leaves the Temple. Thus the Temple is left desolate. At the same time the ark gets translated up to Heaven. God will not let it stay in the Temple when the Beast is there.

The ark is a picture of the throne of God. It is a living picture, or let's say instrument, of the throne of God. To allow the Man of Sin to enter the Temple with the ark present, and then desecrate it, would be like having Satan take over the Heavenly throne of God, which has always been Satan's chiefest desire. Thus God and His ark have departed by the time the satanic Man of Sin enters.

The indignation of the Lord now begins.

Revelation 12 - Highlights

After covering the end of the Tribulation in Revelation 11:15, and then the end of the universe in 11:17, the Lord now returns to where He left off in Revelation 11:13. Revelation 12 covers the wife of God the Father. The woman who broke the heart of the true Almighty God of the universe.

> [9]And they that escape of you shall remember me among the nations whither they shall be carried captives, because **I am broken with their whorish heart,** which hath departed from me, and with their eyes, which go a whoring after their idols: and they shall lothe themselves for the evils which they have committed in all their abominations.
> (Ezek. 6:9)

I find it an amazing thought that the God of creation, the Most High, the all powerful, the all knowing, the all present God who is never weary and never faint, had a time where He was broken. Have you ever been brokenhearted? Have you ever had someone that you loved and cared for turn away from you and break your heart? The God of the universe has, and if you have had that happen to you, then you have a God who knows and understands how you feel.

We know that Jesus Christ was a man of sorrows and acquainted with grief. But this verse in Ezekiel is referring to God the Father, for Israel is the wife of God the Father. It is an amazing thought to think about God the Father weeping with a broken heart. There is not another religious book or religion that ever portrays their god in that fashion.

Here in chapter 12 God is going to bring Israel back into fellowship with Him. There is no doubt He is greatly looking forward to this moment, just as I am sure Jesus Christ is greatly looking forward to being with His bride, the Church, as well.

I'm not going to go verse by verse through this chapter, for this book is not a commentary on the book of Revelation. But there are some things that I need to mention.

> ⁶And the woman fled into the wilderness, where she hath a place prepared of God, that **they should feed her there a thousand two hundred *and* threescore days.** (Rev. 12:6)

The fleeing of the Jews into the wilderness happens in two steps. The first step is with a very small remnant of Jews who have had access to the information found in the Gospel of Luke, or are reading the Gospel of Luke.

> ²⁰¶ And when ye shall see **Jerusalem compassed with armies, then know that the desolation thereof is nigh.**
> ²¹Then let them which are **in Judaea flee to the mountains; and let them which are in the midst of it depart out; and let not them that are in the countries enter thereinto.** (Luke 21:20-21)

262

There is a remnant of Jews who have been reading the Scriptures. Even though the Jews do not recognize the New Testament, nevertheless the New Testament is just as much the Holy Scriptures as the Old Testament. A small remnant of Jews will recognize this, or at least recognize that what is written in these writings is coming true right before their eyes.

As they hear the news of armies arriving to surround Jerusalem, they leave all of their possessions and head to the wilderness. This group of Jews is able to gather their family and depart.

Then there are the Jews who wait, for whatever reason, until the image of the Beast is being set up in the Temple. This takes place immediately after Moses and Elijah are killed and ascend into Heaven. This matches Matthew:

> [15]When **ye therefore shall see the abomination of desolation**, spoken of by Daniel the prophet, **stand in the holy place**, (whoso readeth, let him understand:)
> [16]Then **let them which be in Judaea flee into the mountains:** (Matt. 24:15-16)

It is interesting to note that the Jews who have the "heads up" to leave are only those Jews who have been reading, or are aware of the New Testament writings. Nowhere in the Old Testament are there detailed instructions given like are found in the Gospels.

A remnant of Jews hide out in the wilderness known as Petra, under the protective hand of God. Did you notice how long they hide out for? Well, look at that! It's for a thousand, two hundred and threescore days, or 42 months, or three and a half years.

The first three and a half years they have been worshipping God in the Temple in Jerusalem, now for the second three and a half years they are going to be in the wilderness.

¹⁴¶ Therefore, behold, **I will allure her, and bring her into the wilderness, and speak comfortably unto her.**

¹⁵And I will give her her vineyards from thence, and the valley of Achor for a door of hope: and she shall sing there, as in the days of her youth, and **as in the day when she came up out of the land of Egypt.**

¹⁶And it shall be at that day, saith the LORD, *that* thou shalt call me Ishi; and shalt call me no more Baali.

¹⁷For **I will take away the names of Baalim out of her mouth,** and they shall no more be remembered by their name.

¹⁸And in that day will I make a covenant for them with the beasts of the field, and with the fowls of heaven, and *with* the creeping things of the ground: and I will break the bow and the sword and the battle out of the earth, and will make them to lie down safely.

¹⁹And **I will betroth thee unto me for ever; yea, I will betroth thee unto me in righteousness, and in judgment, and in lovingkindness, and in mercies.**

²⁰**I will even betroth thee unto me in faithfulness: and thou shalt know the LORD.**
(Hos. 2:14-20)

In verse 14, the allurement is that she is running for her life. The allurement is the safety that is provided in the wilderness, although I must say that these Jews have a love for the truth, and thus a love for Jehovah. These are the few who have their God, and what He wrote to them, as their number one priority. Thus they are rewarded with a personal fellowship and protection with their God for three and a half years.

In verse 17, knowing what you know about Israel now and what is going to happen to her in the near future, you can see that from here on the names of Baalim will be removed from the mouths of the Jews, the nation of Israel. When the remnant of Jews are in the caves of Petra, they will not desire the false gods any longer. They will love their true God, Jehovah, and He will speak comfortably to them, vs 14. This starts at the half way point of Daniel's 70th week.

> [12]¶ Therefore rejoice, *ye* heavens, and ye that dwell in them. **Woe** to the inhabiters of the earth and of the sea! for **the devil is come down unto you, having great wrath, because he knoweth that he hath but a short time.**
> [13]And when the dragon saw that **he was cast unto the earth**, he persecuted the woman which brought forth the man *child.*
> [14]And to the woman were given two wings of a great eagle, that she might fly into the wilderness, into her place, **where she is nourished for a time, and times, and half a time, from the face of the serpent.**
> (Rev. 12:12-14)

In verse 12 is found the third "woe."

In verse 14 it is speculated by some that the two wings of a great eagle is a large transport jet. This might be true, though it is conjecture. Others speculate that the eagle is a reference to the USA, but I doubt it. As fast as this country is embracing wrong, and as active as this country is in bringing in the one world government, I doubt by then the USA will be friendly to Israel, but that is just my opinion. Also, the amount of light this country is rejecting puts it directly in the crosshairs of judgment and deception brought on by God Himself. (2 Thess. 2:10-11)

Once again, in verse 14 you have three and a half years mentioned as, **"...a time, and times, and half a time."** God mentions the timing of the Tribulation in generic time, times, and He mentions it as days, and as months. The Lord is very set on getting the point across that His "time frame" is three-and a half years. He does this because He does not want, in any way, to be associated with the second half where Satan is in charge of the Temple and has the world worshipping him as God. It is a time of tremendous blasphemy. This is why the seven years is not mentioned as seven years. He mentions it as two, three and a half year periods because they are so very different.

> [15]And **the serpent cast out of his mouth water as a flood after the woman,** that he might cause her to be carried away of the flood.
> [16]And the earth helped the woman, and the earth opened her mouth, and swallowed up

266

the flood which the dragon cast out of his mouth.

¹⁷**And the dragon was wroth with the woman, and went to make war with the remnant of her seed, which keep the commandments of God, and have the testimony of Jesus Christ.** (Rev. 12:15-17)

This event takes place in the middle of the Tribulation as the remnant of Jews are fleeing for their lives. This is not a reference to the flood that takes place at "the end."

²⁶And after threescore and two weeks shall Messiah be cut off, but not for himself: and the people of the prince that shall come shall destroy the city and the sanctuary; and **the end thereof *shall be* with a flood,** and unto the end of the war desolations are determined. (Dan. 9:26)

The flood of Daniel 9:26 takes place in "**...the city and the sanctuary...**" and takes place at the end.

The flood of Revelation 12:17 takes place outside of Jerusalem as Israel is fleeing into the wilderness. It is here that the earth opens her mouth and swallows up the water. The two floods are not the same.

In reference to Daniel 9:26, Brian Donovan says this:

The "flood" of the verse is found in Revelation 12:15. When during the tribulation, Satan tries to drown out the Jewish remnant fleeing his wrath, but this does not come till "the end." *(Donovan, Brian, (2016), The Revelation of the Seventy Weeks, Published by Brian Donovan, 1130 Jo Jo Road, Pensacola, FL 32514, Bible Baptist Bookstore, pg 40)*

He has this wrong because he is not rightly dividing the time of the Tribulation. The flood of Revelation 12 takes place in the middle of the Tribulation. The flood of Daniel 9:26 takes places at the end. They are not the same.

One last thing though, in regards to the flood that the Dragon casts out of his mouth. Why water? Why is it water that comes out of his mouth. In Job 41 he is a fire-breathing Dragon, but now here after he is cast down to the earth, he is spewing water out of his mouth. Isn't that strange? You might think that he gets "burned out." I don't have an answer, but I thought it was interesting none the less. No doubt that the Dragon is limited as to what God will allow him to do to Israel. He can only get so close to the woman. So he sends water to drown her out. For the Jews who did not heed the words of God ie. the Truth, the Dragon goes back and makes war with them. He has access to them, whereas he does not have access to the Jews inhabiting the wilderness.

[17]And the dragon was wroth with the woman, and **went to make war with the remnant of her seed**, which keep the commandments of God, and have the testimony of Jesus Christ. (Rev. 12:17)

There are Jews that are left behind in Jerusalem and Israel. The remnant that runs to the wilderness have the best chances of survival, for they are in God's perfect will. As we already read in Hosea, the Lord speaks comfortably to His bride in the wilderness. Those Jews left everything at the drop of a hat and ran. They were the "extreme fanatical Jews." And they end up right in the middle of God's perfect will for their lives. It pays to be extreme when it comes to living for and service for your Lord Jesus Christ.

The Jews that don't make it to the wilderness are going to be attacked relentlessly by Satan himself. He is going to make Adolf Hitler look like a novice by the end of the Tribulation.

Revelation 13 - Highlights

Revelation 13 picks up just after Moses and Elijah have been killed, which is half way through the Tribulation. The Mark of the Beast has not yet been implemented, nor the image unto the Beast. This is where in the time frame of the Tribulation all of that begins.

The Ark of the Covenant has been taken up to Heaven. God has left the Temple. Moses and Elijah have ascended up to Heaven as well. A remnant of Jews have fled into the wilderness. The world has turned to the Beast and is worshipping Satan and the Beast as God. All who don't go along with the worldwide movement will be persecuted and killed. I am glad that I will not be there!

> ²And the beast which I saw was like unto a
> leopard, and his feet were as *the feet* of a
> bear, and his mouth as the mouth of a lion:
> and the dragon gave him his power, and his
> seat, and great authority. (Rev. 13:2)

The Beast is an integrated animal. When you mix animals together, in other words you integrate them, you end up with a Beast. It has no identity, and it can't function properly for it is not put together the way God designed it or intended it to be.

We are watching this happen in society right before our eyes. Men are trying to be women, and women are trying to be men. People and children are trying to be animals, and science is trying to make animals like people. The effort today is to integrate all life together with the thought that it will speed up evolution and make things better. But in reality it devolves all life into an amalgamated mess with suffering and sorrow being left in its wake. As it says in Job 41:22 "**...sorrow is turned into joy before him.**" The more suffering in the world, the more joy Satan gets out of it.

> ³And I saw one of his heads as it were
> **wounded to death; and his deadly wound
> was healed:** and all the world wondered after
> the beast.
> ⁴And **they worshipped the dragon which gave
> power unto the beast: and they worshipped
> the beast, saying, Who** *is* **like unto the
> beast? who is able to make war with him?**
> (Rev. 13:3-4)

270

> ⁵And there was given unto him a mouth speaking great things and blasphemies; and **power was given unto him to continue forty *and* two months.** (Rev. 13:5)

Well, look at that! He continues 42 months. You see, he had already been leading the world for 42 months, for he confirmed a covenant with the Jews for "one week." Now he is going to continue for another 42 months. A total of seven years, for it is Daniel's 70th week. But this second half is the time of the Lord's indignation. He no longer is dealing with the world through men. He is now going to deal with man directly, or by angels, and in anger, though still with the desire for people to repent and turn to Him. And many will during this time period.

> ¹⁴And **deceiveth** them that dwell on the earth by *the means of* those miracles which he had power to do in the sight of the beast; saying **to them that dwell on the earth, that they should make an image to the beast, which had the wound by a sword, and did live.**
> ¹⁵And he had power to give life unto the image of the beast, that the image of the beast should both speak, and **cause that as many as would not worship the image of the beast should be killed.** (Rev. 13:14-15)

So you now have an image of the Beast, and all peoples upon the face of the earth are to make an image of the Beast. This is the overspreading of abominations

271

that I mentioned in Daniel 9 and Matthew 24. Satan is the ultimate rebellious one, so he has images of himself erected and thus breaks the second commandment. Then he commands the world to worship him as God, which blasphemously breaks the first commandment as well.

> [45]And he shall plant the tabernacles of his palace between the seas in the glorious holy mountain; **yet he shall come to his end, and none shall help him.** (Dan. 11:45)

In Daniel 11 there is verse after verse on the workings of the Antichrist, but then at the end there is a little postscript: "yet he shall come to his end, and none shall help him."

Here is another scripture like it:

> [12]How art thou **fallen from heaven, O Lucifer,** son of the morning! *how* art thou cut down to the ground, which didst weaken the nations!
> [13]For thou hast said in thine heart, **I will** ascend into heaven, **I will** exalt my throne above the stars of God: **I will** sit also upon the mount of the congregation, in the sides of the north:
> [14]**I will** ascend above the heights of the clouds; **I will** be like the most High.
> [15]**Yet thou shalt be brought down to hell, to the sides of the pit.** (Is. 14:12-15)

There is Lucifer saying "I will, I will, I will, I will, I will," ... and then God says: **"Yet thou shalt be brought down to hell, to the sides of the pit."**

Seven Years

Book 2
The 70th Week

This book will be more of a free-written overview of the Tribulation. There will be times where I quote the scriptures outright, but I am going to try to write this more in a story style. The technical details will be combined with poetic license to where it will be more readable, and hopefully more understandable.

Seven Years

First Half

As a young kid, I had the pleasure to have been born and raised in Tuolumne County, California. The southern end of the county is actually part of Yosemite National Park, and it takes little more than two hours to drive to Yosemite Valley. Wildlife photographers call it the most photographic five miles on earth. The beauty is such that words could never do it justice.

Perhaps you have seen pictures of Half Dome or El Capitan, which are two of the most well-known granite mountains in all of the park. When in the valley, your eyes are lifted upward to behold them in all of their grandeur. And then there are the waterfalls with the misty water vapor that sprays out at the bottom of them, and when the mist is pierced with the golden beams of sunlight, beautiful rainbows emerge. Then there also is the crystal clear snow water that flows through the middle of the grassy valley. So clear you can see the bottom with the rainbow trout darting from boulder to boulder. And there are many other sights I could go on to describe. But later in the spring, when the snow has been cleared away from the high country road, you can drive up to a place called Glacier Point, and from here you can see out over the whole area of the valley. It is almost like viewing the valley below from an airplane you are so high. Your eyes can also look out to the tops of the Sierra Nevada mountain range with its snow capped peaks, with other large waterfalls splashing cold clear snow water as it cascades downward finally to end up in the Pacific Ocean. From this high vantage point, you have the opportunity to behold the whole area in all its beauty like an overview.

So with this said, let's get into the overview of what we have already studied in particular.

Conditions after the Rapture

It will be a day just as any other day. People will have arose from sleep and gotten ready for the day. Children will go off to school, adults will go to work, those on welfare will still be in bed. For others on the other side of the globe, they will have come home from work and with supper now ended, they will have gotten ready to go to sleep for the night. But one day, some time soon, Jesus Christ is going to come and call all born-again souls up to meet Him in the air. This is our Blessed Hope, and to love His appearing will gain for you a crown at the Judgment Seat of Christ. (2 Tim. 4:8)

With no warning at all, the saints will hear the sound

of a trumpet, a shout from Jesus Christ, and the voice of the archangel. (1 Cor. 15:50-53, 1 Thess. 4:14-17). The dead in Christ shall arise. Then there will be another trump which will be the last trump. At the sound of the last trump, the dead in Christ, along with those who are alive at the time of the Rapture, will be changed in the twinkling of an eye. At that moment we will all receive our new bodies. We will put on incorruption. Then we all are caught up together to meet the Lord Jesus Christ in the air. In a flash there will be millions of saints who will leave this earth. To the lost, they will immediately disappear and it will sound like thunder. What kind of effect will it have on the world?

We know that salvation is a free gift, and based upon various religious surveys, (yes, I know they are not the most trustworthy) a conservative estimate is that one-forth of the population of the USA professes to be born again. Worldwide that percentage drops even more, but even if you were to estimate 10% of the world population to actually be born again, that means out of 8,092,835,813 as of Friday, February 23, 2024

(Current World Population, worldometers.info/worldpop-ulation/#:~:text=8.1%20Billion%20(current),currently%20living)%20of%20the%20world., viewed 5/10/2024)

809,283,581 people will leave the earth in a moment. But if one fourth of the adult population in America was to leave, along with even more if you include born-again children, then you have about 100 million people who will vanish from the nation. Do you realize what that will do to the country? It would destroy the country.

Not only will the sheer number of people who vanish

be a blow to all operations of the nation, but usually --though not absolutely-- the Christian workers are the best workers. As a rule they are honest, can think for themselves, and work harder than the average lost person. So for the most part, the best of the work force will vanish.

There have been a number of books and movies made about this very thing, but still it is something to consider. What would it be like for a husband to lose his wife, or a wife to lose her husband? All of a sudden they are gone, and where they stood or were lying down are left nothing but the clothes that they were wearing.

The Bible says that flesh and blood shall not inherit the kingdom of God. (1 Cor. 15:50) At the Rapture the flesh is changed, so it is likely that the blood is left behind. Wouldn't that be a sight? Everywhere a Christian was there are some clothes and blood on the ground. That would shake you up, especially if it were someone you loved.

I don't know why I think about this, but in the age in which we live it truly is amazing what modern medical science has been able to do. With all of the advancements there are people now with metal shoulders, hips, and knees, as well as plates, screws, pins, glass eyes, posts as teeth, and pacemakers. I have this image of some guys out eating in a restaurant when the Rapture takes place. Out of the party of four, let's say, only one of the guys is saved. And it just so happens that he had been in a bad accident, so he has a glass eye, an artificial hip, and an artificial knee.

Boom! In the twinkling of an eye, he is gone. The other three jump out in shock as they hear his parts clang on the floor. And then they look at his plate and his eyeball is rolling around or sitting in his french fries looking back at them. Boy, that would shake up your day, wouldn't it?

The greatest typology of a Christian who is alive at the time of the Rapture and disappears, is the man Enoch.

> [23]And all the days of Enoch were three hundred sixty and five years:
> [24]And **Enoch walked with God: and he was not; for God took him.** (Gen. 5:23-24)

Enoch is the only man in the Bible who will never die, and as such he is the greatest type of a Christian who is alive at the time of the Rapture, for they will never die either. From the text it just reads that Enoch walked with God and then he was gone. That's how it will be for the born-again Christian. You will be going about your daily life when you will hear a trumpet sound and your name will be called. After your name is called, you will hear, **"Come up hither,"** and boom, you will be gone.

> [5]By faith Enoch was translated that he should not see death; and **was not found**, because God had translated him: for before his translation he had this testimony, that he pleased God. (Heb. 11:5)

Don't you know there are going to be people looking for their loved ones, and they are not going to find them? What about the children? This is always a

281

controversial subject, but I will tell you what I see from the word of God.

We know that when Jesus Christ comes, He comes with and for those who have believed the gospel and have been born-again.

> ¹⁴**For if we believe that Jesus died and rose again, even so them also which sleep in Jesus will God bring with him.** (1 Thes. 4:14)

He is coming for and calling out of this world His bride, which is the Church. But what about the children?

Well, there is a verse that gives a clue as to the children who have not yet reached the age of accountability. For a saved mother or father who has children who are not saved, it can really be a fearful time thinking that they could be left behind at the Rapture.

> ¹⁴For the unbelieving husband is sanctified by the wife, and the unbelieving wife is sanctified by the husband: else were your children unclean; but **now are they holy.**
> (1 Cor. 7:14)

It doesn't say that the unsaved spouse of a Christian is saved. It says that they are sanctified. That means spiritually they are set apart from the rest of the lost by the spiritual condition of their saved spouse. And then it says concerning the children, "**...but now are they holy.**"

What it looks like to me is that if one of the parents, or both are born-again, then the children who are under the age of accountability, will go up at the Rapture. I do not believe all the children of the world go up at the Rapture. The verse does not say that. The verse is only referring to those children whose mother or father, or both, are saved.

Are those children in the body of Christ? No! But they are holy, and under the age of accountability, and "...sin is not imputed where there is no law." (Rom. 5:13) David said, concerning his newborn son that died, **"...I shall go to him, but he shall not return to me."** (2 Sam. 12:23) As to the older children who have reached the age of accountability, they will not go up in the Rapture.

Now Momma or Daddy, don't let the Devil beat you up to where you are living in fear for their lives every day. Don't try to push them into Heaven under your power.

I remember hearing a preacher one time say that when his kids would come to him and tell him, *"Daddy, I want to get saved."* He would then ask them, *"OK, are you a sinner?"* Usually they would reply, *"No."* Then he would answer them, *"Well then, you have nothing to worry about."* And then with a serious tone, he would tell them, *"But don't sin, because if you sin then you will go to Hell."*

He said after about two weeks he would notice they would have a very serious look on their face. They then would come to him and say, *"Daddy, I want to get saved."* He would reply, *"OK, are you a sinner?"* And they would get a tear in their eyes and say, *"Yes, I am a sinner.*" Then he would tell them all about the Saviour and pray with them to get saved.

With a major portion of the population gone in a moment, and twice the number who are left behind in mourning, it will be a time of much sorrow and confusion. This is why the Lord says, when the disciples asked Him what was going to be the sign when all these things happen, the first thing He says is, "... **Take heed that no man deceive you.**" (Matt 24:4)

The Temple Built and the Law

What I have just described has to do with the physical actions that will take place at the time of the Rapture and immediately thereafter, but spiritually there will be things taking place as well.

God will return to and reinstate the Old Testament laws for Israel. Why? Because God will be dealing with Israel once again. He had left Israel for 2,000 years and treated them equal to the rest of the world with regards to salvation. Today, in this Church Age, a Jew gets to Heaven the exact same way as a --to them-- Gentile dog. This hits them in their pride, for they take great pride in proclaiming that they are God's chosen people. Well, they are God's chosen people...nationally. But in the Church Age, salvation is not through the nation of Israel any more. Salvation is through, and only through, Jesus Christ. With regards to salvation, there is neither Jew nor Gentile. We are all sinners in need of the Saviour, Jesus Christ. Either you come to Him and be born-again, or you go to Hell. It doesn't matter what your blood line is.

But once the Rapture takes place, and the Church is removed, this signals the Church Age is over. Then the time of Jacob's trouble begins, and the Old Testament law is re-instituted but because it's after Calvary there is one more thing required. You now have to keep the commandments of God AND have the faith of Jesus Christ.

> ¹⁷And the dragon was wroth with the woman, and went to make war with the remnant of her seed, **which keep the commandments of God, and have the testimony of Jesus Christ.** (Rev. 12:17)

> ¹²Here is the patience of the saints: here *are* they that **keep the commandments of God, and the faith of Jesus.** (Rev. 14:12)

In order to be able to properly do this, the Temple of God has to be present for the Old Testament sacrifices to be offered. (Yes, I know for some of you reading this, I just wrote heresy. But if you are going to rightly divide the scriptures as well as believe what you are reading, then that is what is going to be needed. If you do not rightly divide the scriptures then you will not be able to literally believe what you just read. You will make it figurative. And you will be wrong!)

Either way there is no doubt that the Temple of God is going to be rebuilt, for it is present in the Tribulation. At the time of this writing (February 2024), the temple is not rebuilt. But there is much talk, and the Temple Mount Jews claim to have all of the materials, garments, articles, and even the red heifers ready. There is no doubt that a certain segment of the Jewish population, especially the Orthodox Jews, are yearning and eagerly awaiting the construction of the third temple. I viewed some articles from the Jerusalem Post, and allisrael.com, and there is much talk about constructing the third temple. Rumor has it as well, that the Israeli Government is budgeting money towards the building of the new temple. This news is concerning to, and infuriates the Moslems in the area though.

(Wouldn't it be interesting if one of the terrorist factions had one of their rockets go off course and hit the Al-Aqsa mosque.)

Whether the temple is built before the Rapture or after, it is going to be rebuilt. If it is not rebuilt by the time of the Rapture, then part of the covenant made for one week will include the rebuilding of the temple. With all of the materials ready, it will not take long for it to be rebuilt.

When the temple is finally rebuilt and the Christians are gone, then at the dedication of the temple, God's presence will once again abide in the Holy of Holies on the Ark of the Covenant. Once His presence is there, worshippers will assemble within the temple to worship Him, to sing praises to Him, and in the court, offer sacrifices to Him. Jews will return to their Old Testament laws and oblations. The temple will become fully functional, just as it was in the time of Solomon.

This all happens about seven months after the Rapture takes place.

Why do I say seven months? Because for the first 220 days of the Tribulation, the sacrifice is not taking place.

(Dan. 8:14, See Chart Dan. 8:14 Prophecy) It is likely that the temple will be built, or at least finished being built in these first 220 days after the covenant is confirmed with the Jews.

Here's an aside to all of this. As a born-again Christian, we are commanded to be looking for our Blessed Hope and glorious appearing of Jesus Christ. (Titus 2) We are not to be looking for the Antichrist. You are not going to be able to see the Antichrist before the Rapture takes place. Why? Because he is not "revealed" until the middle of the Tribulation, and we will have been in Heaven for three and a half years by then.

If there is one thing that you and I can be aware of and looking for, it is the rebuilding of the Jewish temple. If construction begins, the spiritual ramifications are immense. For one, the amount of fulfilled prophesy will be enormous, thus proving without any shadow of a doubt, that the word of God is actually God's holy words. The world will not care by then because they will be so hardened by sin that it won't matter to them. It will mean nothing to them. But if it takes place during the last moments of the Church Age, it will be the single greatest signal that our time here on earth is over.

Confirmation of the Covenant

²⁷And he shall confirm the covenant with many for one week: (Dan. 9:27)

The disappearance of many people at the Rapture will bring in a great amount of confusion worldwide. Immediate loved ones will search and mourn;

acquaintances will wonder what happened as well. The missing workforce will bring about troubles in commerce and travel. Frustration, confusion and sorrow in much of the world will take place. There will also be those who celebrate the disappearance of the Christians.

Out of the confusion will rise up a world leader, to whom people all over the world will gravitate to for comfort and leadership. He will bring a certain return of normalcy to the world, and with it a confidence and trust in him to work things out.

It will likely be a Roman Catholic Pope that will emerge as the world leader, as well as a comforter to all whose loved ones have vanished. We know that Revelation 17 is a direct description of Rome and the mother of harlots. We also know that the Pope has been active, in organizing a one-world religion and church.

The Abrahamic Family House
Also referred to as the one world church
This quote is from their own website:

The mission of the Abrahamic Family House builds on that historical legacy and is inspired by concepts laid out in The Document on Human Fraternity signed by His Holiness Pope Francis and the Grand Imam of Al Azhar His Eminence Dr. Ahmed El-Tayeb in 2019, and particularly the belief that open dialogue, understanding, and acceptance are paramount to addressing the many challenges humanity faces today. *(The Abrahamic Family House, Diverse in our Faiths. Common in our Humanity. Together in Peace., Abrahamic Family House, https://www.abrahamicfamilyhouse.ae/about-us#origin, viewed 5/10/2024)*

Isn't that interesting! Here is the Pope right in the center of establishing the one-world religion, faith, and church. And this is in our time. Ah, brother and sister, you had better have your spiritual bags packed and ready to go because it won't be long and we are "outta here!" The hand writing is on the wall, as they say, though that idiom itself is from the book of Daniel. (Dan. 5:5)

As some politicians say, *"Don't let a good catastrophe go to waste:"* So the Pope strides onto the worldwide scene with a message of peace and hope. He comes in speaking flatteries. (Dan. 11:21) To further quell the situation, He will confirm the covenant with the Jews and allow them to build their temple and to worship Jehovah in Jerusalem. The Jews can make their sacrifices, but only in the inner court of their temple, and they can worship their God in their temple. The compromise will be: though contrary to the law of Moses, the Gentiles will only be allowed into the outer court, but no further. To the Jews and the law of Moses, the Gentiles should not even be allowed in the outer court. This agreement will last for 7 years, at which time there will be a renewal or a renegotiating of the agreement. Upon agreement of the Jews and the representatives of the nations, the covenant is signed into effect.

289

As the signatures dry on the paper, the final week of the time of Jacob's trouble begins.

Deception becomes the norm as false Christs and false prophets abound. Lying signs and wonders are performed to deceive people into believing lies. At the root of it all is greed and the love of money.

In this age the fake "healers" abound while raking in millions of dollars. People flock to these fake healers and end up disappointed and worst of all, deceived by the devil. But in the Tribulation, the deception will be magnified to a much greater extent. Fake miracles of healing, protection, and wealth are promised to those who will give their money to the fakers.

Lies, cheating, bribery, and more become commonplace. Hearts of people become deceitful. Marriages are destroyed, as well as relationships between loved ones. **Because iniquity shall abound, the love of many shall wax cold.** (Matt. 24:12)

The only ones who will escape the tremendous deception of this time are those who cling to the words of God. Those --though labeled extreme, fanatical, or lunatic-- will be the ones who see through it all, and it will be because they loved the truth more than they loved pleasure.

Many people will no longer be able to weep, even at the most horrible scenes. It is a time of extreme selfishness. And while all of this coldness of hearts grows worldwide, yet up in the city of Jerusalem in the temple a strangely glorious event takes place.

It now has been approximately 220 days since the confirming of the covenant. The temple is finally ready.

With all of the preparations made, with the priests

cleansed, with the animals inspected thoroughly to be free from all spots and blemishes, the time comes for the dedication of the temple. An event that many said for over 2,000 years would never take place, yet the time has arrived. It is a time of dismay to many worldwide, yet a thrill and ecstasy of those dedicated orthodox Jews in Jerusalem. To them, what the world thinks means absolutely nothing. All they are concerned with is to obey Jehovah. At this time they still do not realize that Jesus Christ is Jehovah, but that realization will happen in the very near future.

With the purification ceremonies performed and the prayers made, along with the shouts of glory and tears of joy, the final sprinkling of blood takes place. Then something happens that perhaps takes many, if not all of those present, by surprise and awesome amazement.

A sound of wind is heard blowing through the temple. That wind then turns into a cloud, a smoke. And then in the holiest of all a light shines behind the curtain, the veil that separates the holy place from the most holy place. The actual presence of God moves into His temple, just like He was in the Old Testament, when Israel was in fellowship with Jehovah as a nation. The temple is now fully functional physically and spiritually.

The last time a Jewish sacrifice in a Jewish temple was performed was sometime before A.D. 70. Almost two thousand years without a temple and sacrifices, yet the Lord had told them this would happen.

[4]For the children of **Israel shall abide many days without a king, and without a prince,**

and without a sacrifice, and without an image, and without an ephod, and *without* teraphim: (Hos. 3:4)

Yes, it has been many days. There have been many days, decades, and even centuries while the Jews have wandered worldwide. It wasn't until 1917 that land in the Middle East was to be established as the homeland for Israel. And it wasn't until 1948 that Israel became a nation once again. The wandering of Jews has been so prevalent that there is a house plant named after them called Wandering Jew. But here, about seven months into the Tribulation, the Jewish temple is completed and operating under the Jewish law.

The Jews without in the court bow on their knees, with their faces all the way to the ground. They are filled with awe, fear, and joy, all at the same time. It's like they have come home after being so long away. Tears flow, hearts are broken with joy as well as repentance, like they have never repented before. For those Jews it is a very real revival that takes place in their hearts.

Then two men show up on the steps of the temple. They are strange-looking men, though the strangeness is not in the sense of weird. It is in the sense of "another world." They are prophets by the name of Moses and Elijah. I'm sure many of the Jews doubt their claim, until the two begin to preach. As they preach some of the Levitical priests remember the following verses:

⁴¶ Remember ye the law of Moses my servant, which I commanded unto him in

Horeb for all Israel, *with* the statutes and judgments.

⁵Behold, **I will send you Elijah the prophet before the coming of the great and dreadful day of the LORD:**

⁶And he shall turn the heart of the fathers to the children, and the heart of the children to their fathers, lest I come and smite the earth with a curse. (Mal. 4:4-6)

While homes are being destroyed all around the world, yet in Israel, and especially around Jerusalem, there is a revival that begins to break out. It is a revival of families. Fathers begin to weep, hug and hold their children. The children begin to weep, hug and hold their fathers and mothers. Though the love of many waxes cold out in the world, yet for the Jews (and Gentiles as well) who will listen to Elijah preach, they begin to melt under the conviction of the word of God. And yes, the Holy Spirit is present to move upon the listeners.

The power of God can be felt and seen in the temple, and word begins to travel. Other Jews begin to migrate to Jerusalem, and the national revival of Israel begins to take place. The nations around them do not like this, as well as people around the world.

Then on a certain day not long after the start of these events, this man called Moses prophesies a plague to take place on America. He stands out in front of the temple, lifts up his right hand high in the air and proclaims the plague to fall upon America.

Some of the passersby look at him strangely, like he

is some nut. A reporter is there and happens to record him as Moses gives the judgement. Instantly news travels around the world, and most of the people are indifferent. Others mock at the news. But within an hour the plague begins to spread and break out in America, just like this man, Moses said would happen. Along with the plague people begin to get sick, suffer and die. Disbelief and shock spreads through the world as they wonder if it is a coincidence or not. Many will not allow theirself to believe that it is real. After all, they are educated with scientific minds. There must be a logical explanation. But whether there is or not, (though we know) the fact remains that people are suffering greatly in America.

Meanwhile, back in Jerusalem, on the streets out in front of the temple, the other man steps out from the temple. He lifts up his right hand to Heaven and loudly proclaims that there is going to be no rain upon the continent of Europe. By now, other reporters have gathered in hopes of catching another scene like the one with this man called Moses. They hear and record this new prophecy as well. Within seconds news travels around the world that another man has stepped out from the temple by the name of Elijah. He has proclaimed that there is not going to be any rain on the continent of Europe.

Within minutes the storm that was taking place over Berlin just stops. The rain stops and the clouds part. So too in other parts of Europe. The rain just quits. One reporter, who is broadcasting live on air talks to another reporter who is live in Berlin.

Jerusalem reporter to Berlin reporter; *"This is Amy in Jerusalem. I am told I am talking to Joe in Berlin, is that right?"*

Joe: *"Yes, this is Joe in Berlin."*

Amy: *"Joe, what time did it quit raining there in Berlin?"*

Joe: *"Amy, It quit raining, all of a sudden at 10:07 A.M."*

Amy, with an expression of credulity: *"Really!? Because that, considering the time difference, is precisely the time this man who goes by the name of Elijah, yelled out that it was not going to rain in Europe."*

Joe: *"Well, Amy, it would be hard to believe he did this, but either way, the rain did stop at the very same moment he pronounced his words."*

Along with these pronouncements from Moses and Elijah, they also give rebukes to the world and proclaimed that the people need to repent and turn to the Lord God Jehovah. Repent or perish! It is time to get right with God. Break up your fallow ground. Turn from the false gods of Tao, Buddha, Krishna, Allah, Kali, and all others. The Lord God Jehovah is the only true God.

With this being proclaimed from these two prophets, the world becomes angry that such an intolerant sermon would be allowed to be preached. The wonder and curiosity of these two men now turns to disdain, mockery and outright hatred.

The plague continues to spread throughout America with people dying, suffering, and moaning from pain. Anger spreads throughout America as they begin to consider that this man Moses might just have caused the plague. It doesn't take long before people talk of traveling over to Israel to kill Moses and Elijah.

[8]All these *are* the beginning of sorrows.

[9]**Then shall they deliver you up to be**

> afflicted, and shall kill you: and ye shall be
> hated of all nations for my name's sake.
> ¹⁰And then shall **many be offended, and
> shall betray one another, and shall hate one
> another.**
> ¹¹And many false prophets shall rise, and
> shall deceive many. (Matt. 24:8-11)

Not only do people talk of killing the two witnesses, but they begin to persecute and kill those who are following the Scriptures. The people who will not do right, which will be the vast majority of all nations worldwide, will be extremely intolerant of those who are doing right. It has always been this way from the time that Cain killed Abel. Abel's works were righteous, and Cain's were not. Cain could not stand to be around Abel and killed him. (1 John 3:12)

Blood begins to flow all around the world. Innocent people who are merely doing right are slaughtered. The murderers are not punished. The killers are even praised for what they have done.

Some Bible scholars have taught that the first half of the Tribulation will be a time of peace, but that is not true. It is a time of an agreement upon a covenant with the Jews, but it is not a time of world peace.

It has now been about a year since the confirming of the covenant, and about five months since the sacrifices started being offered. The first attempt to kill Moses and Elijah takes place. In front of the Temple stands the two prophets preaching to the world. A crowd of people is gathered around and listening to them preach. Out of the crowd some people shout insults. Others quietly say, "Amen," to the sermon. As they continue to preach, from the midst of the crowd out steps a gunman. Pointing his gun at the prophets, he shouts, *"We are sick of your intolerant preaching."* As he starts to pull the trigger, fire comes out of the mouths of the prophets and burns him up on the spot.

Those around him get singed and jump backwards with screams and gasps of horror as they witness what just happened. In front of them, smoldering on the sidewalk, are the remains of a badly-blackened and charred body, with smoke ascending from the carcase.

Some standing nearby the scene think of movies they had seen on TV, and then realize that this was real, very real! The crowd goes silent in disbelief. Like a bright burst of light piercing through an utterly dark night, the prophets --back to back-- cry out the same message, *"Break up your fallow ground, for it is time to seek the Lord Jehovah."*

A few understand the message while most of the people conceal a silent rage of rebellion within their souls. They don't like the message, but they now have a new found fear and respect for these two "men." And so ends the first year of Daniel's 70th week.

Worldwide the anger of the rebellious, wicked populace is taken out on those who have the faith of Jesus Christ and keep the commandments of God. Their heads are cut off and their blood is used for communion in their satanic Roman services, while their flesh is eaten as well. (Ps. 16:4, Isa. 6:13) A frenzied gurgle of hideous laughter and glee is loudly heard coming from the devilish revelry in their ungodly worship services. Instead of repenting and getting right with their Creator, they are defiantly stiffening their necks against the truth of the word of God.

More and more attempts are made upon Moses and Elijah. Each time the perpetrators get burned up with fire coming out of the prophets' mouths.

The next day the two anointed ones stand forth and proclaim a new round of plagues and earthquakes that are going to hit various places on the earth. Along with that Moses pronounces the waters of Australia are going to turn to blood. Reporters record the proclamations, which are in turn broadcast worldwide. The number of skeptics has greatly decreased, yet there is still a diligent inquiry to find out if what they just said will come to past.

As the reports start to come in, people are stunned as the plagues, earthquakes and waters turning to blood happen exactly as the two prophets proclaimed. Along with the proclamation is the message to turn from your sins and do works meet for repentance. With that message comes a deep anger that sizzles within millions of people. Hatred for Jehovah and these two prophets continues to grow. Governments hold special sessions to deal with this problem. The distress of nations grows dramatically.

The relief the world sensed when all of the born-again Christians disappeared is very short-lived. They realize that there is a new "menace" now to deal with, and it is far worse than those Christians who were preaching the love of God. This new religious group is preaching the judgment of God, and with their message is a power, the likes of which the world had not ever remembered.

It has now been a couple of years since the covenant was confirmed, and there is a very interesting thing that takes place in your King James Bible. There are only two times the word "exploits" is used in the Bible and there are the following.

> ²⁸Then shall he return into his land with great riches; and his heart *shall* be against the holy covenant; and **he shall do *exploits***, and return to his own land. (Dan. 11:28)

> ³²And such as do wickedly against the covenant shall he corrupt by flatteries: but **the people that do know their God shall be strong, and do *exploits*.** (Dan. 11:32)

These are the only two verses where this word is used and it is never used in the singular form. In Dan. 11:28 it has to do with the world leader who confirmed the covenant with the Jews. While the two witnesses have been sending plagues, earthquakes and disasters worldwide, the "prince" (also known as the "Man of Sin"), has been traveling the world and exploiting his position for financial gain. He has gotten great riches.

As he has traveled, he has also sought to quell the anger nations have towards each other in order to "keep the peace." Along with the distress of nations, he has been confronted about the Jews and the two witnesses. As time goes by, he becomes more and more angry with the Jews, and it is likely he regrets ever having confirmed the covenant with them.

Then you have the use of the word "exploits" in Daniel 11:32, and here it is used for the people of God. These are the ones who are living for Jesus Christ and keeping the commandments of God. (Rev. 14:12) The exploits they are performing are not making them rich, nor are they doing it for that reason like the prince is. The exploits done by the people of God are heroic deeds in the face of death. While saints are being persecuted and killed, other saints are standing up for Jesus Christ knowing that they too are going to be killed. It is very similar to the martyrs who have died while being tortured for Jesus Christ. As an example I find the following story a magnificent example of a Godly mother and son:

Symphorium 275 AD

"The Judge said: "Why didst thou not honor the mother of the gods, or worship her image?"

Symphorian answered: "Because I am a Christian, and call only upon the living God, who reigns in heaven. But as to the image of Satan I not only do not worship it, but, if you will let me, I will break it in pieces with a hammer."

The Judge said: "This man is not only sacrilegious at heart, but also obstinate and a rebel; but perhaps he knows nothing of the ordinances or decrees of the Emperor. Let the officer, therefore, read to him the decrees of the Emperors."

The decrees having been read to him, Symphorian said: "I shall notwithstanding never confess that this image is anything but a worthless idol of Satan, by which he persuades men that he is a god; while it is an evident demonstration of their eternal destruction for all those who put their trust in it."

"Upon this confession, the Judge caused him to be scourged and cast into prison, to keep him for some other day. Some time after, he had him brought again before his judgment-seat, and addressed him with kind words, saying: "Symphorian, sacrifice to the gods, that thou mayest be promoted to the highest honor and state at court. If not, I call the gods to witness that I am compelled this day, after various tortures, to sentence thee to death."

Symphorian answered: "What matters it, if we deliver up this life to Christ, since, by reason of debt, in any event we must pay it to him? Your gifts and presents are mingled with the sweetness of the adulterated honey, with which you poison the minds of the "unbelieving." But our treasures and riches are ever in Christ, our Lord, alone; and do not perish through age or length of time; whereas your desire is insatiable, and you possess nothing, even though you have everything in abundance. The joy and mirth which you enjoy in this world, is like fine glass, which, if placed in the radiance and heat of the sun, cracks and breaks in two; but God alone is our supreme happiness."

After Symphorian had said these and like things before the Judge, Heraclius, the Proconsul, pronounced sentence of death upon him, saying: "Symphorian, having openly been found guilty of death, because he hath blasphemed against the holy altars, shall be executed with the sword."

"When this godly confessor was led to death, to be offered up to Christ, his mother called down to him from the wall of the city this comforting admonition: "Symphorian, my son! my son! remember the living God; let thy heart be steadfast and valiant. We can surely not fear death, which beyond doubt leads us into the true life. Lift up thy heart to heaven, my son, and behold him who reigns in heaven! To-day thy life will not be taken from thee, but be changed into a better one. If thou remainest steadfast to-day, thou shalt make a happy exchange: leaving this earthly house, thou shalt go to dwell in the tabernacle not made with hands."

"Symphorian, having been thus strengthened by his mother, was taken out of the city, and beheaded there, having commended his soul into the hands of God, in the time of Emperor Aurelian, and Heraclius, the Pro-consul, at Autum in Burgundy. His dead body was buried by certain Christians. *(Van*

Braght, Thielem J., The Bloody Theatre, or Martyrs Mirror of the Defenseless Christians / who baptized only upon confession of faith, and who suffered and died for the testimony of Jesus, their savior, from the time of Christ to the year A.D. 1660, SYMPHORIAN, A PIOUS CHRISTIAN, BEHEADED FOR THE NAME OF THE LORD JESUS, AT AUGUSTODUNUM, NOW CALLED AUTUM, ABOUT A. D. 275, Elkhart, Indiana, Mennonite Publishing Company, 1886, Downloaded from: https://www.gutenberg.org/cache/epub/65855/pg658 55-images.html, viewed 5/10/24)

[32]...but the people that do know their God shall be strong, and do *exploits*. (Dan. 11:32)

This is the kind of exploits the people of God will be doing during the Tribulation. And I must confess that Symphorian's mother was quite a mother!! Her son was going to be killed, and she is exhorting him to stay true and stand for Jesus Christ. Amazing! Yes, these are deeds of exploits for the first definition of the word according to Webster's 1913 is: A deed or act; especially, a heroic act; a deed of renown...

During the Tribulation, there will be many saints who will perform exploits in the face of persecution and death.

In the meantime, the prince (who has not been revealed yet as the Man of Sin), will begin to undermine his own agreement with the Jews. He resents having ever made the covenant with them.

[30]For the ships of Chittim shall come against

303

> him: therefore he shall be grieved, and return, and **have indignation against the holy covenant:** so shall he do; he shall even return, and **have intelligence with them that forsake the holy covenant.** (Dan. 11:30)

As the plagues and disasters continue, so too the animosity towards the Jews grows as well. The opposition to the Jews, and especially Moses and Elijah, is outright hatred to the extreme.

More and more people attempt to kill Moses and Elijah, and each time they get burned up. Very organized attempts, very sophisticated attempts with many people are tried, but to no avail. Each and every time the people end up burned to death.

With the hatred against the Jews and Jewish sympathizers growing, some people begin to turn on their own. Families are broken by betrayal. Children turning their parents in for following Jesus Christ. Jews begin to turn against the temple and the Orthodox Jews. It is these that the man of Sin seeks to have intelligence with. There is likely money and riches offered for their betrayal.

During worship times, Moses and Elijah return inside the temple and stand before the Lord of all the earth. The Lord likely gives them commands of what He wants next, though the plagues and disasters are at the discretion of Moses and Elijah. (Rev. 11:6) It is likely that the Lord gives them heads up on what is coming in the way of more assassination attempts.

It has now been almost three years since these two prophets began their worldwide ministry. People around the world are dying, and being tormented by the plagues, pestilence, earthquakes and water turned to blood.

What about that? What about the water being turned to blood? Why would the Lord do that?

> ⁴And the **third angel poured out his vial upon the rivers and fountains of waters; and they became blood.**
>
> ⁵And I heard the angel of the waters say, Thou art righteous, O Lord, which art, and wast, and shalt be, because thou hast judged thus.
>
> ⁶For **they have shed the blood of saints and prophets, and thou hast given them blood to drink; for they are worthy.** (Rev. 16:4-6)

According to the Lord, they earned it. By shedding the blood of the saints, they earned the right —or as the Bible puts it— they are worthy to be drinking blood. Can you imagine being in famine and pestilence (Luke 21:11) and all there is to drink is blood? Don't you know those rebellious people will be furious at God and the saints!

By the end of the first half of the Tribulation, nations who had been at war with each other will become friends. Why? Because enemies will come together when they seek to kill off the saints, just as Pilate and Herod became friends when they worked to crucify Jesus Christ.

> ¹¹And Herod with his men of war set him at
> nought, and mocked *him*, and arrayed him in
> a gorgeous robe, and sent him again to Pilate.
> ¹²And **the same day Pilate and Herod were
> made friends together: for before they were at
> enmity between themselves.** (Luke 23:11-12)

The coming together of the world will begin towards the end of the first half of the Tribulation. You must realize by the end of the first half there is merely a couple weeks to go when the world comes together and shouts to the Beast, "He is God! He is our god!"

At this time right before the end of the first half, armies have amassed and are traveling towards Jerusalem with one intent: to kill Moses and Elijah, and probably the Jews associated with them.

For 2,000 years God has given the world, during the Church Age, the love of God. He has sent missionaries and preachers worldwide to proclaim the Gospel of the grace of God.

> ¹⁶For **God so loved the world, that he gave
> his only begotten Son,** that whosoever
> believeth in him should not perish but have
> everlasting life. (John 3:16)

But the Church is now gone. Though the love of God is still manifest through the words of God in Bibles, yet the dealings from the Father through His men has turned to strong warnings of judgment, and the need to repent, to **"...break up your fallow ground, for *it is* time to seek the Lord..."** (Hos. 10:12). Along with the

306

harsh messages are plagues, earthquakes, pestilence, famines and more. The message from Heaven is not merely landing upon ears, but it is also affecting the bodily comforts by inflicting pain, hunger and dehydration.

So now, after three and a half years, the world is clearly divided. The vast majority is mad at God, but a small minority is heeding the admonitions from God through His men. They repent and live for Jesus Christ, and keep the commandments of God.

The alignment of the world has formed. Adamic, natural (i.e. "organic") man, in his depravity has decided to shake his fist at the God he hates, and basically challenges Him to a fight. And that fight is on its way.

Isn't it strange how people get mad at God? People all over the world fight against their Creator. Even Christians will do this. I must remind myself that I could quite easily end up like this if I am not careful. What is strange though is this: do you really believe that you will win?

I know one person who really believes that he will win. Lucifer!

[15]**Yet thou shalt be brought down to hell, to the sides of the pit.** (Is. 14:15)

Seven Years

Middle of the 70th Week

The middle of the Tribulation is one of the most clearly defined points in this Bible study. It is known as the, "...**midst of the week...**" in Daniel 9:27. God very plainly splits the week in the middle, thus creating two halves of the seven-year time frame.

The beginning of the Tribulation is not as easy to determine, though it is likely, dispensationally speaking, to begin right after the Rapture, which marks the end of the Church Age. But the Rapture has no time frame on it as well. We do not know when the Lord will come and call His bride, the Church, out of this world. So the end of the Church Age is unknown to the Church, and thus the beginning of the Tribulation is unknown to all except God Himself.

The middle of the Tribulation is plainly given, which we will see, as there are many events that take place in a matter of days, right in the middle of the Tribulation.

Seven Years

At the center of the events that take place in the midst of the week is the Jewish temple. If you understand what happens in and at the Jewish temple in the midst of Daniel's 70th week, you will have a very good understanding of the entire Tribulation.

Up to this point in the Tribulation, the Jewish Temple, (which is located in Jerusalem,) has had Jews in the temple worshipping the Lord God Jehovah. (Rev. 11:1) Gentiles are not allowed to be inside the Temple, nor are they allowed inside the inner court. Only Jews are allowed. The outer court and Jerusalem are given to the Gentiles, and they are allowed to roam around on that soil. (Rev. 1:2). But inside the temple during this time is the presence of the Lord God Jehovah in the most holy place. That is why it says that the two prophets stand before the God of the earth. The Lord's presence is in the temple just the same as it was in the Old Testament.

This is very important for it proves that the worship here is not of the image of the Beast for it has not been set up yet. At this point the Mark of the beast has not been instituted in the Tribulation. The Man of Sin, the Antichrist, has not been revealed yet to the world. Up to this point, he is a man of worldwide leadership and politics, but it has not been revealed yet who he is. (2 Thess. 2:6)

We are now at the midpoint of the week.

> ²⁰¶ And **when ye shall see Jerusalem compassed with armies, then know that the desolation thereof is nigh.**
> ²¹**Then let them which are in Judaea flee to**

310

the mountains; and let them which are in
the midst of it depart out; and let not them
that are in the countries enter thereinto.
(Luke 21:20-21)

[The following is poetic license, otherwise known as
fiction. I am writing it as an illustration for those who
may not understand so far what all is taking place.]

It was late afternoon, and the 3 p.m. prayer time was
over in the temple, but the orthodox Jewish men were
not in a hurry to leave. As the hatred for the Jews grew
around the world, the men found themselves growing
closer to each other, for it was there, in the temple,
where they fit in. It was where they "belonged" as God's
chosen people. With the latest news broadcast, they
"hung around" to see what the other men thought. The
news was that many nations were sending armies to
surround and attack Jerusalem. These Jewish men
had no illusions to how they were perceived by the
world. They knew full well that the world hated them,
their two prophets, and their God, even though He is
the God and Creator of the world. But the world had
greatly shifted over the past three years. Ever since
Moses and Elijah started preaching and plaguing the
world.

Among the gathering of men in the temple was a
Jewish man by the name of Aaron Goldstein. Aaron
had showed up to the construction site of the temple
shortly after the Christians had all vanished. Then
when the temple was finally dedicated, about seven
months after the Christians vanished, Aaron was

311

present at the dedication. But Aaron did not completely fit in with these men, even though he was fully Jewish and observed the laws as well as any of them. He did not fit in because of what he kept telling the others, but they did not like what he had to say and did not want to hear it. To the rest of the men, he was extreme and a borderline heretic. More than once he was close to being kicked out of the temple. Why?

Well, before all of the Christians had vanished, Aaron had worked for a couple of years with a Christian by the name of Charles Smith. Charlie claimed to have been sent by God from the United States to talk to Jews in Jerusalem about Jesus and the upcoming events.

At the time Aaron wasn't all that interested in religion and brushed Charlie off as a nuisance. Aaron had been approached more than once by missionaries and considered them to be well-meaning pains in the neck. But over time, and having to work daily with him, Aaron began to see Charlie differently. Charlie had a knack, a gift as it were, for talking to Jews, and Aaron began to like Charlie. Aaron even started listening to what Charlie was talking about. He realized that, because he —Aaron— was a Jew, he was right in the center of Charlie's conversations. Then one day they stayed outside of work and talked for a long time. Something had changed in Charlie as he seemed much more serious and concerned, especially for Aaron and his wife and children.

This day they clocked out from work, and Aaron was looking forward to going home to his wife and children. As they reached their cars, Charlie stopped Aaron. He noticed that Charlie was more serious than usual;

Charlie began, *"Aaron, I heard that the construction of the Jewish temple has begun."*

Aaron nodded his head in happy agreement, *"Yes, you are right. It has finally begun in earnest. I hear they are attempting to construct it in less than four months. It is a very exciting time to be a Jew. We haven't had a temple for almost two thousand years."*

"Aaron," Charlie's voice now spoke with a serious tone, *"With the temple being built, I want you to know that in a short time I, and all of the true born again Christians are going to vanish. We are leaving this earth to meet Jesus Christ in the air. But that is not the main thing that I want to tell you."*

With a quick but firm response, Aaron cut off the conversation. *"Charlie, you have already gone over the being born again stuff, and I told you that I am not interested. It's after work, and I am ready to go home to my family."*

Realizing that Aaron was wanting to end the conversation, Charlie became urgent in his voice, *"No, no, I understand. I am not going to talk to you about the need to be born again right now. I know you have heard it all and I have given you pamphlets about salvation, but that is not what I want to talk to you about right now."*

Charlie continued speaking with all seriousness, *"Aaron, after I vanish, along with all of the other Christians, there is going to come a world leader to get things back in order because there is going to be a lot of confusion and chaos worldwide. But the Jewish temple is going to be dedicated and fully functioning. It might take about seven months to complete. At that time two of your greatest prophets are going to return."*

Aaron, wondering if Charlie had finally lost his mind, asked with a look of incredulity, *"What? Who do you claim is going to return?"*

Charlie, eager to explain replied, *"Moses and Elijah are coming back to smite the world with plagues, turn water to blood, and many other kinds of disasters. But the world is not going to repent. They are going to hate the Jews, as well as Moses and Elijah."*

Aaron didn't know what to think. Shaking his head he asked, *"Wow! Charlie, Where do you get stories like this?"*

Trying to calm himself, Charlie then answered, *"It's in the Christian Scriptures. Oops, I mean in the Christian writings, since I know you don't like it when we call our Bible the Scriptures, even though they truly are Scriptures. But I know it's getting late and you want to go home, so let me just give you a couple things that you need to know, because it won't be long and I am going to vanish out of here."*

Aaron still didn't know whether to take him seriously or not, but something seemed to resonate within Aaron that what Charlie was telling him was true so he begaan to listen more intently. And Aaron had worked with him long enough to know that Charlie lived what he "preached" and wasn't some weirdo who had been chanting in the bushes.

Charlie went on, *"After three and a half years, the world is going to be furious at Israel, and especially at the temple where the two prophets preach from because of the disasters that they will be bringing to people all over the world."* Moving closer with his Bible now open, Charlie showed him, *"Aaron, look right here:*

314

20¶ And when ye shall see Jerusalem compassed with armies, then know that the desolation thereof is nigh.

21Then let them which are in Judaea flee to the mountains; and let them which are in the midst of it depart out; and let not them that are in the countries enter thereinto. (Luke 21:20-21)

"There is going to come a day about three and a half years after I vanish out of here, that Jerusalem is going to be surrounded by armies. When you see this beginning to take place, you need to gather up your family and flee to the mountains. Specifically, you need to go south of the Dead Sea to the wilderness mountains of Petra."

Something like a sword pierced through Aaron Goldstein at hearing all of this. This was different than the born-again stuff Charlie had been telling him for the past couple of years.

Charlie continued to show him the Scriptures, *"Aaron, check and see how many times God mentions Selah in the Hebrew Bible. And then look at what He is talking about. It is at Selah that Israel is going to be brought back into fellowship with Jehovah. Israel is His bride. Now look right here in the Hebrew Scriptures:"*

14¶ Therefore, behold, **I will allure her, and bring her into the wilderness, and speak comfortably unto her.**

15And I will give her her vineyards from thence, and the valley of Achor for a door of hope: and she shall sing there, as in the days

315

of her youth, and **as in the day when she came
up out of the land of Egypt.** (Hos. 2:14-15)

[19]And **I will betroth thee unto me for ever;
yea, I will betroth thee unto me in
righteousness, and in judgment, and in
lovingkindness, and in mercies.** (Hos. 2:19)

"Aaron, you are a Jew, and your God is coming soon."

Aaron nodded and turned to open his car door. _"Well,
Charlie, that is amazing, but I have got to get home."_

Charlie now pleaded with him, _"Just one more thing.
Hear me out. Just one more thing."_

Aaron by now was losing his patience and just wanted
to get home. He stopped and turned back to Charlie,
"Alright, one more thing. What is it?"

Charlie, after praying for one more opportunity then
quickly spoke, _"Look right here at what it says."_

[15]**When ye therefore shall see the
abomination of desolation, spoken of by
Daniel the prophet, stand in the holy place,**
(whoso readeth, let him understand:)
[16]**Then let them which be in Judaea flee into
the mountains:**
[17]**Let him which is on the housetop not
come down to take any thing out of his
house:**
[18]**Neither let him which is in the field return
back to take his clothes.** (Matt. 24:15-18)

"Aaron, for the Jews who don't leave when the armies

surround Jerusalem, then this is what they are commanded to do. This is in the Christian Scriptures, in the 24th chapter of the book of Matthew, don't forget that. Do you still have the Christian Bible that I gave you?"

Aaron nodded that he did still have it.

"Good, don't lose that. But the Jews that don't leave and remain in Jerusalem, especially those in the temple, there will come a day when the two prophets get killed and then a man is going to walk into the temple and set up an idol of himself in the holy place."

Aaron Goldstein's eyeswidened, and he exclaimed, "God forbid!"

Charlie tapping the page of his open Bible went on, "Yes, I know, but according to the Christian Scriptures, it is going to happen. And when it does, those Jews will not have time to gather their families, they are commanded to flee and to take nothing with them. It is best to leave when you see the armies coming in. Aaron, do you understand what I am telling you?"

Aaron looked at Charlie dumbfounded, and a little bit shaken. He could tell Charlie was dead serious in what he was saying. "Yes, Charlie, I hear and understand what you have just told me, but I don't know if I believe it."

Charlie replied, "When you see it take place, you will remember this conversation, and you have the Scriptures to read as well. Here, I wrote the Bible references on this paper for you to look up on your own. Aaron, don't lose this. Your life and the lives of your family will depend upon it."

When Charlie mentioned the lives of his family it caught Aaron's attention. He knew Charlie meant well, and it meant something to Aaron that this man would care for his family as well. Whether what he was saying was true or not, Aaron didn't know. But the concern for his family moved Aaron in his heart. He made sure he didn't lose that paper.

So they departed, and over the next days when opportunity would allow, Charlie would mention this to Aaron with other truths as well.

Then, just as Charlie had told Aaron, Charlie vanished and was gone. And so were the other born-again people.

It was a day just like any other as Aaron Goldstein and Charlie Smith arrived for work. A few hours had passed when all of a sudden there was a sound of the loudest thunder that Aaron had ever heard.

Windows were shattered. (Psalm 29:5) Workers fell to the floor and crawled under desks and tables. Then a lady who was kneeling under a work table, screamed as a trickle of warm red blood flowed across the carpet and touched her hand. Not knowing what it was she looked and then saw the pile of bloody clothes, shoes, phone and watch lying on the floor. Realizing her co-worker was gone, she let out another scream that filled the office.

As Aaron looked around to try to figure out what was happening, the thought came to his mind like a flash of light. He remembered what Charlie had told him, that he was going to be leaving very soon.

Aaron looked over to where Charlie worked, and on the floor were the pile of his clothes with blood flowing from under them. He was in shock. He hadn't believed Charlie and thought him to be strange, yet now the conversation returned to his memory. His thoughts raced trying to remember the Scriptures Charlie had told him of. Aaron thought to himself, *"Could it be true? Was Charlie right? It...it must be true."* Aaron was bewildered, astonished and then became very serious in his mind. He thought about his wife and children.

The work place was closed for the day. Aaron got in his car, but the streets were a mess. Slowly he made his way home to his wife and children. Coming in the house, he was met by his wife Elizabeth, his son Isaac, and his daughter Abigail. With a swell of emotion, he threw his arms around them all, bringing them into a family hug. Then he began to talk to his family as fast as he could:

Fearfully excited, he said to them all, *"I think Charlie was right. Honey, do you remember that man I told you about from work? The one I kind of like, but I thought he was crazy?"*

Elizabeth looked directly at Aaron with all seriousness. *"Yes, I remember. You mean the man that kept giving you those pamphlets. Wasn't he the one that gave you that book. Didn't he give you the Bible?"*

Aaron was relieved that she remembered. *"Yes, that's the man. Elizabeth, he told me that he was going to vanish one day, and when all that thunder happened I looked over to his work place and he was gone. All that was left was his clothes and his blood."*

Elizabeth shrieked with astonishment. *"What? His blood and clothes were on the floor?"*

Aaron, hurried off to the bedroom, but spoke over his shoulder. *"Yes, He's gone! They closed the office down and sent us home."*

Digging around in the bottom of his closet, Aaron found the Bible that Charlie had given him a few years earlier. He had placed the paper Charlie gave him with the verses to read in the Bible as well. Now he looked over the paper with all respect and extreme curiosity. Thinking out loud, a whisper of words quietly rolled from his lips, *"Could it be true? Is this Christian Bible the Scriptures as well as the Jewish Scriptures? How could that be?"*

As Aaron's eyes met the pages, he sat down on the floor and began to read the verses Charlie had marked for him to read. The first Scriptures he read had to do with the calling out of the body of Christ in 1 Thessalonians 4 and 1 Corinthians 15. Then he read about the armies surrounding Jerusalem, and the idol being set up in the temple.

As he read more and more, he could see it all beginning to take place right in front of his eyes. He thought to himself, *"Whether these are the words of God or not, one thing is for sure, what this book predicted has just come to pass. I am going to pay attention to the other things it has to say, and I don't care if the rabbis don't believe it."*

With the Christians gone, many people rejoiced. To them it was *"Good riddance!"* Though the world had changed in a moment, it seemed as if prophets were every where claiming to be someone special. Along with these "prophets" came miracles and wonders to show the supposed proof of their words.

Not only were there all of these preachers, but a world leader had come on the scene. With his coming came an agreement that the Jews had the right to build their temple and worship their God the way they wanted to. It was called a holy covenant.

At this point Aaron Goldstein made up his mind that he was going to be a dedicated, faithful Jew in attendance of prayers and worship in the Jewish temple just as soon as it was finished and dedicated. Aaron made his way to the site where the temple was under construction. There he and other Jews gathered and prayed for God to bless the constructing of the temple, and that it would be completed soon.

Then he noticed two older men. They were rugged, dressed in robes with lively bright eyes that seemed to pierce right through him when they looked at him. Then they moved on, so Aaron asked some of the men, *"Who are those two men?"* But before he finished asking, he remembered what Charlie had told him. Moses and Elijah would be returning.

One of the men answered his question in a strange way. *"Well, Aaron, those two men claim to be Moses and Elijah."* They did notice that the building of the temple prospered when those two showed up. One of the rabbis spoke up and said, *"It's just like it was in the days of Ezra. When they were building the temple, they prospered under the prophesying of Haggai and Zechariah."*

It was about seven months after the Christians vanished that the temple was complete. Aaron was in deep thought when he remembered Charlie telling him it would be about seven months. Looking down at the ground, he shook his head in wonder, *"How did he know that?"*

Finally the day came for the dedication of the temple, and Jews came from all over the world. Here was a miracle. The Jewish temple was once again built and operational according to the Scriptures. While the other religions did not like the fact of the Jews having their temple again with daily sacrifices being offered, yet they could do nothing about it. They had to abide by the holy covenant that had been confirmed and signed.

Upon entering the inner court of the temple, Aaron was in awe. He knew many of the men who were present because they had all gathered outside and prayed while the temple was being built. But there were some new faces so he introduced himself and soon became well known amongst them all.

It had been a mere nine months since the Christians vanished, and only two months since the temple was dedicated and the daily sacrifices were instituted. But Aaron thought much about what Charlie Smith had told him as well as warned him of what was going to happen to Jerusalem and the temple. He wondered what the Orthodox Jewish men of the temple would think so he brought the subject up one day.

The men immediately scoffed, especially when Aaron mentioned what was written in Luke and Matthew in the Christian writings. One of the men almost spit on the temple floor when Luke's and Matthew's writings were mentioned, but feared when he realized he was in the Temple of God. Yet Aaron Goldstein did not stop bringing things up.

Though the men listened to this with some amusement, yet a few others said that they had heard these things as well, which silenced the others. They then added that it was the Christian writings which they did not believe.

Moses and Elijah began to plague the world and as they did, Aaron remembered again what Charlie had said to him, about the prophets, and how the world was going to hate them and the Jews. By now Aaron was reading his New Testament Scriptures as well as the Old Testament Scriptures. Because he loved the truth and diligently read the Scriptures, over the next months Aaron watched it all begin to take place. He could clearly see things take place just like it said it would in the Bible.

That day was one of many such days. It was a day when someone tried to kill Moses, but Moses burned them to death with the fire that came out of his mouth. The attempts to kill one, or both of the prophets were growing stronger and more frequent, yet the two prophets were unmoved by it all. They smote the world even more with plagues, droughts, pestilence, earthquakes and turned water to blood.

Once again in the temple, Aaron told the men that the world was going to hate them even more, and that it was going to get to the point where armies from all over the world were going to come and surround Jerusalem. To this the two prophets agreed.

Then Aaron Goldstein showed them the verses in the Gospel of Luke chapter 21. The Jewish men did not like it, but they had gained enough respect for Aaron that they actually read what it said in Luke. The verses troubled them, and they did not want to believe it so they turned away.

It had now been three and a half years since the Christians had vanished when Aaron then showed them the Scriptures in Matthew. Once again the men turned away, though in their hearts and minds there was a great troubling that seems to stab them with the thought, *"What if these writings were true?"*

News then hit the airwaves that armies were getting ready to come and attack Jerusalem. That morning in the temple after prayers the men gathered to talk about the news. Among them was Aaron Goldstein who spoke up and said, *"Men, in the Christian writings in the book of Luke this is mentioned and we are told to flee when the armies surround Jerusalem. So we   —"*

But before he could say more, the men cut him off and would not hear any more of it. They sternly declared, *"We are Jews and don't listen to heretic writings."*

Upon hearing this Aarons' heart sank down low. He knew what was coming because he now believed the New Testament Scriptures and was diligently reading them. He was also making sure his family all understood them as well. To Aaron it was so clear to see, but his fellow Jews were still filled with pride and would not listen. A tear filled his eye because he knew the danger that was soon to arrive and how they could easily avoid it all, but they would not listen to the Scriptures. To this Aaron looked down at his Bible and closed it. When he looked up, many men had turned their backs on him and departed.

There was one man across the temple court who was watching Aaron. As their eyes met, he nodded in agreement. It brought a strange comfort to Aaron, as it seemed to let him know that he was not the only one.

Two days passed. Upon rising early that day and after hearing the reports coming over the news, Aaron Goldstein knew that it was time to gather his family and leave. The scriptures he had read over and over confirmed this. He had prepared his wife and children for this time and they were ready, though hearts were heavy upon having to leave it all.

This was their home that they were leaving. Not only that but their actions were all based upon a book that Christians wrote, and many of their friends said those Scriptures were lies. But Aaron and his family could see all of the events that had unfolded which were described in those writings. What's more, they could see what was getting ready to happen with the armies arriving on the shores of Israel and heading towards Jerusalem. The choice was clear, but it was still hard to leave everything based upon some writings that some claim were wrong. But Aaron encouraged them all. He wept with them as they walked out of their bedrooms with the few clothes and shoes they brought with them. It was time to go.

Loading up what they needed, the Goldsteins departed by faith, listening to what God said in His words. Turning southward on Highway 40 they headed to the place called Selah Petra. What lay ahead for them they did not know.

As they drove along the highway, in the distance they saw a man on the side of the road hitchhiking. He turned around and was facing them as they approached him. He seemed in earnest and was flagging them to stop. Aaron wondered if he should or shouldn't stop and offer the man a ride. They had room for one more and something seemed to give them all peace about giving the man a ride, so they stopped and he got in.

Pulling out and getting back on the road the man spoke up and light-heartedly introduced himself. *"I'm Starlie Beam. Are you guys headed for Selah Petra?"*

Aaron stuttered his answer in surprise, _"Y..ye...ye... yes, that is where we are headed. How did you know?"_

Starlie smiled. _"I just know these things. You are going the right way and doing the right thing. I know it's hard but believe me, you will not regret it."_

His words were a great comfort, yet they were still amazed that he knew what they were doing. All fear of this man fled away. The ride even became enjoyable in spite of having just left everything.

Aaron wondered, but was too afraid to ask, _"Could this man be an angel?"_

As soon as Aaron thought this, the man, who sat up front with Aaron, turned his head, looked at Aaron and smiled.

✱✱✱✱✱✱✱✱✱✱✱✱✱✱✱✱

Meanwhile, back in Jerusalem things are continuing to heat up at a rapid pace.

The nations are now furious and burning with hatred against the Jews in Jerusalem, and especially against those two prophets who have been tormenting the world with plagues and disasters. (Rev. 11:10) Armies from all over the world begin to arrive in Israel. The latest weaponry is brought with the determination to kill Moses and Elijah. The leaders are blind with hatred that these two narrow minded men would dare to proclaim that all of the "good people" of the world need to repent and accept Jehovah as the true God of the world. The battle becomes a religious war, and those kind of wars are the bloodiest.

The Man of Sin, though not yet revealed, has begun

to side with the armies and the nations against the Jews. (Dan. 11:30) As he sits on his throne in Rome, prior to this he had integrated the nations religiously into one big conglomerate spiritually satanic mess. Now he follows intently and publicly on the latest events as they transpire. As the battle gets ready to begin, he flies to Israel to be there.

Army after army begin to surround Jerusalem with the main purpose of killing those two prophets.

All over the world, the people watch the events unfold, and as they do the people align themselves more and more on the side of the armies against the Jews. More and more people worldwide are filled with hatred for the God of the Jews. Deceptive miracles and preaching abound which fuels the great turning away of the masses from good and right. Good is now evil, and evil is now good. Included in this great turning are many Jews. There is a turning, a falling away from all forms of right and true godliness towards the ungodly influences of the Dragon.

The Chinese and the Japanese rejoice because for thousands of years they have worshipped the Dragon, and now for the first time, in their eyes, the world is seeing that they are right. In their perverted thinking, it is the Dragon that should be worshipped. Well, they will get their desire, but oh, what an eternal price they are going to pay!

For the Jews in Jerusalem, and especially in the temple, the tension and turmoil is extreme. They cling to the stories in the Scriptures, such as David and Goliath, or Joab and Abishai against the Ammonites, when Joab said, "Be of good courage, and let us play the men for our people, and for the cities of our God: and the LORD do that which seemeth him good." (2 Sam. 10:12)

The Jews are vastly outnumbered. Yet they continue with a resolute determination to stay true to their God, Jehovah. After all, they have seen Moses and Elijah whip everyone that has come against them in the last three years. Perhaps they have gained a confidence in the two prophets that sustains them at this time. Along with the two prophets, God's presence is in the temple. They cling to this and trust, but there is one great problem for them that they do not realize. The New Testament, the Christian writings which warn them of what is coming and instructs them in what they are supposed to do, they will not heed nor read. Those writings are the only Scriptures that warn them of the coming judgments.

Armies are now arriving into position for the battle against Jerusalem and the two prophets. It is a David and Goliath battle once again, except this time God is not with "David" i.e. the Jews, that remain in Jerusalem.

****

As the Jews assembled to worship the Lord, they noticed that some of their members were missing. When they asked where they were, the reply struck fear into their hearts.

Joseph Bauer looked over to John Finklestein and asked, *"Where is Aaron Goldstein?"*

With a look more serious than he could have ever imagined, John replied, *"Well, you know Aaron was always kind of extreme. And he would read the Christian Bible, too. You know how he would talk to us about it? He said that before all of these Christians vanished, that he had a Christian man who constantly told him what was going to happen, and even showed him from his book that he claimed was the word of God. Aaron told me that when we started building the temple that the Christian he worked with wouldn't shut up about how he was going to vanish one day soon. He told me everything that Christian had said was coming true exactly like he said it would."*

Joseph, while ignoring the Christian part, replied with a small grimace, *"Yeah, I know he would talk and talk about it all, and it would bother me. He wouldn't shut up about it."*

John spoke ernestly, *"Well, he showed me where it said that when you see Jerusalem compassed about with armies, we were supposed to flee. He said we should be like Lot leaving Sodom, and don't even look back. Well, Joseph, with the armies beginning to surround Jerusalem, Aaron took his wife and kids and left everything. Word has it that he is heading to Selah Petra."*

Joseph took a deep breath, as he looked around the temple he, *"Do you think we should do the same?"*

With a long stare, it was obvious John didn't know what to say.

Others began to gether around the two men. John, upon realizing others were listening, as well, seemed to set his jaw with a stoic resolution. *"This is our temple,*

329

and we have seen God work many wonders in the past weeks. I am here to stay. I am not going to desert my God or His prophets and run."

To this the listeners quietly said, "Amen," as they all got prepared to worship and pray in the temple.

****

Starlie spoke up and said, "This is a good place to stop and park the car." Aaron and his family looked around at a landscape of gently rolling, rocky, and sandy wasteland. A couple of miles off in the distance, jagged, rocky mountains, abruptly sprang up. Aaron parked the car and turned the motor off. The silence in the car was broken by Starlie, "You all are going to be alright, I promise you. But you're going to need to get going so you can make it by nightfall."

With that said, Starlie opened the door and got out of the car with a grin. Looking over to Aaron he said, "Well, it's been a really enjoyable ride with you all. Now what you want to do is hike toward that opening in the mountains over there and hike along into the city. There is only one way and you will be fine." With a slight pause he added, "You know, there are not very many who have done what you just did. But I want you to know that you will not regret what you have done in the least bit."

Elizabeth spoke up and her question was curious. "How do you know this?"

Starlie then looked at her with a gentle and kind face. "I just do, you will see. Now, you had better get started if you want to get in there before dark."

Aaron was quick to ask, "Aren't you coming with us?"

Starlie calmly replied, *"There's no need. You have made it."*

With a wave of good-bye, they started on their trek towards the opening in the mountains that Starlie had showed them. It had been less than a minute since they started walking. Isaac turned around to see Starlie one last time, but he was no where to be found.

"Dad," said Isaac quickly, *"Where did Starlie go?"*

Looking back, all they could see was a flat, wide open desert area. It was miles in size. Their car was parked by itself, with a few other cars scattered around the area. There really was no place for Starlie to conceal himself, yet he was gone.

Elizabeth spoke up, *"Do you remember reading somewhere in the Bible about entertaining angels unaware?"*

Aaron face wore a startled look as he remembered the verse. *"Yes, I do remember that verse. I wonder if that was an angel?"*

Their hearts seemed to leap with excitement as Elizabeth answered, *"I think Starlie was an angel. He had to be. He knew too much not to be. Wow! Honey, we are on the right track. Thank you for believing and obeying God. Now, Let's get to the city."*

And off they walked with a new found hope and peace in their hearts.

After walking for a bit, they soon caught up with another family just ahead of them. And though not very many people were to be seen, yet there were a few walking towards the same opening between the steep, rocky mountains.

Aaron with a hesitation struck up a conversation with the man of the family. *"Have you ever seen Petra before?"*

The man looked at him, *"No, we thought we would like to finally make ourselves come down here and see it. We've heard a lot about it though."*

Aaron now began to wonder if this man and his family were simply tourists. He then thought to himself that if they were tourists, this is the wrong time of day for tourists to come out here. But curiosity compelled him to ask, *"Are you Jewish?"*

The man sharply turned and looked at him, and for a minute Aaron thought that he had made a big mistake in asking that. Nervously looking around, the man then queried, *"Why do you ask?"*

Aaron with a slight boldness answered, *"Well, it's the wrong time of day for a tourist to be out here, and I've heard rumors that Jews are going to be staying out here for a while."*

The man started to relax just a bit, nodding his head. *"Yes, I've heard that as well."*

Aaron, remembered again what he had heard from Charlie, as well as what he had read on his own in the Scriptures. Could this man also know about the Jews living in Petra for the last half of the Tribulation?

Aaron smiled. *"My name is Aaron Goldstein. This is my wife, Elizabeth and my son, Isaac, along with my daughter Abigail. What's your name?"*

"My name is Michael Cohen, and this is my family." A smile broke across his face as he now seemed more relaxed. *"And Yes, we are Jewish, as I can tell by your name, you are too."*

332

Aaron replied, *"Yes, we are. I was worshipping in the temple in Jerusalem, but when I saw the armies—"*

Michael blurted out before Aaron could finish his sentence, *"Yes! The armies, it was time to run for the mountains. And in the Scriptures it seemed like we should to go to Petra. And then on the way down here a —"*

Aaron then excitedly jumped into the conversation. *"Did you picked up a man hitchhiking who guided you down here?"*

Michael's reply was immediate, *"Yes, I think he was an angel."*

This answer filled both families with wonder. So the two families rejoiced as they walked along, secure in the assuance that they were doing what God truly wanted them to do.

Looking around Michael asked, *"Do you think the rest of these people are Jews?"*

To that, Aaron replied, *"I think it is very likely."*

Scattered here and there were other families, totaling maybe 100 people in all. And all of them were heading towards the narrow gorge that wound its way into the rock city called Petra.

They had stepped out by faith, based upon what they had read or heard from Christians, as well as seeing the fulfillment come to pass with the gathering of the armies around Jerusalem. They had been watching closely the news reports as the armies and nations announced what they were getting ready to do. As the armies left their nations bound for Jerusalem, some of the Jewish families recognized what was happening and left all of their material possessions behind. They did not fully know what was getting ready to happen. And they did not realize that they were in actually saving their own lives?

The Battle Begins

Back in Jerusalem, as well as all of Judaea, the vast majority of Jews have remained there, along with the faithful who are still in the temple. The two witnesses, Moses and Elijah, are before the altar and praying. They are not scared in the least. They are ready to fight and to obey God and His word.

It is a strange thing to think about, but the two witnesses are very spiritual men. They know the Lord and they know the Scriptures very well. So they will know that they are going to end up dead in this upcoming battle. Other than Jesus Christ, I'm not sure if there is anyone in the Bible who, from the Scriptures knew exactly when and how they were going to die.

God gave Peter a glimpse of how he ––Peter–– was going to die, telling him it would be when he was old. But Peter did not know exactly when that was going to be. (John 21:18)

Because it is Moses and Elijah, they have already seen Heaven, Jesus Christ, and eternity. I would guess there is a certain excitement that they are going to be getting out of this wicked world and going home once and for all.

Armies are now surrounding the city, and the battle is getting ready to begin. A few more Jews have read the book of Luke and with trembling hearts they decide to exit the scene. With a precarious trip ahead of them, they leave to shouts behind them. Shouts of _"Cowards!" No faith, ungodly, go ahead and leave God's house."_

In the twilight of the evening they cautiously make their way out through the streets of Jerusalem. They also head to their homes. They quickly get their families together and head out for the wilderness. At first they have great fear and mixed emotions, but the farther they go the more peace they have. The guilt and uncertainty that consumes their emotions now bit by bit is easing. A calm assurance seems to be born within them the farther away from the city they go.

Each family meets someone who helps them in their trek. One Jewish family drives along slowly, cautiously and picks up a man who is waving his arms for a ride. They stop and offer him a ride. Once in the car, He looks over at the man who is driving the car and introduces himself, *"Hi, my name is Starlie Beam. You cut it quite close, didn't you?"*

The startled Jewish man then replies, *"We…We… Well, I guess I did. I wasn't sure what to do and…"*

Starlie spoke up. *"It's OK, you did the right thing. You need to go to Selah Petra, and I will guide you there."*

It's an hour before dawn when the battle in Jerusalem begins. Shells begin to land in and around the city. Squads of men with armored vehicles move towards the temple. Word arrives at the office of the prince that the battle is beginning. Outwardly he has appeared to try to diffuse the situation, but inwardly he is glad it is beginning. He is looking forward to when these two men who have created havoc worldwide will finally be removed. Though he is not even sure of this, as they have been victorious over every attack against them up to this point.

In front of the temple a blast of light is seen as Elijah

speaks; a bright, piercing flame burns up those in the first attack.

The temple at this time still has the presence of God in it, so any shells, bombs or attack upon the building is quenched. Through this whole battle, the temple remains intact. It is not destroyed. Moreover, the Man of Sin desires it should not be destroyed, for he wants to enter that temple himself.

Billows of smoke rise from the streets of Jerusalem as Moses and Elijah thwart attempt after attempt to kill them. Other parts of the city are on fire and being destroyed from the attack. Israel fights back valiantly, but the onslaught is so great they cannot keep up.

The battle continues for some time, and Moses and Elijah are holding their own. The enemies from the nations of the world are not making any headway in the goal of killing these two powerful prophets.

It is now three and a half years into the seven-year Tribulation. Down, down, down through the ground into the depths of Hell, a cage is opened. The gates of brass swing open as well, and the Beast ––with a gutteral growl of laughter–– begins to rise. (Rev. 13:1) Up to the surface of the earth, he ascends with a menacing power that is beyond what the two witnesses have encountered in all of their battles.

As the Beast reaches the surface of the earth he goes into the body of the prince.

[The same thing happened to Judas at the Last Supper. As they are eating Jesus tells the disciples, **"One of you shall betray me."** (John 13:21) Then they all begin to ask Him, **"Is it I?"** (Matt. 26:22) The apostle

John was leaning upon the Lord's breast, and he looked up to Him and asked, **"Who is it Lord?"** And the Lord answered to John, **"He it is, to whom I shall give a sop, when I have dipped it. And when he had dipped the sop, he gave it to Judas Iscariot, the son of Simon."** (John 13:26). **"And after the sop Satan entered into him. Then said Jesus unto him, That thou doest, do quickly."** (John 13:27)]

The pope--prince then becomes very angry and eagerly desires to go and fight Moses and Elijah himself.

[Why do I say he is a pope?

Because the pope, and throughout the centuries the popes, have claimed openly to be a substitute christ. "Vicarius Christi," which is one of the official titles for the Pope means, "substitute christ."]

> The Pope stands in the place of Jesus Himself as The "Vicar of Christ on earth." He is the head of the Catholic Church and Her nearly 1.3 billion Catholics, and is responsible for the Salvation of all the Souls throughout the entire world. *(Christ By The Sea, The Pope & The Papacy, christbythesea.net/the-pope-the-papacy#:~:text=The%20Pope%20stands%20in%20the,belie ve%20that%20Jesus%20chose%20St.,viewed 5/10/2024, 1:14P.M. CST, This is a Pro - Roman Catholic website:)*

With all the fury of Hell, the Beast storms down the streets as a roaring lion to where the prophets are. The scene is like something out of the Marvel Comics Universe. Streams of fire shoot out of the mouths of Moses and Elijah. The Beast dodges and blocks the streams, only to fire back at Moses and Elijah. What his weapon is, I do not know. Does he fight fire with fire? Maybe. But I do not know for sure.

Attack and defend, advance and withdraw --all takes place on both sides. Until in a blast of fire, light and heat, both sides fall down motionless.

As the news gets out, orders are given and all bombardment stops. The battle is over and done. Soldiers first, and then others gather around and see the two witnesses lying on the ground. Not all that far away is the prince lying on the ground as well. One of his arms is severely mangled, and the right side of his head is bloody with his right eye blown out.

How long do people stop and stare at the scene, I do not know. Reports are broadcast that the two witnesses are dead, and so is the prince. Worldwide there is a mixed emotion, yet an inward sigh of relief because the two that tormented the world are now dead.

As news reaches all the way around the world in a matter of minutes, cheers and shouts of joy are heard as well. People flood out into the streets and start dancing, laughing and praising the Beast and the Dragon, for finally killing the two prophets. The time of day does not matter. The news is met with such joy that those who are asleep in their beds get up and rejoice for the death of the prophets.

People are so happy they feel like sending gifts one to another. They are not celebrating a birthday. They are celebrating a death-day: The demise of the two prophets of God. And with the celebration comes an attitude of death towards the Lord God Jehovah.

Worldwide, the people are convinced, *"We now know who the true God is, and it is the Dragon and his prince. Our allegiance is now to the Dragon and his prince."*

This point in the Tribulation is the zenith of the world's falling away. There is a complete worldwide shift; the world sides with and worships Satan in the form of the Beast and the Dragon. It's the satanic trinity so if you worship one, then you are worshipping the other.

Worldwide the prince, though dead at this point, is esteemed a hero who gave his life for the good of all mankind. Reports go out about how no one was able to defeat the two prophets, but the prince sacrificed himself for us all. He is hailed as a hero of heroes.

Perhaps three days and three nights go by, since Satan seeks to counterfeit Jesus Christ. It is three days and nights of party, orgies, and celebrations. Music plays all over the world. Gifts are sent all over the world. To the carnal, self-loving citizens of the world, it is what they imagine to be Heaven on earth. No work and all play. If an election were to be held at the end of the three days and nights, the Beast would get ninety-eight percent of the vote. Virtually all the world goes after the Beast, as well as the Dragon. (Rev. 13:3-4)

Cameras are now pointed towards the dead bodies of Moses and Elijah. Worldwide people look at their dead bodies and rejoice. With shouts of *"I'm so glad they are dead! The prince, he is my hero. I just wish he would not have died."*

Some Jews come out to gather the bodies of Moses and Elijah in order to bury them but they are blocked immediately. The Jews say they want to bury their bodies, and those around pointedly shout back, *"No! We want to see the birds and dogs come and eat them. The bodies stay where they are, you can't move them. Let their sight be a reminder that the prince is our hero and even our god. Leave those bodies alone and get out of here! Go back into the temple of your weakling God."*

With that the Jews retreat back into the temple.

Three days and nights go by. The prince's body has been taken up and prepared for a heroes burial that is to be broadcast worldwide. Weeping and mourning break out all over the world as the funeral proceeds. Then all of a sudden in the casket, the prince begins to move. First his head, then he moves a leg, and then he opens his one good eye. Cameras and lights are turned on him as he sits up in the coffin, shakes himself, and declares, *"Who is a savior like me?"*

Through the streets, over the internet, and around the world shouts of joy ring out, *"Heeee's Aliiiive!!! Our prince, our savior, our king is alive."* Joy is now flowing throughout the world. Joy and happiness, even on the streets of Jerusalem.

Cameras are still pointed towards the dead bodies of Moses and Elijah. Worldwide people are still gazing at their dead bodies and still rejoicing over their deaths. They never tire of shouting, *"I'm so glad they are dead! The prince, he is my hero."*

The worldwide shift at this time grows even stronger. The world falls away from any acknowledgement of the true God. They all now accept Satan, the Dragon as their god. The world with many of the Jews falls away, and the culmination of it is the celebration and the sending of gifts one to another. It only makes sense that the world would celebrate as they accept the god of this world as their true god.

Meanwhile, the bodies of Moses and Elijah have lain in the streets now for three and a half days. People still walk by and rejoice just to see their dead bodies. Cameras are still broadcasting a live stream their dead bodies lying in the streets of the city, "**...which spiritually is called Sodom...**" (Rev. 11:8)

All of a sudden Moses and Elijah begin to breathe. They come to life and stand up on their feet. It's been twelve hours since the Man of Sin came to life. Great fear falls upon those around them who are watching. (Rev. 11:11-12). They then ascend up to Heaven in the sight of all of their enemies.

In the same hour there is an earthquake and 7,000 men end up dead. Like a thief who gets caught in the act, the enemies of the Jews begin to praise and to glorify the Lord Jehovah, but it is only a short lived repentance. (Rev. 11:13)

Somewhere in this time frame, something extraordinary happens.

For three years the Jews have been worshipping in the temple and keeping the law of Moses just as they did in the Old Testament.

During the first half of the Tribulation, when the temple is being used for the worship and obedience to God, you should realize that in the holiest of all there is the Ark of the Covenant, also known as the Ark of His Testament. That is where the presence of God is when the temple is in operation. And whether it is at the same time as when Moses and Elijah get caught up to Heaven, I am not sure, but I do know that the Ark gets translated up to the third Heaven.

> ¹⁹And the temple of God was opened in heaven, and **there was seen in his temple the ark of his testament**: and there were lightnings, and voices, and thunderings, and an earthquake, and great hail. (Rev. 11:19)

That Ark is a picture of the throne of God. That ark has had the presence of Almighty God upon it. It is the throne of God that Satan has always wanted to take over. So the Man of Sin would love nothing more, while under the inspiration of Satan himself, to walk into the holiest of all and desecrate the Ark. In a very strong way it would signify Satan destroying the throne of God in the third Heaven. So God raptures the Ark out of the world and up into Heaven.

It will not remain forever in Heaven because we will be bringing it back with us at the Second Advent. The Ark will then be placed in the Millennial temple, in the most holy place. It will reside in the temple which is in the city that bears the Lord's name, which is Holy. That is why it is capitalized in Daniel 9:24.

The Man of Sin is Revealed

> ¹⁷Woe to **the idol shepherd** that leaveth the flock! **the sword** *shall be* **upon his arm, and**

> **upon his right eye: his arm shall be clean dried up, and his right eye shall be utterly darkened.** (Zech. 11:17)

This shepherd is an idol shepherd. He is worshipped. This is the Man of Sin. He is the one who has a withered arm and his right eye is darkened. It is likely that he is blind in his right eye, and possibly wears a patch over the eye.

It is 2024 as I write this, and more often than in the past years, you will see references to Satan, or people with their right eye blind, patched or covered. As I did a quick search I found that most of the photos with people covering one eye had the right eye covered, but not all. Many had the left eye covered instead of the right. But the act of covering one eye can stem from this verse.

Around the USA there are popping up After School Satan Clubs. In the logo of the club is a cartoon caricature of a man with two horns coming out of his head. His left hand is holding up two fingers, just like a pope holds up (The sign of the bowman; the sign of death. For further study see *Mark of The Beast* by Peter S. Ruckman, Bible Baptist Bookstore) and his left eye is darkened. *(The Satanic Temple, After School Satan, https://thesatanictemple.com/pages/after-school-satan, viewed 5/10/24)* But from the viewers perspective it is the right eye. The problem with the logo is that it is not HIS right eye that is darkened, it is HIS left eye. But the Bible says HIS right eye shall be darkened.

If you will just go with your King James Bible you will get it straight.

So most of the pictures of people covering one eye, it is with their right eye covered —which would be the correct way to do it if you wanted to proclaim that you are following Satan.

> [4]And **they worshipped the dragon** which gave power unto the beast: and **they worshipped the beast**, saying, Who *is* like unto the beast? who is able to make war with him?
> (Rev. 13:4)

> [8]And **all that dwell upon the earth shall worship him, whose names are not written in the book of life** of the Lamb slain from the foundation of the world. (Rev. 13:8)

> [4]Who opposeth and exalteth himself above all that is called God, or that is worshipped; so that **he as God sitteth in the temple of God, shewing himself that he is God.**
> (2 Thess. 2:4)

Ah, yes! There you have it. He shows himself as God so that he will demand to be worshipped. This brings us to the middle of the 70th week. At this point we are three and one-half years into the week, and the information given in the word of God is specific in nature and leaves no doubt about what is going to happen. This is the great dividing of the week by God to let you know that the second half has elements that are completely opposite of the first half.

Let me connect the scene from where I last left off.

The Man of Sin resurrects from the battle three days and nights after he was killed. The world, while still celebrating the deaths of Moses and Elijah, are now ecstatic over the news that their hero is alive. Then twelve hours after his resurrection, Moses and Elijah come to life and are then raptured up into Heaven. The same hour that takes place, there is an earthquake and 7,000 people end up dead.

Now you must admit there is quite a bit of detail that the Bible gives you concerning these things. This is not confusing or mystical. All you have to do is rightly divide the Scriptures and believe what is written as it is written. There is no need to go to any Greek or Hebrew manuscripts. You have all of the information preserved perfectly for you in English. The problem is with those who read it, and with bad hearts refuse to believe the Bible for what it says.

After the short-lived fear of God subsides from those who lived around the area of the earthquake, the world continues on in their party.

Word gets out that there is a large image of the Man of Sin being built and will be completed within a day or two. This news reaches the Jews who remain in the temple, as well as throughout all of Judaea.

For those Jews who have been reading the Gospel of Matthew, they know exactly what this means. They know that image is going to be set up in the temple. It is amazing to realize that the only Jews who escape the wrath of Satan (through the person of the Man of Sin) are the Jews who will have loved the truth and will recognize the New Testament Scriptures as the truth. The New Testament is the only place in the Bible where the specific commands (Matt. 24:15) are given to show the Jews what they need to do, as well as all of the nations of the world.

In the temple, as well as all around Judaea, tempers begin to rage as New Testament reading Jews try to warn family and friends concerning what is about to happen. As they show them the Scriptures in the New Testament, other Jewish persons reject it as heresy. Fathers and sons, wives and husbands, daughters and mothers are torn apart. Only those who place the words of God above all else are the ones who will escape. It is a time of sifting for the nation of Israel.

By this time now there is no longer any way to delay a decision. You are either for God or you are not. You are either going to believe the words of God, including the New Testament, or you are not. By believing the words of God, there will be a leaving of loved ones. This is why the Lord wrote the following words:

> **³⁴Think not that I am come to send peace on earth: I came not to send peace, but a sword.**
> **³⁵For I am come to set a man at variance against his father, and the daughter against her mother, and the daughter in law against her mother in law.**
> **³⁶And a man's foes** *shall be* **they of his own household.**
> **³⁷He that loveth father or mother more than me is not worthy of me: and he that loveth son or daughter more than me is not worthy of me.**
> **³⁸And he that taketh not his cross, and**

followeth after me, is not worthy of me.
[39]He that findeth his life shall lose it: and he that loseth his life for my sake shall find it. (Matt. 10:34-39)

It is now time for all the people of the world to choose Jesus Christ. To not choose Him is to end up dead, sooner or later, as you will see later in this book. By the end of the Tribulation, the only people who will survive will be those who loved the truth, including the New Testament, and were willing to obey the truth regardless of who or what it would cost them.

Meanwhile, back in Jerusalem the Man of Sin has a plan for all of the world to behold. The image is now ready to be set up. The theme song has now been written and is ready to be played worldwide. The Man of Sin is ready, and even believes that he is God. And the world is slobbering hungry to have him ascend the world stage as their true god.

The morning has dawned and cameras are filming. The parade begins with the Man of Sin being carried upon the shoulders of "the faithful." He is smiling at the crowds and waving, while dressed in his long white robe. His darkened eye is covered with a gold patch that sparkles in the sun shine. On his head is a golden crown with an inscription which reads, Filii Die. (The "Vicarius" has been removed) In his other hand he holds a golden scepter. People line the road and begin to throw their coats and garments onto the road in front of him. Others fall down and worship him as he is carried by.

Behind him, borne on a trailer being pulled by regal

horses and draped by a gorgeous purple and scarlet covering, is the golden image of the Beast. It has not been seen yet. Only the world has heard about it. Today is the unveiling of it.

Onward the procession slowly maks its way towards the Jewish temple. No longer will it be for the Jews. Today the Gentiles will take over the temple.

The theme song continues to play on all kinds of instruments. Psalteries, harps, sackbuts, cornets, flutes, along with guitars, drums and keyboards. A fabulous praise band also plays the worship music. As the tempo builds, people begin to be slain in the spirit and fall down on the ground, foaming at the mouth.

As the procession at last approaches the temple, something happens inside. Up to this point the temple had been bright with light as well as filled with joyful music and singing. A peaceful spirit also resided inside. But now something changes.

As the Jews see the image on its way, some of them warn the others that it is time to flee to the wilderness. Many do not yield. But a remnant from all parts of Israel now run for their lives. They don't stop for anything, and they don't look back. They run as fast and as hard as they can.

Upon reaching the southern part of Israel, they begin to notice other Jews running too, so they band together. Little by little their Jewish flock grows as they make their exodus from their homeland. They have left early enough to not be hounded too much.

Back in Jerusalem, the temple becomes strangely dark, and it grows cold and clammy inside. The Ark has ascended to Heaven. The candlestick has burned out. Desolation takes over the temple for God has departed.

The front doors swing open, and a blast of music fills the court. Then men bring the image of the Beast inside and set it up in the holy place. Along with that, a golden throne is brought in and placed in the holiest of all, behind the veil. Perhaps the veil is torn down so that the world can see their god sitting upon his golden throne in the Temple of God.

The Man of Sin is lowered from the shoulders of his followers, and walks upon the robes of the faithful. He wears his eye patch, and he shows his withered arm as a badge of honor. Upon entering the temple, the music plays and people fall to the ground and worship his holiness, their new god. Waking into the holiest of all, and with the image now standing in the holy place, he proclaims to the world, "I am God. I have defeated God and his weakling servants. I am the one to be worshipped. We have begun a new world of hope, joy and love for all."

With that the theme song plays again and all of the people fall down wherever they are and worship the Man of Sin. Those who do not fall down and worship are immediately marked and warned that if they do not worship the Man of Sin they will be killed. There are no exceptions.

This is now the last possible opportunity for the Jews to exit and to run for their lives. Yet most of the Jews set their jaws, stiffen their necks and will not budge. They are staying put in their homeland. Those Jews still remaining in the temple are immediately killed, to the cheers of all those watching.

The ones who flee at the last minute, perhaps flee to the Ben Gurion Airport that is thirty miles away. They have heard there is a transport waiting to take them to safety.   As room on the plane quickly fills up, it is time to take off.   Others have just arrived but it is too late. The plane is full, the door is closed.   Just in time it takes to the air like a bird with two great wings, and heads south.

Landing out in the desert, the people exit and make their way for Selah Petra. The closer they get to Petra, the more peace they have.   A calm assurance is beginning to fill each heart, though many are weeping because of the loved ones they have left behind.

As they walk, the others who left a couple days earlier catch up with them as well, and they become one flock of people with one thing in common. They believe the words of God, and act upon them in spite of the cost. God is first in their hearts.

****

But alas, what has happened to Aaron Goldstein and his family?

Aaron and his family finally made it to Selah Petra in the wilderness. In the book of Luke, it says that when they see the armies surround Jerusalem, they are to flee into the mountains. But in Revelation 12, it says that they flee into the wilderness; in Hosea it says that they are allured into the wilderness. So how do they know where to go?

When the Lord says that He will allure her (Israel) into the wilderness **"as in the day when she came up out of the land of Egypt"** (Hos. 2:15), for a Jew there is no doubt about where that is. It is the land of Edom which is south of the Dead Sea, and just north of Ezion Geber

350

which is at the northern tip of the Red Sea.

There is a strange wording found in Hosea 2:14, when the Lord says that He will **"allure her, and bring her into the wilderness."** And then in Hosea 2:19 the Lord says that He will, **"...betroth thee unto me..."** What you have is Jehovah God in love with His bride (which is Israel), and she is finally back in love with Him. This remnant of Jews will love Him completely, and unreservedly. The names of Baalim will have been taken out of the mouth of Israel, just as He said He would in Hosea 2:17: **"I will take the names of Baalim out of her mouth..."**

There in the wilderness for three and a half years the remnant of Israel will be nourished and loved on by God the Father, her husband. They will be in very rough physical surroundings, but it will be very wonderful spiritual communion with Jehovah.

It is amazing to think about, that God the Father was broken over Israel's whorish heart. (Eze. 6:9) His bride whom He loves deserted her husband and committed adultery against Him. For 2,000 years He cast her aside, but here He is now bringing her back into love with Him.

The allurement into the wilderness is their love for their God and His words, for it is His words that saved their lives. The presence of God that was only experienced in the temple is now with all of the remnant of Israel in the wilderness mountains, just like it was when they came out of the land of Egypt. I know Israel murmured and complained in the wilderness, but now all such murmuring is gone. The love and desire to be with God, and where God's presence is, is what allured them to Selah Petra, for that is where God will be. And that is where they will be nourished and protected from the dragon. (Rev. 12:14)

As Aaron and his family arrived into the rock city known as Selah Petra, there was a peace and a calm assurance that was guiding them all along the way. Something inside of him just knew that what he had done was right. He had brought his family, and he was in the first group that arrived.

Walking in and out of the caves and rock structures which had been dug into the sides of the vertical rock walls of the mountains, Aaron sought to find the right place for him and his family to abide. With his reading of the New Testament, he knew that they would be there for three and a half years.

Aaron, thinking out loud, whispered to himself, _"We need to make the best of it that we can. We are going to be here for a while."_ And with that he brought his family to the inside of a cave with a flat smooth dirt floor. He gathered his wife and children around, telling them that this would be their new home for a few years. Then he stepped out of the cave and looked around at the other Jews who were arriving.

He noticed a man with his family walking in his direction. As the man got closer, Aaron looked and recognized him from the temple. He was the one who had looked across the room and nodded his head when Aaron was showing the others the Scriptures in Luke 21. Running over to him, Aaron hugged him with great joy. Looking at him he asked, _"Are we the only ones who left when as the armies were surrounding Jerusalem?"_

With a compassionate sadness, the man replied, _"I'm afraid we are."_

Aaron looked down and shook his head in despair. *"I tried to tell them... then after a short pause ...but at least you are here. And what is your name?"*

Gathering around him was his wife, two boys eight and ten years old, and a girl of four. The man introduced himself, *"I am Judah Cohen, and this is my wife Sarah, and my boys, Samuel and Elijah, and my daughter Ruth."*

Aaron in turn introduced his family as well. *"This is my wife Elizabeth, my son Isaac and my daughter Abigail."*

The children looked at each other. As their eyes met they could see that each was feeling the same thing. The fear and hurt, as well as the leaving everything that they knew. Instantly there was a close bond between them. It was such a comfort to know that they were not alone in their trials.

Aaron asked, *"So how long do you think it will be before the idol is set up in the holy place?"*

Judah looked at him and a small shrug. *"Oh, I am not sure, but I don't think it will be all that long. Once those armies start the battle it will be only a matter of a day or so. I figure, it won't be too long before the rest of the remnant come running here."* And he was correct.

****

As things are forming for the one world religion and the worshipping of the Man of Sin, there is a battle that takes place in Heaven. Michael and his angels fight with the Dragon and his angels. **"...neither was their place found any more in heaven..."** (Rev. 12:8)

Satan first gets cast out of the third Heaven. (Ezek. 28:16) He then gets cast out of the second heaven. (Luke 10:18) He then gets cast out of the first heaven. (Rev. 12:9). From there he gets cast into the bottomless pit at the Second Advent. (Rev.20:1-3) Then his final casting down is into the Lake of Fire. (Rev. 20:10)

So at this point then, Satan has been cast out into the earth, and he is furious.

Have you ever seen someone like that? God deals with them over and over and all they do is harden their-self against God. Do you realize the way to win in life is to submit to Jesus Christ?

If you are a soldier, or someone who was in the military, then you have been trained not to surrender. As a soldier in battle that is how you should be --full of courage and moral fortitude to press on in the battle. But, please, hear what I have to say.

If God is dealing with you, there may be a thought or belief that if you break or surrender that you are losing. But that is not so. If you are saved, then you know how to surrender, because that is exactly what you did when you got saved. When you don't --or won't-- surrender to Jesus Christ, you are acting just exactly like Satan. AND YOU WILL LOSE THAT BATTLE. If you are saved, no, you won't go to Hell, but between now and Heaven you can get beat up really badly by Jesus Christ. But He is doing it out of love.

A True Story

As the cocky young man walked into the tent, he looked around at the chairs that had been set up for the church revival service. Most of them were empty because his friend had brought him to the meeting early in order to introduce him to the speaker.

The speaker was an ex-gang member who had been the leader of the gang. But he had gotten saved and was now in the ministry. He took one look at this cocky young man and "had his number."

Upon being introduced, the preacher, --a clean cut, but big strong burly man, shook the cocky young man's hand. He looked him in the eye and said, *"It's good to meet you."* But he would let go of the young man's hand.

The young man, who had already been witnessed to days earlier, tried to pull his hand away but couldn't. Inside he flared with anger, getting ready to hit this man with his free hand.

Then the preacher, still looking at him in the eye, said sternly, *"Why don't you just give up!"*

Becoming even more angry, the young man wanted to fight back, but something inside wouldn't let him.

The preacher continued, *"Don't you think it's about time you got saved? You need to give up."*

With the Holy Spirit working as well, the young man broke and fell to his knees and got saved. To this day he is a pastor and serving Jesus Christ. The day he surrendered to Jesus Christ is the day that he got the victory —the greatest victory of his life. He was born again.

Dear reader, are you fighting God? Maybe you don't even know that you are. Why don't you ask Him, "God, am I fighting you in anything?" When the Lord shows you, just repent and surrender to Jesus Christ.

If He is leading you in a direction that scares you, then tell Him that. Be honest. If He is leading you to a higher level of walk that to you is beyond what strength you have, then tell Him that.

There have been times where I have seen what God wanted me to do, and it looked so high that I didn't know how I could ever achieve it. So I told him so. I prayed and said, *"Dear Lord Jesus, I want to be there, but I don't have the strength. I will try, but God, I need you to get me there, because I can't do it."* And God got me to where He wanted me to be. It wasn't me. I did not have the strength. Jesus Christ got me there, by His grace.

Enough preaching for now, so let's get back to Satan coming down to this earth in the middle of the Tribulation.

The main remnant of Jews are now walking through the desert to get to Selah Petra. They have gotten off the plane. The other Jews who had come by car, bus, or on foot, have arrived as well and have consolidated into one larger group of people.

Their assembling together was a great encouragement to everyone the same way it was for the Goldstein family when they met the Cohen family. There were many hugs given and tears shed.

The day was drawing on, and still they had a ways to go. As they walked through the desert, all of a sudden they heard a sound coming from behind them. Turning around and looking back, all they could see was a wall of water coming towards them at 60 miles an hour. Screaming and running as fast as they could, they tried to find safety, but to no avail. With all hope gone, it looked like the whole flock was going to be wiped out. But just before the water reached them, there was a rumble in the earth. The shaking and shockwaves of the earthquake caused some of the people to stumble and even fall down. And then the earth opened up a very deep and wide crack in front of the flood of water, causing the water to fall into the earth and the flock of Jewish people to run on in safety.

That flood had come from the Dragon himself, for he drank up Jordan and spit it out in an attempt to kill those Jews. But God thwarted him, which made the Dragon furious. (Job 40:23, Rev. 12:15) Turning around, he went back to Israel, and made war with the rest of the Jews who were still back there. Oh, what a sad time they are going to have over the next three and a half years!

> [12]¶ Therefore rejoice, *ye* heavens, and ye that dwell in them. Woe to the inhabiters of the earth and of the sea! for **the devil is come down unto you, having great wrath,** because he knoweth that he hath but a short time. (Rev. 12:12)

Heaven is rejoicing because the Dragon is cast out, but on the earth the world is worshiping the Dragon as God. What an amazing contrast! (Rev. 13:3-4)

Oh Lord, let me always view life and things in light according to your holy words, and let my heart be aligned with Heaven!

The Mark of the Beast

The time has now come when "...he who now letteth, will let, until he be taken out of the way." He has now been taken out of the way, and the Satanic trinity is no longer "incognito." Satan is openly ruling and reigning on the earth from Jerusalem. Because of this, freedom and the Laodicean civil rights have ended. It is now a time of absolute control, and the first act is to control and track everyone through a mark in their forehead or in their right hand. (Rev. 13:16-17) This is known as the Mark of the Beast, and no man can buy or sell without the mark.

If you take the mark, you can have a great time. You can eat and drink, buy and sell, get married, build buildings and enjoy yourself. (Luke 17:28, Matt. 24:38) There is just a couple of problems for those who take the mark of the Beast. The first of which is the fact that if you take the Mark of the Beast, then you have sealed your fate. You will die in your sins and go to Hell. (Rev. 14:9-10). The second problem with taking the Mark of the Beast is that you will get a grievous sore upon your body. (Rev. 16:2)

You will notice that in the verses I have given as reference, it says these things happen to those who take the Mark of the Beast, and who worship his image. If a person does one, then they will be doing the other as well.

The taking of the Mark of the Beast is a personal declaration of allegiance to him, which is in essence a declaration of allegiance to Satan. They are placing their lives, food, pleasure, wealth, and security into the hands of Satan. Lest this seem strange, you should know that there are many today who are already doing this in secret. It is common to hear of entertainers who have done this very thing. They sell their soul to the Devil for fame and fortune. So this is nothing new.

I have a book (and actually more than one) in which are court records of witches giving testimony. Without torture and they testified that they signed an agreement with "the man in black" and after having their finger pricked, they then sign their name with their own blood. The purpose was the promise that they would have food, wealth, fun, and be able to take vengeance upon those with whom they are mad at.

It is very interesting to note that when they call for the man in black, they call out the name "Robin." Then the man in black comes. Does that sound like someone you might have heard of? A "hero" in black who has a helper by the name of Robin?"

Court testimony of Elizabeth Style of Stoke Twister, County of Somerset, England, 1664 (5th Examination)

5. Exam. Elizabeth Styles her confession of her Witchcrafts, Jan. 26 and 30, and Feb. 7, 1664, Before Rob. Hunt Esq; She then confessed, that **the Devil about 10 Years since, appeared to her in the shape of a handsome Man, and after of a Black-Dog;** that he promised her Money, and that she should Live gallantly, and have the Pleasure of the World for 12 Years, if she would with

her Blood sign his Paper, which was to give her Soul to him, and observe his Laws, and **that he might suck her blood.** This after four Solicitations, and the Examinant promised to do; upon which, he prickt the fourth Finger of her Right-hand, between the middle and upper Joint, (where the sign at the Examination remained) and with a Drop or two of her Blood, she signed the Paper with an [O] Upon this, the Devil gave her Sixpence, and vanisht with the Paper.

That since he hath appeared to her in the shape of a Man, and did so on Wednesday Seven-night past, but more **usually he appears in the likeness of a Dog, and Cat, and a Fly like a Millar, in which last he usually sucks in the Poll about four of the Clock in the Morning** , and did so Jan. 27, and that it usually is pain to her to be so suckt.

That when she hath a desire to do harm, **she calls the Spirit by the Name of Robin, to whom when he appeareth, she useth these words, O Satan give me my purpose !** She then tells him what she would have done. And that he should so appear to her, was part of her Contract with him.

Pg 75

The Man in black, sometimes plays on a

Pipe or Cittern, and the Company dance. At last the Devil vanisheth, and all are carried to their several homes in a short space. At their Parting they say [**A Boy! Merry meet, merry part.**]

That the reason why she caused Elizabeth Hill to be the more tormented was, because her Father had said, she was a Witch.

(Glanville, Joseph, Saducismus Triumphatus: , Third Edition, 1700 AD, Part 2, Relat. III: Which containeth the Witchcrafts of Elizabeth Style of Bayford, Widow, Pg 73, 75,https://archive.org/details/saducismustriump00gla n/page/n427/mode/2up, viewed 5/10/24). (Capitalization and punctuation is preserved in the quote, just as found in the book.)

This is merely one account of stories of people who sold their soul to the Devil for comfort and vengeance. Many are doing this secretly in the age in which we now live, but in the near future, when the Man of Sin is revealed, people will openly take the mark as a sign of allegiance to the Beast.

Something else that is interesting is the fact that those who sell their souls to the Devil, they end up with a grievous sore upon their body. This sore has been called a "witches Teate." It is spelled in various ways such as tit, teat, or teate. It is a mark upon the body, usually in a covered part of the body, and it is the place where the Devil, or his devils come and suck the blood of the person or witch.

Daemonology, Second Book, The description of Sorcerie and Witchcraft in speciall

Chapter 2

The following quote I have updated some of the spelling since the Old English is a bit difficult to read and understand, and left whole words in with definitions in parenthesis.

The context is the Devil taking someone in allegiance to him.

> At which time, before he proceed any further with them, he first persuades them **to addict themselves to his service**: which being easily obtained, he then discovers what he is unto them: makes them to renounce their God and Baptism directly, and **gives them his mark upon some secret place of their body, which remains sore unhealed**, while his next meeting with them, and thereafter ever insensible, how soever it be nipped or pricked by any, as is daily proved, to give them a proof thereby, that as **in that doing he could hurt and heal them; so all their ill and well doing thereafter, must depend upon him.** And besides that, the intolerable dolor (pain and suffering) that they feel in that place, where he hath marked them, serves to waken them, and not to let them rest, while

their next meeting again: fearing lest otherwise they might either forget him, being new Prentices, and not well enough founded yet, in that fiendlie folly: or else remembering of that horrible promise they made to him, at their last meeting, they might skunner (loth themselves) at the same, and preasse (fight or strive) to call it back.

(James I, King of England, Daemonologie, 1597, Daemonology, Second Book, The description of Sorcerie and Witchcraft in speciall, Chapter 2, downloaded from https://www.gutenberg.org/cache/epub/25929/pg25929-images.html, viewed 5/10/24)

A Guide to Grand-Jurymen:

By a Witches mark, which is upon these baser sort of witches, and this by sucking, or otherwise by the Devils touching, **experience prooveth the truth of this**, and innumerable instances are brought for examples. **Tertullian found this true, and saith, It is the Devils custom to mark his: God hath his mark for his, Ezeckiel 9. Rev. 7 and 14, The beast will have his mark Rev. 13. (Who is the Devils Lieutenant) so the Devil himself will have his mark...** *(Bernard, Rich of Batcombe, A Guide to Grand-Jurymen, Second Edition, 1630, Printed by Felix Kyngston for Edw. Blackmore, Chap. XVIII Of the maine point to convict one of witchcraft, and the proofs thereof, pg 214, downloaded from https://archive.org/details/bim_early-english-books-1475-1640_a-guide-to-grand-jury-me_bernard-richard_1630/page/212/mode/2up, viewed 5/10/24)*

Now in regards to the Mark of the Beast, some have postulated that by taking the mark you will get leprosy, and I am not completely ruling this out. All the word of God says though, is that those who take the mark are given **"...a noisome and grievous sore."** (Rev. 16:2) But it does not say what that sore is, so it is conjecture to say what the sore actually is.

The problem with the sore being leprosy is the fact that leprosy is not a sore. It is an infection that deadens the nerves so there is no feeling. This is why so many people with leprosy have lost fingers, toes, and extremities. When they hurt themselves, they don't feel it, thus causing damage and loss of the extremity.

The Bible says that those who take the mark get a sore upon them. Those who take the Mark of the Beast are pledging their allegiance and worship to the Beast and the Dragon, or Devil. Since they literally are selling their souls to the Devil, I think it is possible that they are given a witches teate by which the Devil can control them through pain or "healing." As King James said in regard to the mark, "he could hurt and heal them; so all their ill and well doing thereafter, must depend upon him." To me this would fit for it being a noisome and grievous sore.

With this Sadducee mentality that we live in today, there are very few people who allow for and acknowledge that there is a very real spirit realm. This modern society, especially the educated bunch, are just like the Sadducees which say that there is "...no resurrection, neither angel, nor spirit..." (Acts 23:8). Thus when you read in modern books and articles about the witch trials and the searching of people for a witches mark, they make it sound ludicrous that such things were ever done. They then claim that the witches teats were nothing more than skin lesions and medically explainable physical conditions. But no, that is not the case. The fact of the witches teat is attested to in many court proceedings where the witch was never tortured to give their information. Yes, some were tortured and in so doing gave testimony to being a witch. The point is though that there were many, many cases where people admitted to being a witch and having a witches teat given them by the Devil when they sold their soul to him.

With Satan openly running the world, and when the people sell themselves to him in order to receive their food and fun, I think it likely that the sore is a witches teat. About 95% of the world takes the mark and are openly living for Satan.

This is not quite four years since the Rapture. For 2,000 years the world had the love of God, but they didn't want that. Now they have Satan and fall "head over heels" for the Devil.

With the instituting of the Mark of the Beast, also comes the set up of the image of the Beast —Satan's "aid to worship." The world is commanded to make an image to the Beast. This creates a vast market and demand for images. The Bible does say that **"...he shall cause craft to prosper."** (Dan. 8:25) And it sure does! From small to large, idols are made.

Do you remember what Rachel did when her father came looking for his images? "...Rachel had taken the images, and put them in the camel's furniture, and sat upon them." (Gen 31:34). And in 1 Sam. 5, you have the statue of Dagon which was quite large.

It's the same as having a statue of Mary. There are statues in front or back yards, and there are statues on the dash of cars, or on the mantle over fireplaces. There are also giant statues of Mary. The largest statue of Mary is in Sitio Montemaria, Barangay Pagkilatan, Batangas City, Philippines and it is 322 feet high. That's appoximately 23 stories high. *(En.wikipedia.org, Mother of All Asia - Tower of Peace, From Wikipedia, the free encyclopedia,https://en.wikipedia.org/wiki/Mother_of_All_Asia_%E2%80%9 3_Tower_of_Peace, last edited on 21 August 2023, Sikimedia Foundation, Inc., viewed 5/10/2024)*

Don't you know that there will be a lot of people made rich in the new global market for images of the Beast?

It really is interesting to see when you read Revelation 18. The merchants around the world are in torments and weeping over the fall of Babylon, but in Heaven it is written, **"Rejoice over her, *thou* heaven, and *ye* holy apostles and prophets; for God hath avenged you on her."** (Rev. 18:20) At the end of the Tribulation, there really is a large disconnect on earth with Heaven. How about you? Are you in sync with Heaven right now?

Remember the prayer that so many churches recite as a vain repetition? **"Thy kingdom come. Thy will be done in earth, as *it is* in Heaven."** (Matt. 6:10). Well, at the end of the Tribulation, earth is totally 180 degrees out of sync with Heaven.

There are individuals scattered around the world who will not take the mark of the beast. And during the Tribulation, there is a very large amount of people who get killed for not taking the mark and who are saved.

They do not die and go to Hell. They join us one day in the Millennium. (Rev. 6:10, 20:4)

All the while though, there is a remnant of Jews living in the caves of Petra and protected by God. As an example of the protection of God, did you notice that when the Dragon cast a flood out of his mouth he did not come any closer to them. He no doubt had the power in and of himself to wipe out the whole bunch of them, but he didn't. Why? Because they were protected by God.

Out there in the wilderness is a group of people who are in line with Heaven. He nourishes them and speaks comfortably to them. Though physically their conditions are not comfortable, yet spiritually they are in fellowship with their God. They left everything out of a love for Him, and He loves them. There is a sweet fellowship that takes place out there in Selah Petra. It is the communion of a people who are brought back into a loving fellowship with Jehovah.

Seven Years

Last Half of the 70th Week

For all those who, from the time of the Cross, have been born again, they are in Heaven and appearing before their Saviour. They must now give an account of the deeds done in their bodies after they were born again. As a reminder of this event, it is the works that are judged, not the person.

As God the Father is nourishing and speaking comfortably to His bride in the wilderness, so too, the Son is dealing with His bride, the Church, as well. Both Father and Son are getting ready, and getting their brides ready for the 1000-year Millennial reign of Jesus Christ upon this earth. You could say that the Millennium is going to be the honeymoons for the Father and the Son.

While this is going on in Heaven, on earth the Dragon is getting his bride ready for Hell. He is also now going to have his moment in the spotlight, so to speak. The

The Tribulation Divided

First Half of the Tribulation	Second Half of the Tribulation
God's Presence in the temple: Rev. 11:1-3	Satan's presence in the temple: 2 Thess. 2:2-4
Ark of testimony is in the temple. Worshipping is according to the law: Rev. 14:12; Dan. 9:27	Ark of testimony is in Heaven: Rev. 11:19
Jews worshipping in the temple: Rev. 11:1-2	Remnant of Jews in the wilderness: Rev. 12
Jews only in the temple: Rev. 11:1-2	Gentiles in the temple: 2 Thess. 2:3-4
Moses and Elijah present: Rev. 11:4	Moses and Elijah in Heaven: Rev. 11:11
God working through men i.e. Moses and Elijah: Rev. 11	God working through angels or directly: Rev. 16
Ark of testimony in the temple: Rev. 11; 14:12; Dan 9:27	Abomination in the temple: Matt. 24:15
No throne to sit on in the temple: Levitical law	Throne for a man to sit on: 2 Thess. 2:3
Sacrifices and oblations made, Altar Rev. 11:1	Sacrifices and oblations not made: Dan. 9:27

last half of the Tribulation is the peak, the zenith, of Satan's attempt to overtly rule the world. This is his moment of glory, you might say. Although he will have another very short-lived time at the end of the Millennium, yet this time here in this last half of the Tribulation is his pinnacle of fame and power, since his fall.

Perhaps it reminds him of the "days gone by" when he sat on his throne and reigned over the sons of God; before he attempted to ascend into Heaven and take over the throne of God. (Isa. 14:13-14) Perhaps he reminisces of those previous times, but more likely he is not.

Satan is anticipating ruling Heaven and earth in place of God; to him, this is the beginning of that very thing. You see, he is greatly deceived. Satan is the epitome of someone who has been deceived by their own sin and rebellious ways. All the Devil would have to do in order to "win" is to not do what the Bible says he is going to do. That would break the word of God, and he would win. But the word of God cannot be broken, and Satan is so deceived that he thinks he "has it in the bag." He fully believes that he is God, and that he is going to win.

Let me clarify some things again. Satan's "reign" through the Beast, during this time cannot occur simultaneously with the ministry of Moses and Elijah. Because the Beast is the one who kills Moses and Elijah, and in Revelation 11 it is written that they minister for **"...a thousand two hundred and threescore days..."** which makes three and a half years. Not only that, but the occupant of the temple is now Satan. The ark has been taken to Heaven, and the presence of God

Problems with the first half of the Tribulation occurring during the earthly ministry of Jesus Christ

1. The occurrence of the "most holy" in the word of God is never in reference to a person. It is always a place or thing, such as a place in the tabernacle or temple.

2. When Judas went out in Matthew 10, there was no confirmation made for one week. One week is nowhere in the passage. The signs and wonders were a witness that Jesus Christ is the Messiah.

3. When Judas went out in Matthew 10, it was at least one year, and up to a year and a half after the Lord started His ministry. The covenant is confirmed at the begining of the week. (Dan. 9:27)

4. Judas did not cause the sacrifices and oblations to cease. Though not accepted by God, yet they are still being made when Paul goes to Jerusalem late in the book of Acts.

5. Judas did not cause the sacrifices to cease. He betrayed the Son of God. The man of sin in 2 Thessalonians 2:3 literally causes them to stop when he walks into the temple, sits down on a throne, and declares himself to be God.

Some things to consider

1. How long do Moses and Elijah prophecy? 3 1/2 Years - "...a thousand two hundred and threescore days"(Rev. 11:3)

2. Who kills Moses and Elijah? The Beast shall kill them. (Rev. 11:7)

3. How long does the Beast "continue" after he kills Moses and Elijah? 3 1/2 years - power was given unto him to continue forty and two months. (Rev. 13:5)

4. That makes a total of 7 years.

has left the temple and gone with His bride into the wilderness. Not only that, but the plagues and disasters that take place on the earth at this time, are no longer brought about by men, i.e. Moses and Elijah; they are now coming directly down from Heaven, either by angels or God himself. There is no way one can properly combine all of these events to occur simultaneously. It just will not work.

With Satan in the Man of Sin now seated in the temple, and with all of the world being commanded to worship him, the second half begins.

As I have studied some on witchcraft in the past, and as I see the Scriptures that relate to the Beast, it shows just how opposite Satan is from the true God. With God there are many times where the Lord does not get what He wants, but He patiently forgives and works things out.

For example when God created the universe, He created it perfectly. And by the way, when God --specifically the Lord Jesus Christ-- creates, He does not create imperfection. When Jesus Christ creates, He gets it right the first time. But sin entered the universe and because of Satan's rebellion, God's creation fell.

Did God want it to fall? No! Did He know that it was going to fall? Yes! But He also knows where we would be today if the creation had never fallen. His foreknowledge did not limit the possibilities that could have happened.

When Adam and Eve sinned, was that God's perfect will? Obviously it was not His perfect will. But God skinned the sheep, clothed Adam and Eve, and went on. Over and over in the book of Judges, Israel rebels against the Lord. He judges them, they repent and He takes them back into fellowship with Him, only to have them rebel again. When you read about how many times in the Bible God does not get what He is wanting, it really is amazing. It is amazing to behold His patience and love for mankind.

The greatest display of this selfless love is Calvary itself, with God as a man being tortured and unjustly crucified for the sins of the world.

On the contrary, it becomes very apparent that with Satan it is all about Satan. He does not care about anybody but himself. He is the opposite of God. Satan wants what Satan wants, and he has zero regard for anyone or anything else.

> [24]His heart is as firm as a stone; yea, as hard as a piece of the nether *millstone.*
> (Job 41:24)

> [33]Upon earth there is not his like, who is made without fear. (Job 41:33)

> [44b]...for he is a liar, and the father of it.
> (John 8:44b)

> [22]...sorrow is turned into joy before him.
> (Job 41:22)

The second half of the Tribulation will all be about Satan, at least that is how Satan is viewing it, for that is how Satan views everything. With his heart of stone, he won't care about the amount of suffering that will take place during the Tribulation. As a matter of fact, the more suffering there is (and by the way it is because of Satan that the suffering is occurring,) the better. The sorrow and suffering that will take place during this time will bring great joy to Satan.

Another thing about Satan is that he does not fear anything, and that includes God Almighty. Satan has no fear of Him, and he has the greatest hatred for and towards God, more than any other being there is.

So after the Man of Sin is revealed in the house of God, the first thing he does is to set up an image in the house of God —an image of himself, the image of the Beast. This breaks the second commandment immediately. Then he has a throne placed in the holiest of all places, sits down in there and commands all to worship him, proclaiming that he is God. This breaks the first commandment, and both of these actions desecrate the temple.

Symbolically it pictures Satan kicking God off His throne in Heaven and Satan taking over. This is exactly what Satan tried to do in the first place when he rebelled.

> [12]How art thou fallen from heaven, O Lucifer, son of the morning! *how* art thou cut down to the ground, which didst weaken the nations!
> [13]For thou hast said in thine heart, I will ascend into heaven, I will exalt my throne above the stars of God: I will sit also upon

the mount of the congregation, in the sides
of the north:
^{14}I will ascend above the heights of the
clouds; I will be like the most High.
^{15}Yet thou shalt be brought down to hell, to
the sides of the pit. (Isa. 14:12-15)

Satan's desire has always been to sit on God's throne
and command all of creation, including God, to worship
him. This is why he offers all the kingdoms of the world
to Jesus Christ in the temptations, and says, "...if thou
wilt fall down and worship me." (Matt. 4:9) That's it
right there, "worship me." That's the heart of Satan;
in the second half of the Tribulation, he will be running
the world under the permissive will of God. What you
must remember is the following verse:

^{18}And Jesus came and spake unto them,
saying, All power is given unto me in heaven
and in earth. (Matt. 28:18)

Any power Satan has, he gets it from Jesus Christ.
Don't ever forget that. Our Lord Jesus Christ is using
Satan to sift the people of the world, to see who will
choose Jesus Christ and right, and who will choose self,
Satan, and wrong, in that order. And there is no way
to be neutral in that decision. A neutral choice is a
rejection of Jesus Christ.

So after Satan, in the Man of Sin, desecrates the
temple, he commands that the world is to be in
allegiance to him. That they are to unwaveringly follow
and be in subjection to Satan. They are to worship him

and him alone. So in order to implement this condition worldwide, a mark is to be placed in the right hand or forehead of the population. It is a mark of allegiance to the Beast.

There will be several different reasons people will be motivated to take the mark. First of all, you have those who are furious at Moses and Elijah for tormenting them, as well as furious at God for sending the two witnesses to trouble their lives. This group of people will readily and very gladly take the mark. They won't even give it a second thought. This will be the vast majority of the world's population.

The second group of people, though not as ready to take the mark as the first, yet they will end up taking the mark. This group are those who realize that they won't have anything to eat if they don't take the mark.

> [4]And Satan answered the LORD, and said, Skin for skin, yea, **all that a man hath will he give for his life.** (Job 2:4)

This group of people will take the mark in order to stay alive.

Now stop and realize that just a little over three and a half years earlier, these people were living in the Church Age. They could have missed all of this if they would have gotten saved, but they didn't. Now they have to choose, and most will choose their belly and physical survival over doing right.

> [9]And the third angel followed them, saying with a loud voice, **If any man worship the**

beast and his image, and receive *his* mark in his forehead, or in his hand,

¹⁰The same shall drink of the wine of the wrath of God, which is poured out without mixture into the cup of his indignation; and **he shall be tormented with fire and brimstone in the presence of the holy angels, and in the presence of the Lamb:**

¹¹And the smoke of their torment ascendeth up for ever and ever: and they have no rest day nor night, **who worship the beast and his image, and whosoever receiveth the mark of his name.** (Rev. 14:9-11)

There is no doubt about what happens to all who take the Mark of the Beast. They first drink of the wrath of God and then go to Hell. They are tormented with fire and brimstone.

In those first few weeks after the Man of Sin is revealed, people line up to take the mark. What's that I hear? Off in the distance I hear something. It kind of sounds like laughter. Yes, I do! I hear laughter. It is a loud, audacious, haughty laughter, and it is coming from the temple. As more and more people damn their souls and take the mark, Satan --in the Man of Sin-- is having the time of his wicked life. He is having more "joy" than he has ever had before as he watches the masses flock to him for survival; as they swear allegiance to him as their god; as they damn their eternal souls by seeking for Satan to keep them alive.

Not only is he laughing at them while on this earth, but he will also see them in Hell and be comforted at seeing them there. The more people with him in Hell, the more comfort he gets. As it has been said before, "Sin likes company."

There is no doubt that Egypt in the Bible is a type of the world, and Pharaoh is a type of the Devil.

> ³¹Pharaoh shall see them, and **shall be comforted over all his multitude,** *even* Pharaoh and all his army slain by the sword, saith the Lord GOD. (Ezek. 32:31)

Satan is the one who is running the show, right out in the open, in the last half of the Tribulation. So one of the first things he does is command everyone world-wide to make an image to the Beast. He knows that wherever the images are set up, God departs from that house and area. Those images are an abomination to God, so this is what is called the overspreading of abominations. And with the overspreading comes the desolations, in the fact that God has departed.

> ¹⁴And deceiveth **them that dwell on the earth** by *the means* of those miracles which he had power to do in the sight of the beast; saying to **them that dwell on the earth, that they should make an image to the beast,** which had the wound by a sword, and did live. (Rev. 13:14)

Worldwide people make images to the Beast. How they make them, I have no idea. It is an image, so it is more than a mere pillar or obelisk. It is a statue similar to the statues, images, and abominations of Mary that you see around the world, except this image to the Beast is in virtually everyone's yard and home. And notice that the word image is always in the singular. It is never plural. It's as if the image is all one, so that when life is given to the image in the temple and it speaks, it looks like all of the images to the Beast speak as well.

A few decades ago this would seem crazy. But now with the Internet, holographic imagery, and artificial intelligence the way it is, there is no doubt it could be done; even without electricity, spiritually this could be done as well. But through this worldwide allegiance, as well as worldwide communication and surveillance (assuming the images can transmit images), there is a firm control that takes place.

An example in the Bible of there being thousands, yet the pronoun "it" is used to describe them, is found in Exodus 12 when God is giving instruction for the Passover lamb. He starts out with the need for "a" lamb (Ex. 12:3), then He refers to it as "the" lamb. (Ex. 12:4) And lastly He refers to it as "your" lamb. (Ex 12:5) By the way it really makes a great preaching outline.

If you want to get to Heaven, then you need a Lamb. A dog, cat, goat, or bull will not do. It must be a Lamb. Then it must be "the" Lamb. There is only one, and that Lamb is Jesus Christ who died and paid for your sins. That is the only sacrifice God will accept. Then you must make Him "your" Lamb. You must receive Jesus Christ into your heart by faith. (Eph. 3:17)

Then in Exodus 12:6-11, the Lord continues on referring to the lamb as "it." Even though there were

380

thousands of lambs killed for the Passover, yet the Lord refers to them in the singular as "it."

This could be the way the Lord chooses to describe the image of the Beast. It could be described in the singular "it," yet there would be many millions of them set up all around the world.

With Jesus Christ --who is the truth-- as well as with the word of God, when both of these are acknowledged and sought, you end up with freedom. **"If the Son therefore shall make you free, ye shall be free indeed."** (John 8:36) When America was founded, it was just past the zenith of the Church Age, and America esteemed the word of God and Jesus Christ for who He truly is. The result was great liberty along with the blessing of God on the land. But when the people of the land departed from the word of God by not reading it daily and not going to Bible-preaching churches, then the moral fiber of the people began to fray and was finally torn. They then turned away from the truth and God. The result was the loss of liberty, freedom and peace, for the Bible says, **"*There is* no peace, saith my God, to the wicked."** (Is. 57:21)

So during the last half of the Tribulation, there is no peace and no liberty. Either you fall in line with the Beast, or you are eliminated. And the method of elimination is to get your head cut off. Either you take the Mark of the Beast and acknowledge him as God, or you cannot buy or sell. Your neighbors and family become your enemies.

[1]¶ Woe is me! for I am as when they have gathered the summer fruits, as the

grapegleanings of the vintage: _there is_ no cluster to eat: my soul desired the firstripe fruit.

^{2}The good _man_ is perished out of the earth: and _there is_ none upright among men: **they all lie in wait for blood; they hunt every man his brother with a net.**

^{3}That they may do evil with both hands earnestly, the prince asketh, and the judge _asketh_ for a reward; and the great _man_, he uttereth his mischievous desire: so they wrap it up.

^{4}The best of them _is_ as a brier: **the most upright _is sharper_ than a thorn hedge:** the day of thy watchmen _and_ thy visitation cometh; now shall be their perplexity.

^{5}**Trust ye not in a friend, put ye not confidence in a guide: keep the doors of thy mouth from her that lieth in thy bosom.**

^{6}**For the son dishonoureth the father, the daughter riseth up against her mother, the daughter in law against her mother in law; a man's enemies _are_ the men of his own house.** (Mic. 7:1-6)

^{12}**Now the brother shall betray the brother to death, and the father the son; and children shall rise up against _their_ parents, and shall cause them to be put to death.** (Mark 13:12)

It is my understanding that Germany was like this under Hitler. Countries under communism are like this as well. In my lifetime, there was a mild form of this during the COVID time with quarantines and all. People became vicious if you didn't have a mask on. They acted like you were going to kill them. That is a small taste of what it will be like when the world is under the operation and control of Satan during the Tribulation period.

Along with the betrayal and the paranoia, there will be the reality that the people are not truly happy. Also those who have taken the mark will be in pain from the sore that forms on their body after they take the mark.

In spite of these conditions, the world continues to go on as if everything is good.

I remember reading a story about the sons of Saddam Hussein. Saddam Hussein was the president of the country of Iraq. In 1990, a coalition of nations united to destroy his reign. There was a perception that Saddam Hussien was an aggressive tyrant who was a threat to the region, as well as the world. Because of this, he and the nation of Iraq were attacked, and the war started.

In the ensuing months, it was obvious that Iraq was losing the war, as more and more territory was conquered by the attacking forces.

Two of Saddam Hussein's sons, one by the name of Uday, the other by the name of Qusay, were getting news that they had to evacuate. The two young men had enjoyed the party life. They frequented the discos and had the pick of any woman they wanted.

383

As they were informed that they had to basically run for their lives, they began to pack just a couple pieces of luggage to take with them. They ended up getting killed; when their luggage was opened, it was revealed that they had packed cologne, dancing clothes, and other things that had more to do with pleasure than it had to do with survival. They didn't want to, and didn't know how to give up the pleasures they had enjoyed.

In this last half of the Tribulation, this is how people are living —just as if all is fine. Eat drink and be merry. But day after day disasters hit that spoil their "fun." The fury they had towards Moses and Elijah now boils over as hatred towards God Almighty.

One of the plagues is when God scorches men with fire, and they blaspheme His name. There is an additional bit of information given: "**...and blasphemed the name of God, which hath power over these plagues.**" (Rev. 16:9) Ah yes! That old Adamic nature that vaunts itself against God.

The next plague is where the angel smites the seat of the Beast with darkness "**...and they gnawed their tongues for pain.**" (Rev. 16:10) That is some darkness to cause people to gnaw their tongues for pain. It gives you a glimpse of what Hell is like, for there is no light in Hell.

Again though, it is recorded that they:

> [11]...blasphemed the God of heaven because of their pains and their sores... (Rev. 16:11)

The second half of the Tribulation is a complete and total rebellion against God by ninety percent of the inhabitants on the earth. Worldwide they openly reject the God of Heaven, and openly they accept and serve Satan, the god of this world.

So, without going into all of the judgments that God brings to the world during this time, we now have come to "**...the end.**" That term is used many, many times throughout the Scriptures. And when that term is misunderstood or misapplied in the Church Age the results are Christians who believe they can lose their salvation.

This is how the Methodists, the Charismatics, and others who are also known as Arminians, arrive at the belief that they can lose their salvation. But as you can plainly see in Matthew 24, "the end" is not a reference to the end of someones' life. It is a reference to the end of a period of time.

> ⁶And ye shall hear of wars and rumours of wars: see that ye be not troubled: for all *these things* must come to pass, but **the end is not yet.** (Matt. 24:6)

> ¹⁴And this gospel of the kingdom shall be preached in all the world for a witness unto all nations; and **then shall the end come.** (Matt. 24:14)

In both of these references "the end" is a reference to a period of time, and that period of time is the 70th week of Daniel's prophecy --which is also known as the time of Jacob's trouble, and is also known as the Tribulation. We are now at "the end" of Daniel's 70th

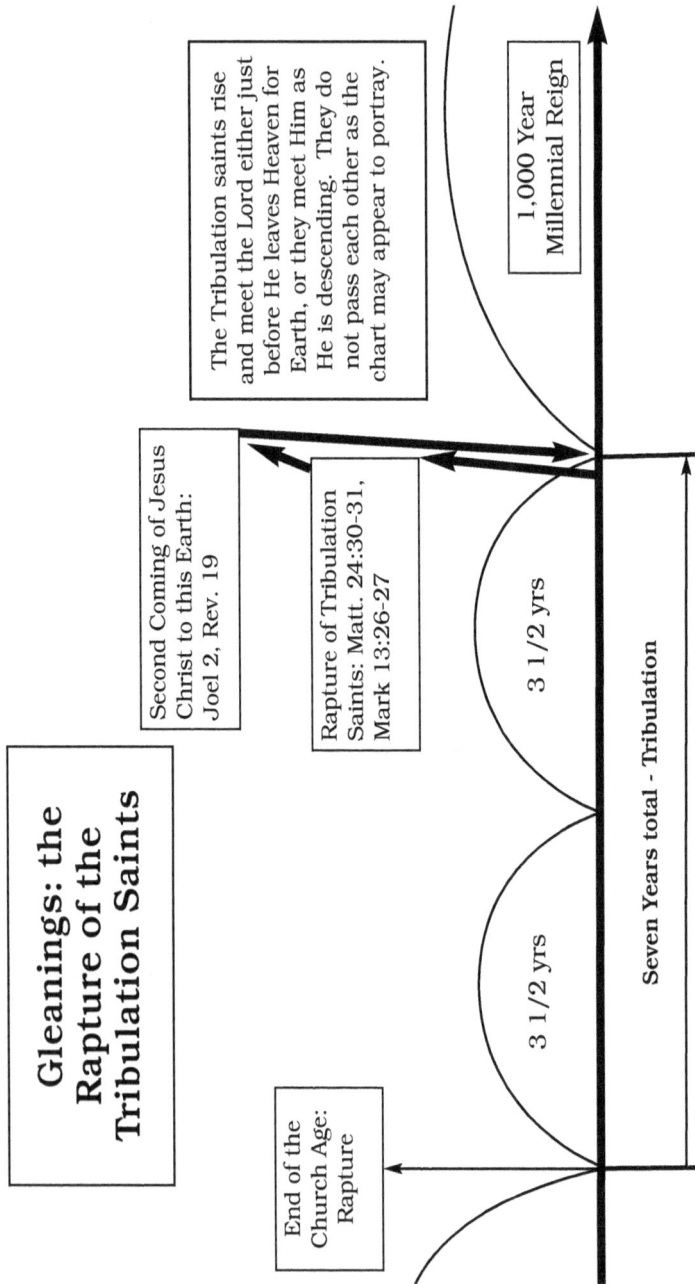

Gleanings: the Rapture of the Tribulation Saints

The Tribulation saints rise and meet the Lord either just before He leaves Heaven for Earth, or they meet Him as He is descending. They do not pass each other as the chart may appear to portray.

1,000 Year Millennial Reign

Second Coming of Jesus Christ to this Earth: Joel 2, Rev. 19

Rapture of Tribulation Saints: Matt. 24:30-31, Mark 13:26-27

3 1/2 yrs

3 1/2 yrs

Seven Years total - Tribulation

End of the Church Age: Rapture

The First Resurrection

Consisting of three events like a harvest, it has First Fruits, Harvest and Gleanings

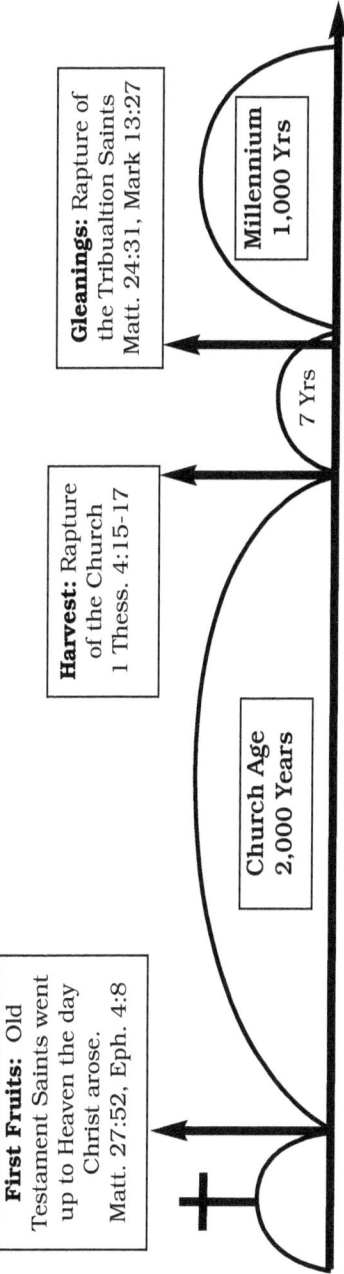

First Fruits: Old Testament Saints went up to Heaven the day Christ arose. Matt. 27:52, Eph. 4:8

Harvest: Rapture of the Church 1 Thess. 4:15-17

Gleanings: Rapture of the Tribualtion Saints Matt. 24:31, Mark 13:27

Church Age 2,000 Years

7 Yrs

Millennium 1,000 Yrs

Rev. 20:5 But the rest of the dead lived not again until the thousand years were finished. **This is the first resurrection.**

Rev. 20:6 Blessed and holy is he that hath part in the first resurrection: on such the second death hath no power, but they shall be priests of God and of Christ, and shall reign with him a thousand years.

387

week. At this point there are actually a number of events or happenings that take place, the first of which occurs right before the end.

There is one event though that needs to be covered now, as it comes just before the end, and possibly occurs right at the end. It is the Rapture of the Tribulation saints. When they are resurrected, then the first resurrection will be complete.

> [29]Immediately after the tribulation of those days shall the sun be darkened, and the moon shall not give her light, and the stars shall fall from heaven, and the powers of the heavens shall be shaken:
>
> [30]And then shall appear the sign of the Son of man in heaven: and then shall all the tribes of the earth mourn, and **they shall see the Son of man coming in the clouds of heaven with power and great glory.**
>
> [31]**And he shall send his angels with a great sound of a trumpet, and they shall gather together his elect from the four winds, from one end of heaven to the other.** (Matt. 24:29-31)

For the past three and a half years, there were those who did not comply with the Beast and take the mark. If they were caught though, they had their heads cut off. (Rev. 20:4) These souls were reserved **"under the altar,"** wherever that is, until the right time. It must be somewhere under ground just as Paradise used to be before it was caught up to the third Heaven. (2 Cor. 12:4) That right time is at the time of the Second Advent. At that time these souls will be raptured out to meet the Lord in the air, just as He is returning to the earth.

The reason for such a late resurrection and meeting with the Lord as He is returning is because this Rapture completes the end of the First Resurrection. As such, this Rapture completes all those who will not be threatened by the second death. (Rev. 20:4)

It is likened unto a harvest with the first fruits of Old Testament saints, (Matt. 27:52), then there is the harvest with the Rapture of the born-again saints (1 Thess. 4:15-17). And here you have the gleanings, which are the saints saved out of the Tribulation. (Matt. 24:31) This last Rapture occurs right as the Lord plants his feet onto this earth for the first time since His ministry about 2,000 years ago.

Those who are "saved" yet still alive on earth at the end of the Tribulation will go on into the Millennium.

Briefly, here are some things to consider that show the rapture of Matthew 24, and Mark 13 is not the same Rapture as that found in 1 Thessalonians 4 and 1 Corinthians 15.

Those who apply the "gathering" of Matthew 24 and Mark 13 to the Rapture of the church as described in 1 Thessalonians and 1 Corinthians 15:51, are wresting the Scriptures. They are not even dividing, let alone rightly dividing, the Scriptures when such a crazy application is put forth. And there are many who are doing this very thing.

The Second Coming of Jesus Christ

The Second Coming of Jesus Christ marks the end of the Tribulation period. "The end" is one of, if not, the most mentioned events in all of the word of God with regard to the Tribulation. "The end" is the other event that clearly marks a point in the Tribulation. The middle is clearly marked, and the end is clearly marked. The end has a number of events that take place which we will cover, but the main event that marks the end is the Second Coming of Jesus Christ to this earth.

The amount of references to the Second Coming of Jesus Christ are more than triple the number of references to the first coming of Jesus Christ. Why is that?

Because the day that God's Son, Jesus Christ, was murdered at the hands of wicked men is not God's favorite event in all of the word of God. The event that God the Father is looking forward to, and the event the Son is looking forward to, and the event the Holy Ghost is looking forward to is the time when God takes over the world. The Devil is then cast into the bottomless pit, and God is married to His bride, Israel, as well as the time that the Son is married to His bride, the Church. Along with those two very special events, is the fact that Jesus Christ will reign on this earth for 1,000 years, which is referred to as the Millennium.

There is no doubt that the marriage of the Father to Israel, and the marriage of the Son to the Church are greatly anticipated by the Father and the Son. You see, back over 6,000 years earlier, and possibly 8,000 years earlier, God created the Heaven and the earth.

Why do I say possibly 8,000 years? And, let me emphasise that this is all conjecture. In other words it is something to think about but as of right now, I do not have Scripture to back it up.

Satan was seated on a throne on this earth according to Isa. 14:13; "**I will ascend into Heaven**, I will exalt my throne above the stars of God." He was reigning over the sons of God on an earthly throne over an earthly kingdom. We do not know how long He reigned before he decided to ascend into Heaven and attempt to take over the throne of God Almighty. If this time was 2000 years, then the parenthetical Church Age has been inserted to replace that time.

This is a very likely possibility in light of the fact that God does not count prophetic time when Israel is out of fellowship with Him. (I know there was no Israel at that time. I am using it as an illustration to show that there are "times" when God does not count the "time.") So if Satan's reign was 2,000 years long, then that time is discarded and the Church Age is inserted, making this period of time a complete 7,000 years. Seven is God's number of completion. So the total time frame would thus be 9,000 years in all. Obviously before the Millennium then it would be without the 1,000 years, which is why I said possibly 8,000 years.

Ok, back to the subject we were on.

So God knew that His creation would fall, and knew what He was going to have to suffer because of it. But if God had not let all that happen He would be alone. But God is love, and how can you exercise love when you are alone?

391

So God allowed the fall, He did not make him fall. Lucifer made the fall when iniquity was found in him.

> [14]Thou *art* the anointed cherub that covereth; and I have set thee *so*: thou wast upon the holy mountain of God; thou hast walked up and down in the midst of the stones of fire.
> [15]Thou *wast* perfect in thy ways from the day that thou wast created, <u>till iniquity was found in thee.</u> (Ezek. 28:14-15)

There it is. In the heart of the anointed cherub is where all of the suffering and sin began.

You know, in the book of Hebrews 12 it is written:

> [2]Looking unto Jesus the author and finisher of *our* faith; who **for the joy that was set before him endured the cross,** despising the shame, and is set down at the right hand of the throne of God. (Heb. 12:2)

God is love, and the greatest portrayal of love the world has ever been shown is the day Jesus Christ died for his enemies on the cross. And on that cross He was going to drink of the cup and suffer the wrath of God poured out upon sin. Yet in the midst of it all, He had joy. The depth of truth, love and the wisdom of God in all of this is far, far beyond what my puny heart and brain can fathom.

But I wonder if the joy that Jesus had during that time was partly because, as God, He was exercising one of His many great attributes, which is love.

Some might take issue and claim that love is God's greatest attribute, but I would disagree. Why? Because in Heaven, they proclaim, **"Holy, Holy, Holy, Lord God Almighty."** The greatest attribute of God is that He is holy.

It has taken over 6,000 years for this time to come about. It is the eternal marriage of the Father to Israel, and the Son to the Church. God will never be alone from here on. After all, He is the One that wrote,

> 18¶ And the LORD God said, *It is* not good that the man should be alone... (Gen. 2:18)

Perhaps I am over humanizing the Almighty, but God is love and He loves to fellowship with you and I, does He not? Does it not grieve the Lord when you sin against Him and your fellowship with your Lord and Saviour is broken? Yes, it does!

So from here on into forever and forever, God will not be alone, and the fellowship with all of His creation will never be broken again. Yes, you can truly say, *"And they lived happily ever after."*

Not only will the Father and the Son be with their brides, but those brides will have freely choosen to be there. In eternity all who are together with God, including the angels, will be there because they **freely chose** to do right. And of course, all who are in the Lake of Fire will be there because they **freely chose** to reject God and His mercy for them.

The Almighty God of creation is so wise! He could have created all beings to automatically love and serve

Him, but how do you truly love a robot? So God created heavenly beings, as well as man, with a completely free will; He knew that iniquity would begin in the heart of Lucifer (Ezek. 28) and then would spread to angels. He created man, knowing that sin would spread to man also. He then exercised the greatest love ever known when He died on the cross. Now after 6,000 years, He has finally come to a major unifying point with His beings. This is why this Second Coming of Jesus Christ to the earth is mentioned far more in the word of God than the first coming. Not only is this a matter of very great importance in the study of rightly dividing the word of God, but more than that, this is a highlight for God Almighty.

So now let us ascend with our minds into Heaven. The first event of the Day of Christ has just finished which is the Judgment Seat of Christ. The Christians have now been reconciled to one another, and they have individually stood before their Saviour and watched their works pass through a fire. Those Christians who served Jesus Christ in their lives, laid up in Heaven gold, silver and precious stones. The other works of wood, hay and stubble were burned up in the fire. Jesus Christ presented crowns to those who did their best to serve Him while in their bodies of corruption. The Judgment Seat of Christ is now over. The second event in the Day of Christ has arrived, which is the Second Coming of Jesus Christ to the earth. It is a great day for the Lord, and all in Heaven are excited.

Millions of very beautiful, brightly-shining, white horses are lining up in ranks and are waiting for the redeemed of the Lord to mount up. Along with these beautiful horses are the exquisitely beautiful unicorns.

> ⁶The sword of the LORD is filled with blood,
> it is made fat with fatness, *and* with the blood
> of lambs and goats, with the fat of the
> kidneys of rams: for the LORD hath a
> sacrifice in Bozrah, and a great slaughter in
> the land of Idumea.
> **⁷And the unicorns shall come down with
> them**, and the bullocks with the bulls; and
> their land shall be soaked with blood, and
> their dust made fat with fatness.
> ⁸For *it is* the day of the LORD'S vengeance,
> *and* the year of recompences for the
> controversy of Zion. (Isa. 34:6-8)

Hundreds of thousands of them are waiting for their Jewish saints to mount up on them as well. These bright, white creatures shimmer with the light of the glory and splendor of Heaven. They have never been outside of Heaven, and with very eager anticipation they paw on the golden street and snort with excitement. Oh, yes! They are ready to get this show on the road, or should I say, they are ready to fly.

> ¹⁴And the armies *which were* in heaven
> followed him upon **white horses**, clothed in
> fine linen, white and clean. (Rev. 19:14)

Excitement builds throughout all of Heaven. Shouts and praise to the Lord our God ring out as the event of all the ages is getting ready to take place. We --the

New Testament saints-- join in on the praising of our God. Babylon has now fallen, and it won't be long before our God, the rightful King of the universe, comes and takes over what is rightfully His.

> ²And he cried mightily with a strong voice, saying, **Babylon the great is fallen, is fallen,** and is become the habitation of devils, and the hold of every foul spirit, and a cage of every unclean and hateful bird. (Rev. 18:2)

As I got ready to write about us returning with our Lord to this earth, this thought occurred to me, *"How do I know we return with the Lord to this earth?"* I have heard that for decades, and I have read many Scriptures that seems to point to the fact that we return with Jesus Christ to this earth, but I thought that I would "nail it down" right here, before I go any further.

Am I really in one of those armies? If you are saved, are you in one of those armies? Well, let's see. What do we know?

We know that we are going to be caught out of this world and forever be with our Lord. (1 Thess. 4:14-17) We know that after the Rapture, there is going to be on the earth a time of great tribulation. During that time in Heaven, the Church (i.e., saved people), is going to be judged at the Judgement Seat of Christ. Then at the end of the Tribulation, Jesus Christ is going to return to this earth and set up His kingdom for 1,000 years. These things we know, and they can be easily found. So now let's study and see if we are in one of those armies that returns with our Lord Jesus Christ.

First of all, we are told that after the Rapture, it is written **"...And so shall we ever be with our Lord."**

> [17]Then we which are alive *and* remain shall be caught up together with them in the clouds, to meet the Lord in the air: and **so shall we ever be with the Lord.** (1 Th. 4:17)

There is no doubt that the Church is the bride of Christ when you read Ephesians 5.

> [30]For **we are members of his body, of his flesh, and of his bones.**
> [31]For this cause shall a man leave his father and mother, and shall be joined unto his wife, and they two shall be one flesh.
> [32]This is a great mystery: but **I speak concerning Christ and the church.**
> (Eph. 5:30-32)

So it can be easily seen that the Church will be with Jesus Christ on this earth since that is where He will be. We are His bride, thus He wants His bride with Him. Amen!

The fact that we will be on this earth during the Millennium is evident as well. Reigning with Jesus Christ is one of the rewards that a Christian earns. (I will be going into great detail on this later in this book.)

To be on this earth during the Millennium is said to be part of the "first resurrection." If you are saved, then you are already seated in heavenly places in Christ

Jesus (Eph. 2:6), and you will never die. Going up in the Rapture is part of the first resurrection.

> **⁶Blessed and holy *is* he that hath part in the first resurrection:** on such the second death hath no power, but they shall be priests of God and of Christ, and shall reign with him a thousand years. (Rev. 20:6)

Now, notice the following portion of scripture. It is a bit lengthy, but it is all one sentence. I wanted to include all of it so as to get the context.

> ⁵*Which* is a manifest token of the righteous judgment of God, that ye may be counted worthy of the kingdom of God, for which ye also suffer:
> ⁶Seeing *it is* a righteous thing with God to recompense tribulation to them that trouble you;
> ⁷And to you who are troubled rest with us, **when the Lord Jesus shall be revealed from heaven with his mighty angels,**
> ⁸**In flaming fire taking vengeance on them that know not God,** and that obey not the gospel of our Lord Jesus Christ:
> ⁹Who shall be punished with everlasting destruction from the presence of the Lord, and from the glory of his power;
> ¹⁰When **he shall come to be glorified in his saints, and to be admired in all them that**

**believe (because our testimony among you
was believed) in that day.** (2 Thess. 1:5-10)

When you read **"flaming fire..."** in verse 8, it is a
reference to the Second Advent. It is not a reference to
the Rapture because at the Rapture there is no flaming
fire, there are clouds. Not only that, but there is no
vengeance from our Lord at the Rapture. The
vengeance of the Lord occurs at the Second Coming of
Jesus Christ. This gives us the context of the sentence.

So now that we have the context of the sentence,
notice in verse 10 that our Lord is **"glorified in his
saints."** The saints, which are all of the saved, are
present with Him at the Second Coming.

> [4]When Christ, *who is* our life, shall appear,
> **then shall ye also appear with him in glory.**
> (Col. 3:4)

Notice in Colossians 3:4 that when Christ appears,
we appear with Him. This is not the Rapture, for in the
Rapture we do not appear with Him, we are caught up
to meet Him. There is a big difference.

And notice what is written in the book of Jude:

> [14]And Enoch also, the seventh from Adam,
> prophesied of these, saying, Behold, **the Lord
> cometh with ten thousands of his saints,**
> [15]To execute judgment upon all, and to
> convince all that are ungodly among them of
> all their ungodly deeds which they have
> ungodly committed, and of all their hard

speeches which ungodly sinners have spoken against him. (Jude: 14-15)

Here again you have judgment executed upon the ungodly, therefore this is a reference to the Second Advent again, and the saints are with the Lord. You are called to be a saint according to 1 Corinthians 1:2 **"...called to be saints, with all that in every place call upon the name of Jesus Christ..."** So the saints are with Jesus Christ at His coming.

[13]To the end he may stablish your hearts unblameable in holiness before God, even our Father, **at the coming of our Lord Jesus Christ with all his saints.** (1 Thess. 3:13)

Ah, yes! That one says it all! Jesus Christ is coming with all of His saints. He does not leave the unfaithful in Heaven for 1,000 years. (Yes, I have heard some teach that!) All of His saints; yes, His entire bride is coming to earth with Him at the Second Advent of our Lord Jesus Christ.

So now that we know that we are ALL returning to this earth with Jesus Christ, let's return to the scene in Heaven as Jesus Christ is getting ready to leave Heaven for earth.

[11]And **I saw heaven opened**, and behold a white horse; and he that sat upon him *was* called Faithful and True, and in righteousness he doth judge and make war. [12]**His eyes *were* as a flame of fire**, and on his

head *were* many crowns; and he had a name written, that no man knew, but he himself.

¹³And he *was* clothed with a vesture dipped in blood: and **his name is called The Word of God.**

¹⁴And **the armies** *which were* **in heaven followed him upon white horses, clothed in fine linen, white and clean.** (Rev. 19:11-14)

The streets are golden, but clear as crystal. Glistening white horses are standing on those streets. There is no darkness and thus no shadows anywhere. The angels are arrayed in white and begin to sing "Alleluia" and praises to the Lord. Then King Jesus stands up from the throne and walks to the head of the great and grand army. Horses, unicorns, and saints await in eager anticipation for the order. With majesty and glory and power, Jesus strides to the front of the column. With a glance back to the throng, He commands, *"Mount up!"*

This is where we, an army of the Lord, each get on our horse for the return to this earth. We have perfect bodies that are just like our Lord Jesus Christ. All of Heaven stands; holy hands are raised in salute as Jesus mounts up and begins to lead His army.

With us is the ark of His testament. It is to be carried by one of the horses and is ready to be placed within the new temple when it gets built.

Another peculiar thing is present as well. It is a large number of horses that have nobody sitting upon them. They are all prepared for riders, but where are the riders? Has someone missed their appointment. No, no one has missed their appointment.

Seven Years

With everyone mounted and ready to go, Jesus shouts and before Him the Heavens split in two like two scrolls. Under all of us is the vast universe of stars, planets and such. We are suspended above it all with nothing under us, but it doesn't matter for we can fly. Like a flood of water that has broken through the bank that held it back, we descend through the galaxies coming ever closer to the planet earth. We are coming with Jesus Christ to take over this earth. It is the great day of the Lord.

The beautiful peacefull doves' eyes (Song of Sol. 4:1) of our Lord have now turned into the fiery eyes of the King of kings seeking vengeance on His enemies. Our Lord is now in a wrathful, holy rage of fury, for this is now His day. He has had enough of the blasphemy that has taken place. He is through with the taking of His name in vain and claiming that He is holy s**t. The rebellion, the idolatry, the murdering, along with all sins, have now come up before our Lord Jesus Christ. In His fury He is going to deal with it all with fire. He is coming to set the world right by force.

There is a great lesson here to grasp. There comes a time in the wickedness of people when they are too far gone to reason with. There is only one thing you can do with them, and that is burn them. Just like Sodom and Gomorrah, the only thing that can be done is to burn them all up and get rid of them. That time for vast majority of the inhabitants of the earth has now arrived.

Down, down through the universe we descend. It could have been done in an instant, but this descent is going to take a little time for the Bible says that every eye shall see Him. So I think it likely that it will take a

402

total of twenty-four hours for the Lord and His armies to arrive on earth.

As we descend through the universe, a strange thing takes place. There is a large group of souls coming towards us. Who are those souls? They are the souls from under the altar. (Rev. 6:9) It's the souls of the saints who had their heads cut off for not taking the Mark of the Beast. Here they come, rising up to meet and to join the armies of the Lord. Oh, that's who those empty horses are for!

It reminds me of Jehu furiously driving his chariot towards the castle of King Joram in 2 Kings 9. The wicked King Joram watches from the tower and sends a man upon horseback to fetch the news. And as the horseman arrives and pulls up alongside Jehu —who is driving furiously— he yells to Jehu, **"Is it peace?"** And Jehu said, **"What hast thou to do with peace? Turn thee behind me."** (2 Kings 9:18)

Seated on His brilliantly white horse Jesus Christ descends from Heaven furious, and with eyes of fire, for the day of His vengeance is here. The saints who were killed during the Tribulation arise and meet us while we descend. They land upon the backs of their beautiful white horses and join us in our return to earth. Nothing, nothing is going to stop us now!

Down, down we fly and enter the "Milky Way Galaxy," coming ever closer to the earth. The people upon the earth see us coming, and the closer we get the larger our army appears. Rebellious pride wells up in the souls of the depraved followers of the Dragon, the Beast and the False Prophet. They are all united in their opposition to Jesus Christ, and they believe that they will defeat Him as well. Such is the effects of sin upon the thinking and mentality of the corrupt mind.

Yet lightly scattered all around on the earth are people, both Gentiles and Jews, who have not taken the Mark of the Beast. They are people who have been reading, believing, and clinging to the written words of God. They have loved the truth more than the pleasures of unrighteousness, and it has not been an easy road for them. They have had to leave everything. Family and friends have turned against them, reporting them to the authorities for not taking the Mark of the Beast.

There have been many forks in the road where they have had to say goodbye to loved ones. From their hearts they have pressed on as the song says, _"I have decided to follow Jesus. Though no one join me, still I will follow. No turning back, no turning back."_ And so they have pressed on, to the point at times of having no strength left.

It has been seven very long and arduous years. In the last six months, they have seen friends and family give up saying, _"The Lord has delayed His coming."_ They then have given in and taken the mark. These know what the results of such an act means, and though they have begged and pleaded with them, yet to no avail. Their loved ones took the mark and will end up in Hell. Yes, these that remain have shed many tears in these last months.

They are lightly scattered all over the earth. Few, if any, remain in the populated areas, for the mark is an obvious sign. Those who do not have it are readily spotted and hounded to death if they won't take the

404

mark. Some try to hide in caves, while others hide in the deserts and plains. Those in the plains barely survive out in the open, due to the attack of animals who are hungry as well. Those in the caves know from the Scriptures what is going to happen to them if they stay there too long. They know the "great" men of the earth are coming, so they will need to flee before those men get there. (Rev. 6:15) It's a very precarious position, but the advantage is they are protected from the animals at night.

For some, it arrives in the day. For others it will be at night. The monotonous burden of enduring the gruesome conditions all suddenly changes as the Heaven departs as a scroll. (Rev. 6:14) Their sullen, sunken, weary eyes immediately are turned skyward and northward. As the Kings, the great men and the rich men run for the caves and rocks of the mountains, the saints inhabiting them flee. They know that the great men would just as soon kill them for looking at them.

Someone exclaims to the rest, *"It's time! We have to go, now!"*

Back in the far side of the cave is an old man lying on the ground. He is weak, with little to no strength left. Coming up beside him is his granddaughter Beth who rouses him. She Bends down close to his ear, and as she gently shakes him, she says, *"Papa, we have to go now."*

The old man's voice is a hoarse whisper. *"Honey, I don't think I can. Dear Lord, help me."*

Rolling slowly onto his side, he is helped up by Beth and another man.

As they exit the cave, they hear the sounds of the elites running up the hill towards the cave. Shouts are heard, *"You _____ no-markers! Get out of there or we will kill you."*

On the side of the mountain are the blackened remains trees that have been burned and scorched to death. The tall branchless trunks are all that remain. They stand on the side of the mountain like sentinels who have lost their armor, guarding a wasted and abandoned kingdom.

At the base of the trunks, weak saints scurry away trying to find a place to rest. In the confusion of the fearful fleeing for their lives, they are unaware of what is happening above their heads.

"Papa," Beth earnestly speaks, *"They say just over the top of the mountain on the other side is a bench in the side of the mountain where we can lie down and rest."*

Upon reaching the pass on the top of the mountain, the old saint collapses on the ground.

Broken heartedly Beth pleads, *"Oh, Papa! Please keep going. It's just a couple bow shots to where you can lie down."*

Tears drop from her cheeks as she notices a strange look in her Grandpa's eyes. When she sees tears welling up in his eyes she asks him, *"Papa, are you in pain?"*

A small smile begins to break across his weathered lips. *"Oh no, I'm not in pain. Far from it."* Lying on his back he points upwards, *"Honey, we made it! We finally made it! Look up in the Heaven. Jesus is coming with His armies."*

Beth looks up and sees the Lord and His armies, and

falls to her knees in joy. Off in the distance she can hear the faint shouts of joy as others see the amazing sight, too. *"Jesus is coming, He is finally coming! Oh, praise be to the Lamb of God, we are saved!"*

Jesus Christ and His armies land on the earth upon Mount Sinai. (Deut. 32:2)

(In Arabia (Gal. 4:25), there is a mountain that stands to this day that is burnt upon its top. At the base of it is an altar with Egyptian cows engraved upon the sides of the altar. There is also a five-story high rock that has a two foot wide crack down the middle of it. The internal sides of the crack have signs of being eroded by water. This information is easily verified by searching the internet with "Red Sea Crossing" or "the split rock of Moses," or other such searches.)

After Jesus Christ and His armies descend upon Mount Sinai, they turn northward. He arrives at the country of Edom. This is where Selah Petra is. It is here that Jesus Christ fights a battle alone. He doesn't want anyone else to be in this battle with Him.

While I described the hiding out of the Jews at Petra with a kind of romantic love story of them with their bridegroom —God the Father— and spiritually it is, yet the physical conditions are anything but romantic. God protects them while they are there, but despite that there is still danger and some of the Jewish remnant end up dead.

> [9]We gat our bread with *the peril of* our lives because of the sword of the wilderness. (Lam. 5:9)

¹⁷For the morning *is* to them even as **the shadow of death: if** *one* **know** *them,* **they are in the terrors of the shadow of death.** (Job 24:17)

The Jews hiding out in Selah Petra will be supernaturally fed, just like there forefathers were fed when they left Egypt. God is going to feed them with manna once again. Manna was like the hoar frost, and they had to gather it in the morning because **"...when the sun waxed hot, it (the manna) melted."** (Ex. 16:21) So the Jews have to go out early in the morning before the sun comes up to collect the manna.

Now there are two possibilities here in regards to the dangers they faced when they went out to collect the manna. And both of these may someday become reality.

The first danger would be that when they went out to collect the manna, it depended upon where they had to go. It was likely out in the desert away from the safety of the rock city, or merely out in front of their caves. Once they ventured out from their caves though, they were in the open and would be an easy target, unless they used the safety of the early morning darkness.

If it were people trying to kill them, gathering in the early hours of the day would be one of the ways to attain a small element of safety.

The other possible danger is that of a deadly shadow; when that reaches a person, it kills them. So as long as they are gathering manna in the twilight of the morning, then there are no shadows, for the sun is not yet up. But once the sun is up, then there is the shadow of death that comes, and those who come under that shadow die.

To me, it looks as though both of these possibilities could become a reality for those Jews. When the Lord arrives in the land of Edom, He personally stomps those who have been trying to kill the Jews in Petra. No doubt the Man of Sin has placed a bounty upon their heads, so that every Jew that is killed brings a good amount of money to the killer. The method of killing would be weapons such as guns, or arrows —weapons for killing individuals. And perhaps the shadow of death could be a weapon that is operated by soldiers who are stationed just outside of Selah Petra during that time. If so, the shadow of death would be powerless to reach the Jews who were hiding in caves. Why? Because inside the caves there are no shadows.

It does seem strange that a shadow could be deadly. When I think of a shadow I think of merely the absence of light, but there is more to it than that. In Acts 5:15, the shadow of Peter had the power to heal people.

But whatever the weapons, and whoever the people are that are camped outside of Petra, it is certain that Jesus Christ is furious with them. He is the Lord God Almighty who spoke the creation into existence. His power is such that He could easily kill all of these people in a moment. That would not be hard for Him to do, so why doesn't He just do that? Why doesn't Jesus Christ just speak and obliterate His enemies in a moment?

Well, you have got to remember that God has emotions and feelings. His emotions and feelings are right and proper, for they are expressed at the right and proper time. Not only that, but His emotions and feelings are just and righteous, whereas sinful man's emotions and feelings are rarely --if ever-- just and righteous.

This is His time to justly exercise vengeance, wrath and fiery righteous judgments upon the wicked. He has been more than patient, more than long-suffering and definitely more than forgiving. But those qualities have now been replaced, and justly so, with wrath, anger and fury.

So the answer to why Jesus Christ does not merely speak and obliterate the enemies of the Jews, who are also His enemies, is because He wants to personally kill them. He wants to personally stomp upon their bodies and have their warm blood splatter upon His clothes. He wants to personally break their bodies and smash their heads in. As He kills them He will be laughing at them, and He mocking them as they scream, cry and plead for mercy. But it will be too late. The mercy for them from Jesus Christ will be long gone. (What I just described, as you will see, is all found in the word of God.)

So as He heads north from Mount Sinai, Jesus Christ makes a beeline straight for Bozrah in Edom. Behind Him are millions of saints upon white horses as well. But this first battle is His, all His. He doesn't want any help, nor does He need any help. He is attacking, destroying, and stomping people in His furious rage and enjoys doing it. His first battle is in Seir, which is also known as Edom as well as Bozrah. It is southeast of the Dead Sea.

Huddled in the caves, the people hear something

strange. Something that they have never heard before.
It is like the sound of many waters. Or is it the sound
of thunder? It is not the sound of horse hooves beating
the ground because the Lord and His army are not on
the ground but flying overhead.

The remnant of emaciated, weak Jews cautiously peer
out from the caves. Looking up into the small bit of sky
they see a miracle. Deliverance! Their Messiah has
returned. The first brave souls that venture out begin
to shout for joy, and tears run down their cheeks. They
then shout to the rest, *"Come see! It's Jesus, Messiah!
We are saved!"* Others begin to venture out to see the
sight, and they, too, begin to shout and praise the Lord.
Others fall on their knees in tears and worship the Lord
with shouts of *"Praise to the Lamb of God!"* With arms
outstretched they bow with their faces to the ground.
Messiah has returned! Oh, happy day!! Over their
heads fly white horses with the sons of God clothed in
white robes.

Not far away in Bozrah is an army of wicked people.
They have tried to kill off the remnant of the Jews, but
the Lord has not let them. Now it is time for the Lord
to kill them off. As He lands, He dismounts His
beautiful white steed and begins to destroy those who
are against Him.

> [1]Who *is* this that cometh from Edom, with
> dyed garments from Bozrah? this *that is*
> glorious in his apparel, travelling in the
> greatness of his strength? I that speak in
> righteousness, mighty to save.
> [2]Wherefore *art thou* red in thine apparel, and

thy garments like him that treadeth in the winefat?

³**I have trodden the winepress alone;** and of the people _there was_ none with me: **for I will tread them in mine anger, and trample them in my fury; and their blood shall be sprinkled upon my garments, and I will stain all my raiment.**

⁴**For the day of vengeance _is_ in mine heart, and the year of my redeemed is come.**

⁵And I looked, and _there was_ none to help; and I wondered that _there was_ none to uphold: therefore mine own arm brought salvation unto me; and my fury, it upheld me.

⁶And **I will tread down the people in mine anger, and make them drunk in my fury,** and I will bring down their strength to the earth. (Isa. 63:1-6)

As Jesus Christ furiously stomps them, blood splatters upon His beautiful white garments. More and more red splatters of blood stain His white robe. They increase until the base of his robe turns full red --now dripping with the blood of the wicked slain. They are made drunk with the fury of the Lord. Staggering, stumbling, falling, puking, and then getting their heads smashed in as the Lord stomps on them, all the while laughing in His furious rage.

As He died alone on Calvary, so also now he destroys them alone in the fields of blood south of the Dead Sea in Edom. Some try to run, but He is faster. They do not escape, for He sees all. As we, the saints of His army look on, we cheer and shout praise to the Lord God Almighty. Hallelujah to the Lamb of God! He is the true Lord God, and this is the time of His vengeance and proof of who He truly is.

The remnant of the Jews at Petra are delivered, and the wicked armies of the Antichrist that were stationed there are destroyed. This is the first victory that takes place when our Lord returns to take what is rightfully his. He created it all, and He is now taking over the earth. All hail the power of our Lord Jesus Christ!

Their Messiah has finally returned as promised.

> [22]Behold, he shall come up and fly as the eagle, and spread his wings over Bozrah: and at that day shall the heart of the mighty men of Edom be as the heart of a woman in her pangs. (Jer. 49:22)

> [12]But I will send a **fire** upon Teman, which shall **devour the palaces of Bozrah.**
> (Amos 1:12)

From Petra, He leaves and heads north on the King's Highway: He crosses the Jordan River where John the Baptist baptized Him 2,000 years earlier. From there, He heads due west to take over Jerusalem. He is flying, and so are we on our white horses.

Our leader, King Jesus Christ, is now red and white with a golden crown upon His head. His feet are stained with blood as well as His garment. I'm sure it felt good to Him to kill those people in Bozrah. The Bible says,

"...the righteous are bold as a lion." (Prov. 28:1) Well, here is the Lion of the tribe of Judah, and He is righteously bold.

> [4]For thus hath the LORD spoken unto me, Like as the lion and the young lion roaring on his prey, when a multitude of shepherds is called forth against him, _he_ will not be afraid of their voice, nor abase himself for the noise of them: **so shall the LORD of hosts come down to fight for mount Zion, and for the hill thereof.**
> [5]**As birds flying, so will the LORD of hosts defend Jerusalem; defending also he will deliver _it_; _and_ passing over he will preserve it.** (Isa. 31:4-5)

Daniel 9:26 says that the prince, which is the Man of Sin, will destroy the temple as well as the city. As Jesus enters Jerusalem, the city is in shambles as well as the temple. The only places that are in good shape are the buildings where the soldiers and the rulers are, and those who are closely aligned with the Beast. This is the seat of His power. This is the city of desolation. Ruins are all that remain of a place when God departs out of it.

The house of God, the temple, is now a shrine to the Beast. A golden statue, the image of the Beast, stands in what used to be the holy place. Around the golden statue is beautiful work. Maybe it's marble of various colors like during the reign of king Ahasuerus in the book of Esther chapter 1. In what used to be the holiest of all sits a golden throne. It is a testimony to the wicked desire of Satan to overthrow the throne of God. This is the closest Satan ever came to achieving His desire to ascend above the heights of the clouds. The closest he ever came to fulfill his desire to, "**...be like the most High.**" (Isa. 14:14) But it is now time for verse 15. You see, there is going to be a payday someday.

Satan has reveled in rebellion and sin for over 6,000 years. Perhaps during that length of time, he was encouraged to believe he was winning, or that God was weak. But now it is payday.

> ¹⁵**Yet thou shalt be brought down to hell, to the sides of the pit.** (Is. 14:15)

Dear reader, you must remember that there is coming a day when every wrong is going to be properly punished, or paid for. Every single one of them. There is no need for you to seek personal vengeance for what has been done wrong to you. That is not to say that punishment should be ignored. No, if legal punishment is due because the law was broken, then it is not wrong to seek that. But you must go as God leads you, and He may lead you to move on and serve Him.

You must remember as well, that there is coming a day when every right will be properly rewarded. Just as no one is going to get away with anything, God also sees what you have done for Him. When all is finished, the Bible says that the councils of the heart shall be made manifest, and every man will have praise of God. (1 Cor. 4:5)

As He approaches the city, people stand to resist Him. This is when He speaks, and a blast goes out of His mouth that literally melts those in front of Him.

> [8]And then shall that Wicked be revealed, whom **the Lord shall consume with the spirit of his mouth, and shall destroy with the brightness of his coming:** (2 Thess. 2:8)

> [12]And this shall be the plague wherewith the LORD will smite all the people that have fought against Jerusalem; **Their flesh shall consume away while they stand upon their feet, and their eyes shall consume away in their holes, and their tongue shall consume away in their mouth.** (Zech. 14:12)

The power and heat of the blast that is projected out of our Lord's mouth is so strong that the people literally melt like wax in a fire. It is at this time that the Antichrist is consumed with the spirit of the Lord's mouth and destroyed with the brightness of His coming.

Along with the Lord literally blowing the wicked away with the breath of His lips, is the fact that this is where we get in on the action. I'm not sure who in the body of Christ has the privilege of fighting at Jerusalem. The reason I say that is because it is only one city, and we will number in the millions. But at this battle we are a very strong people who will be set in battle array. (Joel 2:1-11; 16) We run along the housetops and enter through the windows like thieves. Before us the people are much pained; after we go through, every thing is left in flames. But there is a very curious statement made about us that I enjoy reading and musing upon.

Picture in your mind the following: first of all remember that we will not be subject to gravity like our enemies will be. We will not be able to die either. Now that is the way to fight a war! So we are running through the houses and slaughtering all of the enemies of the Lord. Maybe there will be some in Jerusalem who have not taken the mark and have survived, but if so, there couldn't be that many. At least I wouldn't think so, not in the seat of the Beast. But notice the following:

> [7]They shall run like mighty men; they shall climb the wall like men of war; and they shall march every one on his ways, and they shall not break their ranks:
> [8]Neither shall one thrust another; they shall walk every one in his path: and _when_ **they fall upon the sword, they shall not be wounded.** (Joel 2: 7-8)

We are going to have bodies just like Jesus Christ.

> [21]Who shall **change our vile body, that it may be fashioned like unto his glorious body,** according to the working whereby he is able even to subdue all things unto himself. (Phil. 3:21)

Not only will we have bodies just like the risen Jesus Christ, but we are going to have the same mentality as our Lord. This is our Lord's rightful day to return with vengeance. And the Lord will possess a fury which is such that He will laugh and mock those whom He is destroying. It is called vengeance. Not merely judgment, but vengeance. There is a difference. Vengeance has anger associated with it. Combined with this anger is personal satisfaction that where you were wronged, you are now allowed and able to inflict the punishment that is due.

So, here we are, the born-again saints of our Lord Jesus Christ. We are the bride of Christ, also known as the Church. We are fighting in this battle as well, and it is a great battle to fight, for we will not lose and we cannot die.

But I have a question. If we cannot die, and we will not break our ranks, and we have bodies just like our Lord, then why do we fall upon our sword? "...**when they fall upon the sword...**" (Joel 2:8) We certainly will not trip, for gravity is irrelevant to us anyway. But if the Lord is vexing and mocking His enemies and laughing at their calamity, then we are likely to have the same attitude.

So as we encounter soldiers who are trying to kill us, we will let them stick us with their sword, or shoot us with 300 bullets, and then laugh as we watch them realize we are immortal. Or since it says "**fall upon,**" we will mock them by falling upon a sword in front of them and then get up unharmed right before their faces. As they realize their doom, we will laugh, mock, and then kill them. This is our day. This is our time. He who laughs last, laughs best. Aren't you glad you're saved?!

418

Dear reader, perhaps you are having a hard time. Maybe people are using you, or you are getting abused at work or home, and you are getting discouraged. Remember, your day is coming. If you are saved, then you are going to fight in this battle and win.

Battle at Megiddo

What I am writing is conjecture. In other words it is a guess, based upon what I have read in the word of God. It is not doctrine, other than the major event of the Second Coming of Jesus Christ. And I can also teach the three battles as certainty. But there is much that I am not certain about. It is food for thought, as they say, something to muse upon.

I do not know the amount of time it will take from the appearance of Jesus Christ to His landing upon the earth, then from His first battle in Bozrah to this second battle in Jerusalem. I know that His appearing could be very quick, for it is said to be like lightning.

> ^{27}For as the lightning cometh out of the east,
> and shineth even unto the west; so shall also
> the coming of the Son of man be. (Matt. 24:27)

There is no doubt the coming referred to there is the Second Coming of Jesus Christ. But it does say that every eye shall see Him. How to reconcile the two, I don't know. I know there is no contradiction to it, and when the light is given it will make sense. I just do not have the light for that right now. Maybe God will give it to you, or you already know the answer. Please fill me in.

I know that there is going to be a battle, a very large battle in the valley of Megiddo. This next thought of mine is only a guess, but maybe the Lord arrives to the earth and every eye sees Him. He next fights in Bozrah, and then there is the battle at Jerusalem, and all of this takes some time.

The stomping of people in Bozrah may take much time, as the Lord is doing it Himself alone. How long will it take Him to stomp and kill all of those in Bozrah? Sure, He could do it very quickly, but with it mentioned about the blood staining His garments, there seems to be the possibility of it taking some time. There is no doubt that He is enjoying inflicting judgment upon those people. (Prov. 1, Isa. 2). Why would He hurry? He has waited 6,000 years for this moment.

The battle at Jerusalem may take some time as well. One way or another, by the time the battle of Armageddon takes place in the valley of Megiddo, there are a whole bunch of people there. They are there assembled with the sole purpose of fighting Jesus Christ and His armies. Obviously they are not in their right minds, but then if they have been following the Dragon, the Beast and the False Prophet, they are definitely not in their right minds. They are totally deceived into thinking that they are going to win the battle.

I'm sure there is an attitude of rebellion as well. The rebellion is such that they would rather die and go to Hell than to live with Jesus Christ. Fools! Complete fools!

I remember hearing a pastor tell me a story of when he visited a lady in the hospital. She was on her death bed, to that there was no doubt. She couldn't speak, but was fully alert and aware.

The pastor slowly and completely went over the plan of salvation. During his explanation, he would stop and ask her, *"Do you understand what I am saying to you?"* She would look him in the eyes and nod her head yes. It seemed to the pastor to be going very well and that she was fully aware of her need for salvation. So after explaining it all to her, he then asked her if she would like to pray and ask Jesus Christ to save her. She looked at him and shook her head slowly from side to side, indicating an answer of *"No."*

This astonished the pastor and he asked her if she understood salvation and what he had told her. She then nodded her head yes. Then he moved in closer with his face about a foot away from hers, looking her in the eyes, asking, *"Do you know that you are going to Hell when you die?"* She nodded her head, yes. He then asked again, *"Would you like to pray and ask Jesus Christ to save you so you can go to Heaven?"* With just a few inches separating them, eye to eye, she slowly shook her head giving once again an answer of, *"No."*

There was nothing more to do, so the pastor left her hospital room, and not long after she died. Hard! So hard!

These soldiers at Megiddo are hard, they are deceived, and it is time for the judgment of the Lamb.

As the Lord enters the valley and engages the armies of the Devil, it becomes apparent that those earthly armies are in very serious trouble. For as they use their weapons against the Lord, they suddenly find out that their weapons have no power whatsoever against the Lord and His army.

> ^{20}And the winepress was trodden without the city, and **blood came out of the winepress, even unto the horse bridles,** by the space of a thousand _and_ six hundred furlongs. (Rev. 14:20)

The Lord is now riding His horse with its feet on the ground. And with each step, wicked enemy fighters are being trampled under foot of His horse. The Bible likens it to a wine press, but the people are the grapes that are being crushed by the horse's hooves which are spurred on by the wrath of almighty God. This is where the saying _"the grapes of wrath"_ comes from. This is the famous battle of Armageddon. It is the battle where the term _"we stomped them"_ comes from. In this battle the enemy will literally be stomped to death. Blood begins to flow. A little at first, and then more and more it begins to fill the valley.

As the enemy sees he is powerless to stop the onslaught of the battle, many of them begin to cry out for mercy. Others openly blaspheme and curse at Him in open rebellion. The Lord in His fury begins to laugh at them all. He begins to mock them as they cry or curse at Him. Yes, the "meek and lowly Galilean" is now mocking and laughing at those He is killing.

> ^{24}Because I have called, and ye refused; I have stretched out my hand, and no man regarded;

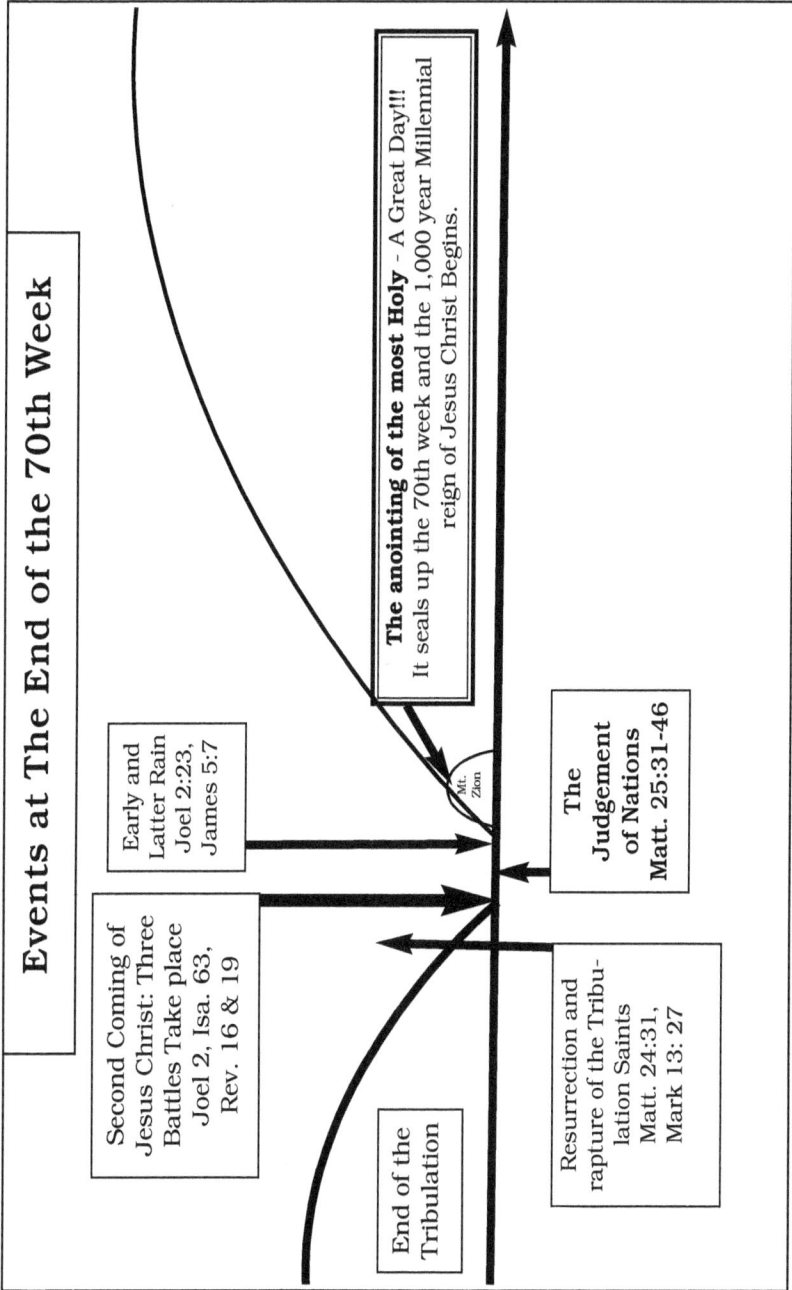

Events at The End of the 70th Week

Early and
Latter Rain
Joel 2:23,
James 5:7

Second Coming of
Jesus Christ: Three
Battles Take place
Joel 2, Isa. 63,
Rev. 16 & 19

The anointing of the most Holy - A Great Day!!!
It seals up the 70th week and the 1,000 year Millennial
reign of Jesus Christ Begins.

Mt.
Zion

The
Judgement
of Nations
Matt. 25:31-46

End of the
Tribulation

Resurrection and
rapture of the Tribu-
lation Saints
Matt. 24:31,
Mark 13: 27

Seven Years

²⁵But ye have set at nought all my counsel, and would none of my reproof:

²⁶**I also will laugh at your calamity; I will mock when your fear cometh;**

²⁷When your fear cometh as desolation, and your destruction cometh as a whirlwind; when distress and anguish cometh upon you. (Prov. 1:24-27)

²The kings of the earth set themselves, and the rulers take counsel together, against the LORD, and against his anointed, *saying,*

³Let us break their bands asunder, and cast away their cords from us.

⁴**He that sitteth in the heavens shall laugh: the Lord shall have them in derision.**

⁵Then shall he speak unto them in his wrath, and **vex them in his sore displeasure.**

⁹**Thou shalt break them with a rod of iron; thou shalt dash them in pieces like a potter's vessel.** (Psa. 2:2-5; 9)

The Lord Jesus Christ is now vexing them in His anger like a cat with a mouse. He is purposefully agitating them. As they plead and beg for mercy, or curse and shake their clenched fist in His face, He laughs and puts a horse's hoof right down on a knee, or a shoulder as a scream of pain splits the air. Then another stomp on the head, and they are done. With that, a loud victory laugh peals out from the Lord Jesus Christ as He rides on into the sea of bodies. People who

424

now are trying to flee have nowhere to go, for it is a valley. Not only that, but the attackers are supernatural.

Then in the middle of it all, the Lord gets off His horse and begins to stomp the people with His own bare feet. As they plead for mercy, He mocks them. With His eyes like fire, He is furious at these wicked people. Yes, He hates them and is now enjoying destroying them personally. This is the other side of the God of love.

Yes, God is love, for the Bible does state that He is. But it also states that **"...our God *is* a consuming fire."** (Heb. 12:29) also **"...he that believeth not the Son shall not see life; but the wrath of God abideth on him"** (Jn 3:36) On this day the wrath of God is going to be exercised on the heathen. Can you imagine the bloody, yet glorious sight?

A soldier, who minutes earlier thought he was so tough with the heart of a lion, has now turned into a fearful wretch with full realization he has no chance of victory. His heart is said to become the **"...heart of a woman..."** (Jer. 48:41) With anguish on his face and fear in his voice, the joints of his knees give out as he trembles for the first time in his life:

"L..L..Lord Jesus, I..I'm so sorry. Please, please I beg of you to forgive me. Oh God, I know I've done wrong. Dear Lord, I..."

The Lord Jesus Christ begins to vex him as He knocks the sinner to the bloody mud with a back hand. A loud *"Ah, Ha Ha Ha..."* goes out of the Lord's mouth. Sarcastically, Jesus says, *"Oh, I fully know you have done wrong. How do you like being on all fours? Finally, you have gotten on your knees."* Then the Lord leans over and says in his ear, *"But it's too late!"* And with that, He puts a foot down on his back that flattens him out, and the other foot slams on his head and crushes his skull in.

Warm, red, blood sprinkles and stains the raiment of the Lord as He moves onward smashing the people in His anger. Back up on his horse, He gallops alone in the middle of the valley, stomping the people.

> [3]I have trodden the winepress alone; and of the people *there was* none with me... (Isa. 63:3)

Ah, yes! The personal satisfaction of proper vengeance is realized. It has taken over 6,000 years to arrive, but at last the Scripture is fulfilled,

> [19]Dearly beloved, avenge not yourselves, but *rather* give place unto wrath: for it is written, **Vengeance *is* mine; I will repay, saith the Lord.** (Rom. 12:19)

The King of glory has returned and captured His kingdom. The Tribulation is now over, and the battles are done. Our Lord Jesus Christ is the conquering King, and victory is His.

In the wake of the Tribulation and final battles, the earth is in shambles. Wars, pestilences, earthquakes, volcanoes, heat --all have taken their toll. Dead fish in the ocean, destroyed buildings, broken sewers, and garbage are everywhere. Dead bodies lie rotting all over the world, with animals gorging them until they can eat no more. Over in Megiddo the stench is horrible.

> [9]And they that dwell in the cities of Israel shall go forth, and shall set on fire and burn the weapons, both the shields and the bucklers, the bows and the arrows, and the handstaves, and the spears, and **they shall burn them with fire seven years:**
> [10]So that they shall take no wood out of the field, neither cut down *any* out of the forests; for **they shall burn the weapons with fire: and they shall spoil those that spoiled them, and rob those that robbed them,** saith the Lord GOD.
> [11]And it shall come to pass in that day, *that* I will give unto Gog a place there of graves in Israel, the valley of the passengers on the east of the sea: and **it shall stop the *noses* of the passengers**: and there shall they bury Gog and all his multitude: and they shall call *it* The valley of Hamongog.
> [12]And **seven months shall the house of Israel be burying of them,** that they may cleanse the land.
> [13]Yea, all the people of the land shall bury *them*; and **it shall be to them a renown the day that I shall be glorified, saith the Lord GOD.** (Ezek. 39:9-13)

Seven Years

It will take seven months to bury the slain at Megiddo:

> [17]And I saw an angel standing in the sun; and he cried with a loud voice, saying to all the fowls that fly in the midst of heaven, **Come and gather yourselves together unto the supper of the great God;**
> [18]**That ye may eat the flesh of kings, and the flesh of captains, and the flesh of mighty men, and the flesh of horses, and of them that sit on them, and the flesh of all** *men,* *both* **free and bond, both small and great.**
> (Rev. 19:17-18)

Israel shall bury them. Not the Gentiles, but the house of Israel. It is a great day for Israel. A long-awaited day, the day that many had said would never come, or that it was only a dream. But it will come, and one day it will be a reality.

The Judgment of Nations

The battles are over and King Jesus has decidedly won every one of them. There was never any doubt that He would win, except in the minds of the depraved deceived armies who were following the Beast.

Still dressed in His garments drenched in the blood of the wicked, Jesus Christ --with His armies behind Him-- ride back into Jerusalem on horseback. The ravages of Satan's reign through the Man of Sin are everywhere, as well as the destruction that took place

428

in the battles of the war to take over Jerusalem. As Jesus Christ stated, **"The thief cometh not, but for to steal, and to kill, and to destroy: I am come that they might have life, and that they might have *it* more abundantly.** (John 10:10) Over the coming years, it will be clearly evident Jesus Christ brings a more abundant life, for the Millennium will be a time of life and peace the world has never seen.

Somewhere during the battle in Jerusalem, or at the battle of Megiddo, Jesus Christ captures the satanic trinity. What a scene that is going to be!!! Can you imagine it?

The power that the Beast used upon Moses and Elijah does not work any more. Why? Because all power is given unto Jesus Christ, in Heaven and earth. The Beast was allowed by God to kill Moses and Elijah thus revealing the true hatred of the people towards their Creator and His servants. Because remember this: they held a jubilant party that lasted for three days after the two witnesses were killed.

Reality is now going to be brought upon the Dragon, the Beast and the False Prophet. The satanic trinity is easily captured. As the chains of God are wrapped tightly around the Dragon, he fights and writhes in defiant fury. Then out of his seething, smoking mouth comes a growling roar that can be heard for miles around. As his back arches in rebellion, he screams, *"I am god! I --I am god! I am goooood!"*

> [8]**They shall bring thee down to the pit**, and thou shalt die the deaths of *them that are* slain in the midst of the seas.

⁹**Wilt thou yet say before him that slayeth thee, I *am* God?** but thou *shalt be* a man, and no God, in the hand of him that slayeth thee. (Ezek. 28:8-9)

And with that he is taken and cast into the bottomless pit. A seal is placed upon the pit and he is there for 1,000 years.

¹¶ And I saw an angel come down from heaven, having the key of the bottomless pit and a great chain in his hand.
²And **he laid hold on the dragon, that old serpent, which is the Devil, and Satan, and bound him a thousand years,**
³**And cast him into the bottomless pit,** and shut him up, and set a seal upon him, that he should deceive the nations no more, till the thousand years should be fulfilled: and after that he must be loosed a little season. (Rev. 20:1-3)

With Satan out of the way (Glory to God in the highest!) it is now time for the Judgment of Nations. A judgment that is little spoken of, but is the third and last event in the Day of Christ. It is written about in Matthew 25 and Joel 3. This judgment is for people on earth who are still alive when Jesus Christ returns.

The first thing that takes place is the gathering of the nations from all around the world. This is the entire population on earth. Every person comes before the King, Jesus Christ.

430

When the Bible says "...**before him shall be gathered all nations...**" (Matt. 25:32), the word "nations" is used as the native Americans use the word by referring to all of the people, not the organization. All the people of the world are gathered before Jesus Christ. It is an ominous judgment!

The criteria used at this judgment is conditioned upon how each person treated the Jews during the Tribulation.

You might remember that when the Dragon came down to the earth knowing that he had a short time, he went to make war with the woman and the remnant of her seed. That was Israel. It was at this time that the Mark of the Beast was instituted. With God sending a strong delusion so that the people would believe a lie, because they received not the love of the truth, I believe about 90% of the world's population takes the Mark of the Beast. By doing this, they not only publicly proclaim their allegiance to the Beast, but they also publicly proclaim their hatred for the Jews. Millions of people are killed during the Tribulation, but being that we are at over eight billion people on earth today, then there are still a good seven billion people left on the earth at the time of the judgment of nations. That means at least six billion people will be taken and:

> [41]Then shall he say also unto them on the left hand, **Depart from me, ye cursed, into everlasting fire, prepared for the devil and his angels:** (Matt. 25:41)

In that first battle that took place in the land of Bozrah, the Lord stained His garments with blood, and specified that He wanted to do it alone. (Isa. 63) In Isaiah 34 there is more information about what took place at that battle. The Lord not only stomped on the enemies of the Jews who were hiding out in Petra, but He also started a fire in the land of Idumea. This fire is said to last for ever and ever. That is a non-ending period.

This fire that He started is an open burning pit that people are cast into at this time and during the Millennium. It is referred to as **"hell fire."** (Matt. 5:22, 18:9, Mark 9:47). It is a pit that people will walk by and look into.

> [24]**And they shall go forth, and look upon the carcases of the men that have transgressed against me: for their worm shall not die, neither shall their fire be quenched;** and they shall be an abhorring unto all flesh.
> (Isa. 66:24)

The location of this pit in Idumea is down around the Dead Sea, and could even end up being at the location of the Dead Sea. This open-burning pit is going to have approximately six to seven billion people cast alive into it. Everyone who took the mark, unless it was a baby or child before the age of accountability, will be cast into that pit of Hell fire. Wow!!

To illustrate the size of this number of people consider the following. If 7 billion take the Mark of the Beast, then I crunched the numbers and it will take approximately 30 days to cast 7 billion people into the fire at a rate of 2,701 souls per second. The rate per second could easily be much greater though.

The earth's human living population that will remain after the judgment of nations will be under one billion, and could easily be around 500,000,000. That is still quite a few people, but a far cry less than the billions who were living before the Judgment of Nations.

Can you imagine the hundreds of thousands of people being cast into the pit of Hell fire by the second? Can you imagine the sound of their screaming and terror as they see where they are going? But the time has come for righteous judgment to be executed. Jesus Christ is just and right. This judgment is done in holiness.

Jesus Christ is cleansing the earth of all who are against Him. Merely seven years earlier they had the love of God preached to them around the world by internet, radio, churches, evangelists, and free Bibles. Not to be forgotten either are the free paper tracts that were given out far and wide. Many of these were thrown onto the ground and walked over. Truth fell in the streets.

Then the Tribulation came with Moses and Elijah, as well as the 144,000 Jewish evangelists going worldwide proclaiming the everlasting gospel.

Ah, yes! They had their chances to repent and receive Jesus Christ as their Saviour. They had their chances to submit to the words of God, but they rejected Jesus Christ. They rebelled against what was right. Payday has arrived. Over seven billion souls go out into eternity by being cast alive into a burning fiery pit. And after they land in that pit, people walk by and watch them burn. That is what the word of God says. You just read it.

With the judgment of the nations finished, so too the Day of Christ is completed. Three judgments, with all three being carried out by Jesus Christ.

Time to Rebuild

The destruction and judgment of people upon the world at this time is now finished and complete, praise the Lord! It has not been all too long since the Lord Jesus Christ has come back with His armies to the earth, but it is now time to repair, recreate, and heal the people and the landscape.

The following is more poetic license, but it is something to muse upon.

Almost all of the remaining Gentiles and Jews alive on the earth will be so because they loved, read and obeyed the written words of God. In order to do this they had to endure grueling hardships. Hunger and thirst would have been a constant trial. Along with all this would have been the reality of watching loved ones and friends get caught and killed for not following the Beast.

Along with the hardships brought on by wicked people, there was also the hardships brought on by natural disasters, plagues, and earthquakes. With all of these trials, it is quite safe to assume there will be many people who by the end of the Tribulation --who have been hiding out in caves and other wilderness places-- will be wounded, weak, and sickly.

At the Judgment of Nations, all the people of the

world have been gathered, and now these who have done right remain alive. I wonder if Jesus will heal them and feed them like He did with the 5,000? I think it likely that He will. And with each life that is restored to health, joy begins to shine forth from the hearts of the healed and fed.

Wouldn't it be a joy if we had the opportunity to heal people during this time? Or perhaps we could feed multitudes as well. Wouldn't that be a joy!

At this point the earth's atmosphere begins to change as well.

> ⁶And it shall come to pass in that day, *that* the light shall not be clear, *nor* dark:
> ⁷But it shall be one day which shall be known to the LORD, **not day, nor night: but it shall come to pass,** *that* **at evening time it shall be light.**
> ⁸¶ And it shall be in that day, *that* living waters shall go out from Jerusalem; half of them toward the former sea, and half of them toward the hinder sea: in summer and in winter shall it be. (Zech. 14:6-8)

Perhaps those living waters will be what heals the wounded and sick. But the light will change and the sun will become seven times brighter and so will the moon. (Isa. 30:26)

Then another event will take place. This time at the end of the Tribulation and the beginning of the Millennium is a time of cleansing. Along with this cleansing, the animals on earth turn vegetarian. The

lion will eat straw like the ox. The wolf and the lamb
shall lie down together. Even the vipers and poisonous
snakes will no longer bite nor destroy upon the earth.
(Isa. 65:25)

One more thing takes place as well: an entire season
of rain shall come down in one month. This is called
the early and the latter rain. This is said to happen in
the first month. Now either that is the month Abib, or
it is the first month of the Millennium. I think it could
easily be the first month of the Millennium.

> [21]Fear not, O land; be glad and rejoice: for
> the LORD will do great things.
> [22]Be not afraid, ye beasts of the field: **for the
> pastures of the wilderness do spring, for the
> tree beareth her fruit, the fig tree and the
> vine do yield their strength.**
> [23]Be glad then, ye children of Zion, and
> rejoice in the LORD your God: for he hath
> given you **the former rain moderately, and
> he will cause to come down for you the rain,
> the former rain, and the latter rain in the
> first** *month.*
> [24]And the floors shall be full of wheat, and
> the vats shall overflow with wine and oil.
> (Joel 2:21-24)

With the atmosphere changing, and the rain coming
down, the blood of the slain soaks into the earth. With
the curse on nature given in Genesis 3 being removed,
the land begins to explode with new life and abundance

of food. There is no longer a need to fear for there will be plenty of food for all.

A bright new earth emerges with joy and light. The bright sun does not burn the skin, yet the plants grow rapidly. And there is one last thing in this time of rebuilding that takes place.

The Great Leveling

> [4]Every valley shall be exalted, and every mountain and hill shall be made low: and the crooked shall be made straight, and the rough places plain:
> [5]And the glory of the LORD shall be revealed, and all flesh shall see *it* together: for the mouth of the LORD hath spoken *it*.
> (Is. 40:4-5)

Verse 4 always reminds me of the the song in Handel's Messiah. As I did a quick search on the internet for this song, I came across someone who asked what was the meaning of this song. The answer given on more than one website was that it is a metaphor that one day there will be equality on earth.

No, that is not the meaning of the song. Not at all! The meaning of these verses are quite literal. In the first weeks of the Millennium, the earth is going to be "landscaped." Do you remember what the Lord said in Mark 11?

437

> [23]For verily I say unto you, That **whosoever shall say unto this mountain, Be thou removed, and be thou cast into the sea;** and shall not doubt in his heart, but shall believe that those things which he saith shall come to pass; he shall have whatsoever he saith. (Mark 11:23)

A similar verse is found in Matthew 21. With these verses in mind, along with Isaiah 40, it looks like we will have the joy of rebuilding this earth. We literally will be moving mountains, raising valleys, and making the crooked places straight. Can you imagine that?!

In the Millennium the landscape is low rolling hills and level plains. The highest mountain will be Mount Zion, which springs up out of Jerusalem. Jerusalem today is at a level of 2,575 feet above sea level. All other mountains will be lower than that. The Himalayas will be leveled and the Mariana Trench will be raised. The Grand Canyon will be filled, and the Rockies and the Sierra Nevada mountains will be leveled.

> [9]¶ O Zion, that bringest good tidings, get thee up into **the high mountain;** O Jerusalem, that bringest good tidings, lift up thy voice with strength; lift *it* up, be not afraid; say unto the cities of Judah, **Behold your God!** (Is. 40:9)

Jerusalem, specifically where the temple will be, will

be the highest place on earth. It will be the highest mountain. Notice there is only one. It is Mount Zion.

Ah yes, Mount Zion! Now comes the final, or you might say, *"The Grand Finale."* Why? Because what you are about to read is very, very grand indeed!

We are now at the very end of Daniel's 70th week, which brings us back to the beginning of the prophecy given by Daniel in Daniel 9:24.

> ^{24}Seventy weeks are determined upon thy people and upon thy holy city, **to finish** the transgression, and **to make an end** of sins, and **to make reconciliation** for iniquity, and **to bring in** everlasting righteousness, and to **seal up** the vision and prophecy, and **to anoint** the most Holy. (Dan. 9:24)

By the end of the Tribulation you are at "the end." This is what's referred to over and over and over again in the books of Matthew, Hebrews, Daniel, James, and others.

And at the end of the Tribulation, Israel and the holy city Jerusalem attain the fulfillment of the seven prophecies given in Daniel 9:24:

1. To finish the transgression: Israel and Jerusalem will have finished transgressing against the Lord God Jehovah. They will never transgress against Him again. It is the Lord who has accomplished the task. He has worked patiently to bring His people to the point where they will never, ever go against Him again.

2. To make an end of sins: Israel and Jerusalem will have finished sinning against the Lord God Jehovah as well. They will never, ever sin against Him again.

3. To make reconciliation for iniquity: Israel and Jerusalem will be reconciled to the Lord God Jehovah. They will forever and ever be in perfect fellowship with their God.

4. To bring in everlasting righteousness: Israel and Jerusalem will be righteous before the Lord God Jehovah forever from this point on.

5. To seal up the vision: The vision concerning Israel and Jerusalem will be finished. All will be fully understood, and all of the vision will have been fully revealed. It will be wonderfully amazing to behold the wisdom and working of God. Ah yes! Hind sight is 20-20 as they say.

6. To seal up the prophecy: And the prophecy concerning Israel and Jerusalem, it will be completely fulfilled. The kingdom has come. David is on the throne. Israel is in their land.

7. The anointing of the most Holy: Ah yes, last --but not the least-- the most Holy is anointed.

This is the event that closes out the Tribulation and ushers in the millennial kingdom. This is a grand event.

This kingdom was attempted in Genesis 1:1, but Isaiah 14:12-15 took place and all of creation fell. So God started over and sought to bring in another kingdom under Adam, but Adam and Eve fell. So now this third try will not fail. Jesus Christ is going to reign on this earth for 1,000 years.

This is what the environmentalists are trying to bring in under their own power. They desire this "earth-friendly" kingdom, but they will never bring it in under their own power. Peace on earth and good will to men will never come in until **"glory to God in the Highest"** comes first. Then, and only then, will there be peace on earth. In the Millennium all of the priorities are right, and a glorious peace comes upon this earth. I can't wait!

COMPARED	
The Gathering	**The Rapture**
Matthew 24 and Mark 13	1 Thessalonians 4
Matt. 24:31 And he shall send his angels with a great sound of a trumpet, and they shall gather together his elect from the four winds, from one end of heaven to the other. Mark 13:27 And then shall he send his angels, and shall gather together his elect from the four winds, from the uttermost part of the earth to the uttermost part of heaven.	1Thess. 4:16 For the Lord himself shall descend from heaven with a shout, with the voice of the archangel, and with the trump of God: and the dead in Christ shall rise first: 1Thess. 4:17 Then we which are alive and remain shall be caught up together with them in the clouds, to meet the Lord in the air: and so shall we ever be with the Lord.
Gathered by Angels	The Lord Himself is coming for His bride
Gathered from the earth and Heaven	Dead in Christ and those alive at His coming are caught up together to meet the Lord in the air.
These meet his angels	These meet the Lord himself who is their Saviour.
These souls are not "in Christ" but are "His elect"	These souls are "in Christ" and thus make up His bride and body: the Church
These are gathered together at the end of the Tribulation	These are caught up and taken out of this world at the end of the Church Age
These souls include those under the altar Revelation 6:9	These include all saved from the dying thief to the last soul saved before the Rapture

The Anointing of the Most Holy

This is the seventh and last prophetical event that seals up and ends Daniel's 70th week. In the sight of God this is an event that He has looked forward to even more than taking out the vengeance on the wicked at the Second Coming. Once this anointing has taken place, the righteous millennial reign of Jesus Christ begins. This is a most important and significant event on God's calendar.

This is not, and can not be in any way the baptism of Jesus Christ. Oh, I know I should not repeat myself, but it must be said again that Jesus is not "most holy." That attribution demeans Him. It implies there is part of Jesus Christ that is not holy, which is blasphemous.

To say Jesus is "holy," which is what they say He is in Heaven, is to attribute the proper accolade to Him ––for He is "holy"! He is not most holy, nor is He "the" most holy. "Most Holy" is a Roman Catholic designation, and there is a celebration each year to celebrate the Solemnity of the Most Holy Trinity.

The Solemnity of the Most Holy Trinity

As early as the 8th century, liturgical prefaces appeared containing references to the doctrine of the Most Holy Trinity. *(Vatican News, Solemnity of the Most Holy trinity, www.vatican-news.va/en/liturgical-holidays/solemnity-of-the-most-holy-trinity.html, Viewed 5/10/24)*

The Solemnity of the Most Holy Trinity: First Sunday After Pentecost

In the West, Trinity Sunday, officially called "The Solemnity of the Most Holy Trinity," is one of the few celebrations of the Christian Year that commemorates a reality and doctrine rather than an event or person. *(Sacred Heart Catholic Church, The Solemnity of the Most Holy Trinity, https://sacredheartfla.org/sunday-mornings/seasonal/feast-days-solemnities/the-solemnity-of-the-most-holy-trinity/, Viewed 5/10/24)*

Of course they do that in an attempt to reverently adore and magnify the Trinity, but in reality they are demeaning and lowering the Godhead. As Bible believers we are to adhere to the Scriptures, and in the Scriptures Jesus Christ, as well as the Godhead, are NEVER referred to as **"most Holy."** They are always referred to as **"holy."** **"Holy, holy, holy, Lord God**

444

Almighty!" In the scriptures "most holy" and "the most holy" are ALWAYS references to a place or thing, with the "thing" being in the tabernacle or temple.

The anointing of the most holy is an event that takes place in Jerusalem in a very special place. As to events that take place from "the beginning" all the way to the end of time, this rates right up there with the best of them all. This is a highlight for our Lord Jesus Christ. This is the fulfillment of **"Thy kingdom come, Thy will be done on earth, as it is in Heaven."**

Satan hates this truth which is why so little has ever been taught on it. And why it has been referenced to another event, place and time.

I have already referenced some of the following, but now we will get into it much deeper and more completely ––well, at least we will try to do our best. We will be studying wonders and truths from the word of God that are very much greater than what these finite minds can handle. Thankfully we have the inerrant words of God for the truths and descriptions of it all.

Modern Jerusalem, ––Mount Zion–– is a mountain. If that mountain stays the level it is today, then the earth will be smooth, for the elevation is 2,575 feet above sea level. After growing up in the Sierras at 4,000 feet above sea level, the height of Jerusalem doesn't seem like much. The Bible does say:

> [9]¶ O Zion, that bringest good tidings, **get thee up into the high mountain;** O Jerusalem, that bringest good tidings, lift up thy voice with strength; lift *it* up, be not

afraid; say unto the cities of Judah, **Behold your God!** (Isa. 40:9)

Perhaps the mountain of the Lord will be much higher than 2,575 feet, but it does give a good amount of room for rolling hills. Gentle streams flow through the shallow valleys; along with the perfect breezes gently blowing across the landscape, birds are singing and peace fills the land.

I remember driving by the Sutter Buttes, which are some mountains of 2,060 feet high just outside of Yuba City, which is just north of Sacramento, California. They jut up in the center of the San Joaquin Valley which is completely flat. As a young boy, I remember riding by and seeing them for many, many miles after we passed them. Little by little, as the farther we traveled away from them, they would "shrink" lower and lower until they vanished from view.

So 2,575 feet is more than high enough, for Mount Zion to become the highest mount in all the earth. All other hills will be lower than Mount Zion during the Millennium. This is quite a thought when you consider the Himalayas, the Alps, the Andes, the Rockies and other mountain ranges. Of course they all can be thrown into the oceans.

I can hear it now: you crazy Christians that believe the Bible. If you throw all of those mountains into the ocean, you will flood the earth from rising sea levels, and no one will be able to live anywhere. You all are so stupid to believe all of that mumbo jumbo.

Well, there is one thing you missed, which is the sun is brighter and it is likely more of a tropical atmosphere. Either the extra water is held in the air, or it is removed since that water was a result of God's judgment upon the earth in the days of Noah. If the curse is reversed, then the water will be removed and placed back where it came from, which many have theorized to be an ice canopy around the earth. This would filter the ultra violet sun rays out so that the people aren't burnt up with the sun being seven times brighter. There is no doubt God removes and reverses the judgements and curses that He placed upon the earth back in the first part of the book of Genesis.

On the top of that mount, there will be a place, a very special place. It will be the place of the temple which will be inside what is called the holy oblation.

An oblation is anything that is offered to the Lord for the ministry. This oblation that will be on the mount is a section of land, and in the section of land will be the temple, which is from where the Lord Jesus Christ will reign over the earth. This temple is where the sons of Zadok will enter to do the service of the Lord. There is quite a bit of information in the word of God about this place.

This piece of real estate, which is referred to as the holy oblation, is 25,000 reeds long from north to south and 25,000 reeds wide, east to west. A reed is said to be six cubits and a handbreadth. (Eze. 40:5) As to the length of a cubit —well, it varies depending upon who you read, so let me give you the following story on how and why I choose the length of the cubit that I do.

Some years back, I think in the late 1980's, there was a man by the name of Ron Wyatt. He was an amateur archeologist, a saved Seventh Day Adventist, and he found Noah's ark. (Look him up on YouTube or Google and buy his videos of his discovery of the ark.) His evidence was so compelling that the Turkish government established Noah's Ark National Park.

When Ron Wyatt found the ruins of the ark, he measured the length and width, but it did not match the length given in the Bible. In Genesis 6:15 it is written that the length of the Ark was to be 300 cubits, and the width was to be 50 cubits. Then he remembered that Moses was "...**learned in all the wisdom of Egypt.**" (Acts 7:22). So Ron Wyatt then recalculated the measurement of the ruins to the standard Royal Egyptian cubit which is 20.6 inches, and it came out exactly 300 cubits by 50 cubits. 20.6 is a common length used for a cubit though the most common measurement is 18 inches. Royal cubits are known to be longer than what is termed the everyday commercial cubit.

I could not find the length of a handbreadth, but with the cubit measuring 20.6 inches, the size of the oblation from north to south is approximately 50 miles, and the width is 50 miles foursquare. (Ezek. 48:20)

> [20]All the oblation *shall be* **five and twenty thousand by five and twenty thousand: ye shall offer the holy oblation foursquare,** with the possession of the city. (Ezek. 48:20)

The total **oblation** is 50 x 50 miles foursquare. Then the size of the **holy oblation** is 50 miles long and 20 miles wide. (Ezek. 45:1-3)

The size of the **most holy oblation**, where the sanctuary will be, is one mile square.

Oblation = 50 x 50 miles

Holy Oblation = 50 x 20 miles

The Most Holy Oblation is 1 mile square

Jerusalem will be the capital of the earth, and mount Zion is the highest mountain in all the earth during the 1,000 year reign of our Lord Jesus Christ. So this oblation will be located within the portion of the city of Jerusalem.

I did a quick measure of the distance from Baytown, Texas to Katy Texas and it is 59 miles. It is solid city the whole way. From Castaic, California to Santa Margarita, California is 100 miles. And it is also solid city for 100 miles. So a 50 by 50 square-mile mountain within the city limits of Jerusalem is very doable, and that is by today's cities. But this is going to be much greater, for it is the city of the great King, Jesus Christ. This area is said to be a city that will have one way streets in it running north and south.

> [9]But when the people of the land shall come before the LORD in the solemn feasts, **he that entereth in by the way of the north gate to worship shall go out by the way of the south gate; and he that entereth by the way of the south gate shall go forth by the way of the north gate: he shall not return by the way of the gate whereby he came in, but shall go forth over against it.** (Ezek. 46:9)

This makes sense because people from all over the world will be coming to worship the King.

> ¹⁶¶ And it shall come to pass, *that* **every one that is left of all the nations** which came against Jerusalem **shall even go up from year to year to worship the King, the LORD of hosts, and to keep the feast of tabernacles.** (Zech. 14:16)

Notice that it says "**...of all the nations which came against Jerusalem...**" These are people who didn't go along with the crowd. These are the ones who didn't take the mark and were saved out of those nations.

> ¹⁷And it shall be, *that* whoso will not come up of *all* the families of the earth unto Jerusalem to worship the King, the LORD of hosts, even upon them shall be no rain.
> ¹⁸And if the family of Egypt go not up, and come not, that *have* no *rain*; there shall be the plague, wherewith the LORD will smite the heathen that come not up to keep the feast of tabernacles.
> ¹⁹This shall be the punishment of Egypt, and **the punishment of all nations that come not up to keep the feast of tabernacles.** (Zech. 14:17-19)

Some of them will come out of duty because of the command to keep the feast of tabernacles, while others

will come just to be near the King of Glory, our Lord
Jesus Christ.

> ²⁰Thus saith the LORD of hosts; *It shall* yet
> *come to pass*, that there shall come people,
> and the inhabitants of many cities:
> ²¹And the inhabitants of one *city* shall go to
> another, saying, **Let us go speedily to pray
> before the LORD, and to seek the LORD of
> hosts: I will go also.** (Zech. 8:20-21)

Here is someone who hears his neighbors are going
to go pray before the Lord of hosts. This is during the
Millennium when the Lord Jesus Christ is physically on
this earth, dwelling in Mount Zion in Jerusalem. They
hear about the trip and say, **"I will go also."** They want
to go.

Have you ever wondered how people will travel in the
Millennium? Will it be cars? Planes?

Well, we know that Jesus Christ with all of His armies
traveled from Heaven to earth in twenty-four hours or
less. Those are some amazing horses! And to have a
horse for every one of us means there are millions of
those horses.

And we know that there are horses in the holy city
during the Millennium. They will have bells on their
bridles with **"HOLINESS UNTO THE LORD"** inscribed
on them. (Zech. 14:20) No doubt that will be a beautiful
sound and sight to see!

It looks like to me that the mode of transportation for
the physical people will be by supernatural horses.
How they can fly swiftly through the air without the

wind knocking their riders off, I have no idea. But it does look as if those horses are the means of transportation.

Because you and I, the sons of God, will have glorified bodies, we will be able to travel unfettered by any physical limitations. Maybe we will be able to transport people as well. Of course this would not be our daily job, at least for those who are reigning over cities. It might be a daily job for the saved who were not faithful in this lifetime. Now that is something to think about! (2 Tim. 2:11-13)

But I digress, so let's get back to the oblation and worship of the Lord in and on Mount Zion in the oblation.

So what must be done before the worship can take place? Three places must be set apart. The first two places are the oblation and the holy oblation. The third place is the most Holy oblation, which includes the temple with its holy place and its most holy place. The temple must be built and anointed before any worship can take place.

> [12]Blessed is he that waiteth, and cometh to the thousand three hundred and five and thirty days. (Dan. 12:12)

After our Lord returns to this earth, there are some times given, and the above time is the longest one of them. It also has a message for those who make it all the way: **"Blessed is he that waiteth."** Why would that be? I am only guessing, but this is probably the anointing of the most Holy, and thus the beginning of the Millennium. When the 1,335 days arrive, it will be time for the grand event.

Have you ever heard, **"Thy kingdom come?"** Have you ever heard, *"Bring in the kingdom?"* Or have you ever heard *"spread the kingdom?"* Those are all references to the kingdom, and the kingdom that is being referenced, though they do not know it for the most part, is the one where Jesus Christ is reigning on this earth. The anointing of the most Holy is the commencement of His kingdom. This event is the one God has been waiting for, and looking forward to for over 6,000 years. Yes, this is a very grand event!!

Here are a list of some of the changes that will take place on the earth at the time of the anointing of the most Holy:

1. Satan is no longer the god of this world for he is in the bottomless pit.

2. This is the beginning of the new world.

3. This is the beginning of Israel in fellowship with God, dwelling in the land with David over them as their king.

4. This is the beginning of the Church reigning on this earth with Jesus Christ.

5. This is the beginning of a time of 1,000 years of peace on earth and **"good will toward men."** (Luke 2:14)

6. This is the beginning of when the natural world i.e. "nature" will all be vegetarians, and the curse will be removed. Roses won't have thorns, and the animals will be tame. A little child will lead a lion or a wolf, or any other animal he or she wants to.

7. This is the beginning of a 1,000 year period of love for each other.

8. There will no longer be weeds, earthquakes, tornadoes, and bloodsucking, flying insects.

9. There will be no food shortages.

10. There will be happy children all over the place living for hundreds of years. They will never be afraid of being kidnapped or harmed in any way.

And it all begins with the anointing of the most Holy. The most Holy is the Lord's house, and the place of the Lord's sanctuary. You might remember that I said the greatest attribute about God is not love, but His greatest attribute is His holiness. Here at the most Holy place the visitors and workers are reminded of the holiness of God.

The horses which are prancing around the streets have bells upon them and written upon those bells is the inscription: HOLINESS UNTO THE LORD. The holy Lord Jesus Christ is in His holy temple. The pots used in the sacrifices are declared to be holy. The ground whereupon the Lord stands and resides is holy. I would guess that all who enter the city will remove their shoes just as Moses and Joshua did when the Lord appeared to them.

Can you imagine walking down the clean streets that have old men and old women slowly strolling along, but is also full of boys and girls playing?

> [3]Thus saith the LORD; I am returned unto Zion, and will dwell in the midst of Jerusalem: and Jerusalem shall be called a city of truth; and the mountain of the LORD of hosts the holy mountain.
> [4]Thus saith the LORD of hosts; **There shall**

454

yet old men and old women dwell in the streets of Jerusalem, and every man with his staff in his hand for very age.

⁵And the streets of the city shall be full of boys and girls playing in the streets thereof. (Zech. 8:3-5)

Along with the innocent and joyful laughter of children ringing out into the air, you also hear the jingle, jingle of the golden bells intermingled with the clippity-clop of horse hoofs as they prance through the streets. Birds sing praises to God, and the fresh clean air kisses your cheeks with a gentle hello as the bright sun is not too hot, but just right to warm the chilly soul. This is the city of the great King, Mount Zion, the joy of the whole earth. And it all begins with the anointing of the most Holy. I love to muse upon what it will be like.

Take your mind back to the end of the Tribulation and the Second Coming of Jesus Christ to this earth. It has been a month or two since His return and the earth is quickly, being transformed.

The inhabitants of the earth who survived the Tribulation without taking the mark are now doing much better. The sick and crippled are healing up well, and the hungry are now "full to the brim." Smiles are returning to the faces which only a few months earlier wore expressions of constant fear, loneliness, and pain.

The sun is shining brighter, the air is smelling cleaner, and flowers are now appearing upon the face of the earth. Fields of black gray ash have turned to bright green with new growth. Streams of water are beginning to trickle through the shallow valleys between the gently rolling hills. It is the dawn of the new world.

With this new dawn of the kingdom, up on the hill of Zion in Israel the new golden house begins to take shape. The gold sparkles brighter by the hour of each passing day. And then, right on time, the moment has arrived for the anointing of the most Holy.

THE ANOINTING OF THE MOST HOLY
A Truly Grand Event!

¹¶ Great *is* the LORD, and greatly to be praised in the city of our God, *in* **the mountain of his holiness.**
²Beautiful for situation, **the joy of the whole earth,** *is* **mount Zion,** *on* **the sides of the north, the city of the great King.**
(Psa. 48:1-2)

The Millennial Kingdom is the time when these verses will be fulfilled, and what a beautiful time it will be! This is a very important event to our Lord God Almighty. He has waited over 6,000 years for this to take place. This is the time when, "Thy kingdom come, thy will be done, on earth, as it is in Heaven."

Notice that the city is in the mountain. No, not literally inside, but it is said to be in the mountain.

⁹¶ O Zion, that bringest good tidings, **get thee up into the high mountain;** O

Jerusalem, that bringest good tidings, lift up thy voice with strength; lift *it* up, be not afraid; say unto the cities of Judah, **Behold your God!** (Isa. 40:9)

If you remember, there is going to be a fifty-mile square oblation for the Lord. To locate all of the information that is given in the word of God, I am not going to do at this time. What I am going to focus upon is what is on top of that mountain. For it is there that the anointing of the most Holy will take place.

Within the city of Jerusalem will be a mountain. On top of that mountain will be a one-mile square gold house. It will be the house of the Lord, also referred to as the sanctuary of the Lord. It will be from where Jesus Christ will reign over the earth for 1,000 years. It is sometimes referred to as a city. But it will cover the entire summit of the "high mountain." It is the city on a hill that cannot be hid.

¹²This *is* the law of the house; **Upon the top of the mountain the whole limit thereof round about** *shall be* **most holy**. Behold, this *is* the law of the house. (Ezek. 43:12)

When I picture the mountain of the Lord, I picture fairly steep sides on the mountain, but that probably will not be the case. It looks like the sides of the mountain are a city, with the top being the temple and house of the Lord. So the base of the mountain may fit within a fifty-mile square. That would be the oblation. With fifty miles north, south, east, and west, the

457

mountain could slowly rise to 2,700 feet. The slope would be such that people could easily live on the incline.

> ^{14}Ye are the light of the world. **A city that is set on an hill cannot be hid.** (Matt. 5:14)

For those Christians who lived for Jesus Christ they will literally be shining for Jesus Christ, and this is the city on the hill. How beautiful it will be! This is where the nations will go up to worship the Lord. The people will literally and individually "...**get thee up into the high mountain.**" (Isa. 40:9)

If you will remember there are two places in the word of God where the Lord appears to Moses and Joshua. (Ex. 3:5, Josh. 5:15). In both places He tells them to take off their shoes for the ground is holy.

After describing the one-mile square "house," He says the following to Ezekiel:

> ^{7}¶ And he said unto me, Son of man, the place of my throne, and **the place of the soles of my feet,** where I will dwell in the midst of the children of Israel for ever, and **my holy name,** shall the house of Israel no more defile, *neither* they, nor their kings, by their whoredom, nor by the carcases of their kings in their high places. (Ezek. 43:7)

Just as was written in Daniel 9:24, Israel and the holy city Jerusalem will no more defile His name as well as the place of His dwelling. This clearly places this at the end of Daniel's 70th week, and the last prophetic event to happen is to anoint the most Holy.

The top of this high mountain is going to be the location where the Lord will **"place the soles of"** his feet.

The top of that mountain is most holy. But that is not all that is holy. The horses that prance majestically up into the high mountain are holy.

Even the pots and pans are holy. Thus you have the holy Lord Jesus Christ sitting upon the holy mountain with holy horses going up and down the mount. The ground is holy, and can you guess what the name of the house is?

Since Solomon's dedication of the temple is a type of the millennial reign, there is some great information to be found.

> [5]Since the day that I brought forth my people out of the land of Egypt I chose no city among all the tribes of Israel to build an house in, **that my name might be there**; neither chose I any man to be a ruler over my people Israel: [6]But **I have chosen Jerusalem, that my name might be there**; and have chosen David to be over my people Israel. (2 Chr. 6:5-6)

> [9]Notwithstanding thou shalt not build the house; but thy son which shall come forth out of thy loins, **he shall build the house for my name.** (2 Chr. 6:9)

One of the titles for Jesus Christ is the son of David. These verses are prophetic of the millennial house that will be built for Jesus Christ. It is built upon the holy Mount Zion.

But notice what it says "**…that my name might be there.**" Notice also that "**…he shall build the house for my name.**" Now, there is one more verse to bring this together.

> [15]For thus saith the high and lofty One that inhabiteth eternity, **whose name *is* Holy**; I dwell in the high and holy *place*, with him also *that is* of a contrite and humble spirit, to revive the spirit of the humble, and to revive the heart of the contrite ones. (Isa. 57:15)

One of the names of the Lord is "Holy." This is why it is capitalized. Thus the name of the house on the top of the holy hill, on the holy mount, with holy horses, and holy pots, and seated upon His holy throne is Him whose name is Holy. **And the name of the house is "Holy." And that holy house of the holy Lord is going to be anointed.**

Another interesting fact concerning Solomon's temple and kingdom is the amount of gold that is present. Gold in the Bible represents deity. It pictures Jesus Christ.

> [20]And all the drinking vessels of king Solomon *were of* gold, and all the vessels of the house of the forest of Lebanon *were of* pure gold: **none *were of* silver; it was *not* any**

thing accounted of in the days of Solomon. (2 Chr. 9:20)

[27]And the king made **silver in Jerusalem as stones,** and cedar trees made he as the sycomore trees that *are* in the low plains in abundance. (2 Chr. 9:27)

When I refer to the city as golden, or the house as golden, then that is exactly what I mean. During the Millennium, the house of the Lord will be gold. Very shiny, pretty gold.

With this new dawn of the kingdom up on the hill of Zion in Israel, the new golden house called Holy begins to take shape. The golden glow and the sparkle becomes brighter by the hour of each passing day. And then, right on time, the moment has arrived for the anointing of the most Holy.

In order to get an idea of what that will be, we must look at the dedication of the temple under king Solomon. That is the type of this very event, and there are a number of things there to see.

[22]And the snuffers, and the basons, and the spoons, and the censers, *of* pure gold: and the entry of the house, the inner doors thereof for **the most holy *place*,** and the doors of the house of the temple, *were of* gold. (2 Chr. 4:22)

[1]¶ Thus all the work that Solomon made for the house of the LORD was finished: and

461

> Solomon brought in *all* the things that David his father had dedicated; and the silver, and the gold, and all the instruments, put he among the treasures of the house of God.
> ²Then Solomon assembled the elders of Israel, and all the heads of the tribes, the chief of the fathers of the children of Israel, unto Jerusalem, **to bring up the ark of the covenant of the LORD out of the city of David, which *is* Zion.** (2 Chr. 5:1-2)

Within the walls of the one-square mile house called Holy, the temple is built which contains the holy place, and the most holy place.

It is now time to anoint the most Holy.

Now assembled are all of the vessels. These include instruments, cups and various other articles, along with the candlestick, the table of shewbread and the incense altar. However, there remains one article of furniture that must be put in the proper place, which is the Ark of His Testimony.

The last we read about it was in Revelation 11:19 ––when Heaven was opened, and the ark was seen in Heaven. God had removed it from being desecrated by the satanic Man of Sin. But that ark has now been brought back to earth with the Lord and His armies, all for the purpose of being placed once again, where it rightfully belongs, in the Temple of God in the most holy place.

Just as the elders and the chief fathers of Israel brought up the ark of the covenant from the city of

David (which is Zion), so too David and the sons of Zadok will bring up the ark of the covenant. There it will be placed in the most holy place in the temple. And with that, loud, royal, majestic music begins to sound out.

> [13]It came even to pass, as the trumpeters and singers *were as* one, to make one sound to be heard in praising and thanking the LORD; and when they lifted up *their* voice with the trumpets and cymbals and instruments of musick, and praised the LORD, *saying*, For *he is* good; for his mercy *endureth* for ever: **that *then* the house was filled with a cloud, *even* the house of the LORD;**
> [14]So that the priests could not stand to minister by reason of the cloud: **for the glory of the LORD had filled the house of God.**
> (2 Chr. 5:13-14)

In 2 Chronicles 6, Solomon prays for Israel and the temple. How far this type can be pressed, I do not know. But either king David prays in the same way, or perhaps King Jesus Christ speaks at the dedication of the temple.

> [1]¶ Now when Solomon had made an end of praying, the **fire came down from heaven, and consumed the burnt offering and the sacrifices; and the glory of the LORD filled the house.** (2 Chr. 7:1)

> ¹⁶For now have I chosen and sanctified this
> house, **that my name may be there for ever:**
> and mine eyes and mine heart shall be there
> perpetually. (2 Chr. 7:16)

This is how the Lord anointed the house of the Lord,
the temple, in the Old Testament. It is a picture of the
millennial anointing and dedication of the temple,
though only a type. There is some information given in
the word of God that I need to bring out now.

King Jesus Christ will enter Jerusalem through the
eastern gate. As He does the earth shines with His
glory. His glory is light that shines out from Him.

> ¹³And in the midst of the seven candlesticks
> *one* like unto the Son of man, clothed with a
> garment down to the foot, and girt about the
> paps with a golden girdle.
> ¹⁴His head and *his* hairs *were* white like
> wool, as white as snow; and his eyes *were* as
> a flame of fire;
> ¹⁵And his feet like unto fine brass, as if they
> burned in a furnace; and **his voice as the
> sound of many waters.**
> ¹⁶And he had in his right hand seven stars:
> and out of his mouth went a sharp twoedged
> sword: and **his countenance *was* as the sun
> shineth in his strength.** (Rev. 1:13-16)

Notice the sound of His voice, for it is as the sound of
many waters.

> ^{2}And, behold, **the glory** of the God of Israel came from the way of the east: and **his voice** *was* **like a noise of many waters: and the earth shined with his glory.** (Ezek. 43:2)

The Lord approaches the eastern gate of Jerusalem and walks in. What He says when He walks in, I do not know. But when He speaks, His voice sounds like many waters. Such as Niagara Falls, or the crashing of the waves at the ocean in a storm. And with His voice, there is a shining brighter than the sun. This is the King of Glory, and He is coming to His home on this earth.

Up the mountain He ascends to His golden city on the Hill of Zion. As He ascends, people fall before Him, while shouts of praise and glorious music sounds out. The cheers of a million voices are heard praising and singing to the Lord of Glory.

> ^{4}And **the glory of the LORD came into the house** by the way of the gate whose prospect *is* toward the east. (Ezek. 43:4)

This house is His sanctuary, His temple, and is most holy. This is the place where the sons of Zadok shall enter with the blood and offer it before the Lord. Only the sons of Zadok are allowed to perform these offerings. Only the sons of Zadok ––of all the priests of the Lord–– are allowed to be in and near Jesus Christ.

> ^{5}So the spirit took me up, and brought me into the inner court; and, behold, **the glory of the LORD filled the house.** (Ezek. 43:5)

465

When the glory of the Lord fills the house, the light --very bright and radiant-- shines for many, many miles all around. This is the house of the Lord and this is the city where the name of the Lord dwells. The name of this city is Holy.

Perhaps then a fire comes down from Heaven and kindles a fire on the altar. A sweet savor once again ascends up to the Father from off the altar. Here in the Millennium it commemorates the sacrifice of the Lamb of God on the cross of Calvary. And the One who sits on the throne now has the scars in His body that shows His love for mankind and declare His obedience to His Father.

So the anointing of the most Holy takes place when King Jesus Christ walks into His house (which is where the temple is), sits down, and reigns righteously for 1,000 years. Remember, when God entered the temple during the reign of Solomon, that was the anointing of the temple. Here in the Millennium, when Jesus Christ walks into His temple and sits on His throne, that is the anointing of the most Holy. While the golden temple already shined with beauty and light, when Jesus walks into His temple the glory that shines is far greater.

It is the event that God has looked forward to for 6,000 years. He has patiently waited to inflict His vengeance in due time. He has patiently waited for the day in which He beholds His Son rightfully sitting upon His golden throne in the city that bears His name which is Holy. You see, the throne, the temple and the city are holy. So the name of the city is the name of our Lord, which is HOLY.

God's will is now going to be done on the earth.

466

[9]¶ After this manner therefore pray ye: Our Father which art in heaven, Hallowed be thy name.
[10]Thy kingdom come. Thy will be done in earth, as *it is* in heaven. (Matt. 6:9-10)

"Hallowed" means holy. Thy kingdom come thy will be done in earth, as it is in heaven. In Heaven they cry out:

[3]And one cried unto another, and said, **Holy, holy, holy, *is* the LORD of hosts: the whole earth *is* full of his glory.** (Isa. 6:3)

[8]¶ And the four beasts had each of them six wings about *him*; and *they were* full of eyes within: and they rest not day and night, saying, **Holy, holy, holy, Lord God Almighty, which was, and is, and is to come.** (Rev. 4:8)

Thy will be done in earth as it is in Heaven. His name is Holy.

[6]But **I have chosen Jerusalem, that my name might be there...** (2 Chr. 6:6)

In the midst of Jerusalem, upon the high mountain is the house of the Lord. It is named Holy. That golden house is most Holy, for it is where the presence of the Lord is!

Seven Years

Bibliography

1. Abbott John S. C., The History of Christianity, Chapter 10, Boston: Published by B.B. Russell, 55 Cornhill, Philadelphia, Quaker-city Publishing-House, San Francisco: A.L.Bancroft & Co., Detroit, Michigan., R.D.S. Tyler, 1872, downloaded from https://www.gutenberg.org/ebooks/59400 (pg 209-212)

2. ABC News, Snake-Handling Pentecostal Pastor Dies From Snake Bite, February 17, 2014&#151, abcnews.go.com/US/snake-handling-pentecostal-pastor-dies-snake-bite/story?id=22551754#:~:text=Pastor%20Jamie%20Coots%20died%20after,during%20a%20weekend%20church%20service., viewed 5/10/2024 (pg 159)

3. Abrahamic Family House, The, Diverse in our Faiths. Common in our Humanity. Together in Peace., Abrahamic Family House, https://www.abrahamicfamily-house.ae/about-us#origin, viewed 5/10/2024 (pg 283)

4. Benecke, Mark (2004). "The Search for Tycho Brahe's Nose" (PDF). Annals of Improbable Research. 10 (4): 6–7: As quoted from https://en.wikipedia.org/wiki/Tycho_Brahe#CITEREF Håkansson2006, viewed 5/10/2024, (pg 35)

5. Berkowitz Adam Eliyahu, Jews begin building Third Temple on Israel Independence Day, https://israel365news.com/352915/jews-begin-building-third-temple-on-israel-independence-day/, May 6, 2022, viewed 5/10/24 (pg 143)

6. Bernard, Rich of Batcombe, A Guide to Grand-Jurymen, Second Edition, 1630, Printed by Felix Kyngston for Edw. Blackmore, Chap. XVIII Of the maine point to convict one of witchcraft, and the proofs thereof, pg 214, downloaded from https://archive.org/details/bim_early-english-books-1475-1640_a-guide-to-grand-jury-me_bernard-richard_1630/page/212/mode/2up, viewed 5/10/24 (Pg 356-357)

7. Brewster David, Martyrs of Science, The, or the lives of Galileo, Tycho Brahe, and Kepler, London: John Murray, Albemarle Street. 1841, Chapter 4, downloaded from: https://www.gutenberg.org/ebooks/25992 (pg 48)

8. Bublack Ulinka, The astronomer and the witch - how Kepler saved his mother from the stake, https://www.cam.ac.uk/research/discussion/the-astronomer-and-the-witch-how-kepler-saved-his-mother-from-the-stake, Published by Oxford University Press on October 22, 2015, viewed 5/10/2024 (pg 49, 50)

9. Christ By The Sea, The Pope & The Papacy, christbythesea.net/the-pope-the-papacy#:~:text=The%20Pope%20stands%20in%20the, believe%20that%20Jesus%20chose%20St.,viewed 5/10/2024, 1:14P.M. CST, This is a Pro - Roman Catholic website. (Pg 331)

10. Current World Population, worldometers.info/worldpopulation/#:~:text=8.1%20B illion%20(current),currently%20living)%20of%20the% 20world., viewed 5/10/2024 (pg 274)

11. Digital Public Library of America, Calendarium naturale magicum perpetuum profundissimam rerum secretissimarum contemplationem totiusque Philosophiæ cognitionem complectens [graphic], https://dp.la/item/571d3c01dfd928389ac6d95279f33 888 / http://www.archive.org/details/calendariumna-tur00meri, viewed 5/10/2024, This is the spelling of his name and the word "invented" in old English. (pg 41)

12. Dao, Christine, 3/01/08, Man of Science, Man of God/ Johann Kepler | The Institute for CreationResearch.pdf/ https://www.icr.org/article/science-man-god-johann-kepler/, Kepler, J. 1619. "Proem." Harmonies of the World., Viewed 5/10/24 (pg 46)

13. Dao, Christine, 3/01/08, Man of Science, Man of God/ Johann Kepler | The Institute for CreationResearch.pdf/ https://www.icr.org/article/science-man-god-johann-kepler/, Epilogue Concerning the Sun, By Way of Conjecture," ibid.. Viewed 5/10/24 (pg 47)

14. Donovan, Brian, (2016), The Revelation of the Seventy Weeks, Published by Brian Donovan, 1130 Jo Jo Road, Pensacola, FL 32514, Bible Baptist Bookstore (pg 27,28,29,30,32,33,44, 51, 52, 84, 86, 100, 262)

15. Dreyer, J. I. E., Ph. D., F.R.A.S., Tycho Brahe, A Picture of Scientific Life Work in the Sixteenth Century, , Edinburgh, Adam and Charles Black, 1890, From the University of California Library, Pg 236 (pg 36, 38, 39, 42, 50, 51)

16. En.wikipedia.org, Mother of All Asia - Tower of Peace, From Wikipedia, the free encyclopedia, https://en.wikipedia.org/wiki/Mother_of_All_Asia_%E2%80%93_Tower_of_Peace, last edited on 21 August 2023, Sikimedia Foundation, Inc., viewed 5/10/2024 (Pg 359)

17. Eschner, Kat, Astronomer and Alchemist Tycho Brahe Died Full of Gold | Smart News| Smithsonian Magazine.pdf, December 14, 2016/ https://www.smithsonianmag.com/smart-news/astronomer-and-alchemist-tycho-brahe-died-full-gold-180961447/ , viewed 5/10/2024 (pg39, 40)

18. Glanville, Joseph, Saducismus Triumphatus: , Third Edition, 1700 AD, Part 2, Relat. III: Which containeth the Witchcrafts of Elizabeth Style of Bayford, Widow, Pg 73, 75, https://archive.org/details/saducismustriump00glan/page/n427/mode/2up, viewed 5/10/24 (Capitalization and punctuation is preserved in the quote, just as found in the book.) (pg 352-354)

19. Guiley, Rosemary Ellen, Occult World, The Encyclopedia of Magic and Alchemy, Brahe, Tycho, Copywrite 2006 by Visionary Living Inc., https://occult-world.com/brahe-tycho/, Viewed 5/10/2024 (pg 43)

20. Himmel Irvin, "And If They Drink Any Deadly Thing, It Shall Not Hurt Them", TRUTH MAGAZINE XVII: 44, pp. 2-3, September 13, 1973, Quoted from: https://www.truthmagazine.com/archives/volume17/TM017691.html, Guardian of Truth Foundation, viewed 5/8/2024 (pg 159)

21. James I, King of England, Daemonologie, 1597, Daemonology, Second Book,
The description of Sorcerie and Witchcraft in speciall, Chapter 2, downloaded from https://www.gutenberg.org/cache/epub/25929/pg25929-images.html, viewed 5/10/24 (pg 355-356)

22. Lamont Ann, Johannes Kepler (1571-1630) Outstanding scientist and committed Christian, https://creation.com/johannes-kepler, Johannes Kepler, quoted in: J. H. Tiner, Johannes Kepler-Giant of Faith and Science, Mott Media, Milford, Michigan (USA), 1977, p. 193., Originally published in Johannes Kepler | Answers in Genesis, Creation 15, no 1 (December 1992): 40-43., viewed 5/10/24 (pg 46, 47)

23. Larkin Clarence, The Book of Daniel, Ch. 9, The Seventy Weeks, PDF, https://www.earnestlycontendingforthefaith.com/, viewed 5/8/2024 (pg 84)

24. Sacred Heart Catholic Church, The Solemnity of the Most Holy Trinity, https://sacredheartfla.org/sunday-mornings/seasonal/feast-days-solemnities/the-solemnity-of-the-most-holy-trinity/, Viewed 5/10/24 (Pg 434)

25. Satanic Temple, The, After School Satan, https://thesatanictemple.com/pages/after-school-satan, viewed 5/10/24 (Pg 337)

26. Scherlis Adam, Parameter Space: The Final Frontier, Tycho Brahe: Wrong, but Points for Creativity, https://adam.scherlis.com/2010/08/04/tycho-brahe/#comments , Posted on August 4, 2010: Accessed 5/10/2024 (pg 44)

27. Staff TOI, The Times of Israel, In extraordinary move, trains to keep running on Shabbat amid war, 13, October 2023, https://www.timesofisrael.com/in-extraordinary-move-trains-to-keep-running-on-shabbat-amid-war/#:~:text=Israel%20has%20never%20had%20official,to%20opposition%20from%20religious%20lawmakers., Viewed 5/10/202) (pg 152)

28. Staniforth Emily, Tillman Nola Taylor, Tycho Brahe: Colorful life, accomplishments and bizarre death, last updated June 21, 2023, https://www.space.com/19623-tycho-brahe-biography.html / Future US Inc, viewed 5/10/2024 (Pg 40,41)

29. University of Oregon, Tycho Brahe, pages.uoregon.edu/jschombe/cosmo/lectures/lec03.html#:~:text=Tycho%27s%20measurements%20were%20used%20to,in%20how%20science%20is%20done., viewed on 5/10/2024 (Pg 37)

30. Van Braght, Thielem J., The Bloody Theatre, or Martyrs Mirror of the Defenseless Christians / who baptized only upon confession of faith, and who suffered and died for the testimony of Jesus, their savior, from the time of Christ to the year A.D. 1660, SYMPHORIAN, A PIOUS CHRISTIAN, BEHEADED FOR THE NAME OF THE LORD JESUS, AT AUGUSTODUNUM, NOW CALLED AUTUM, ABOUT A. D. 275, Elkhart, Indiana, Mennonite Publishing Company, 1886, https://www.gutenberg.org/cache/epub/65855/pg65855-images.html, viewed 5/10/24 (Pg 295-298)

31. Vatican News, Solemnity of the Most Holy trinity, www.vaticannews.va/en/liturgical-holidays/solemnity-of-the-most-holy-trinity.html, Viewed 5/10/24 (pg 434)

32. Vines James, Agent, Heavenly Intrigue: Johannes Kepler, Tycho Brahe, and the Murder Behind One of History's Greatest Scientific Discoveries, https://www.publishersweekly.com/9780385508445 / viewed 5/10/2024 (pg 43)

33. Weisstein, Eric W., Eric Weisstein's World of Scientific Biography, Brahe, Tycho (1546–1601), Retrieved 13 August, 2012., Tycho Brahe - Wikipedia.pdf / https://scienceworld.wolfram.com/biography/Brahe.html, viewed 5/10/2024 (pg 40)

Seven Years

Other Works by Ken McDonald

All works are available
through bookstores and online.

1. Here Comes The Bride

A Critique of the Baptist Bride Heresy
An in depth study of the teachings of the Baptist Briders.

2. Pursuit - (Out of Print)

One Man's quest to find God's perfect will for his life
My personal testimony, along with my family, of trials and
blessings as I sought to find God's perfect will for my life.

3. Good Vibrations

Overcoming Spasmodic Dysphonia
After losing my voice due to preaching, I was diagnosed
with Spasmodic Dysphonia. This is a detailed account of
what I did, and the exercises I did in order to restore my voice
back to a functional working condition.

4. Defiled

The Spiritual Dangers of Alternative Medicine
This book is born out of personal experiences my wife and
I had while using Alternative medicine. This is an in-depth
study of the spiritual side of Alternative medicine. Highly
documented and compared with what the word of God states.

5. Aromatherapy
From a Biblical Perspective

Due to the prevelence of Aromatherapy use in the churches I wrote this to show the dangers of it, and to show God's attitude towards it from the word of God.

SERMON IN A BOOK SERIES

1. Jesus, Talk to Me
Have you ever desired to get the Lord's attention?

Four examples in the word of God of how God reacts to certain people and how to get His attention.

2. Dealing With Bad In-Laws
A Bible Study on Jacob and Laban

There are Biblical limits to how much authority in-laws have in a family. This book shows what they are, and what to do if in-laws are overstepping their boundaries.

3. Even As God
Healing Relationships Biblically

How God deals with His children and how He wants you to deal with those who have genuinely wronged you. Does God have children He loves, but is not in fellowship with?

4. Four Sides of Calvary
Our Lord's Battle on the Cross

A detailed running description of what our Lord suffered on the Cross for those six hours.

5. The Sons of Zadok

What Will you do for 1,000 Years?

One day, Jesus Christ will return to this earth and set up a Millennial Kingdom. The Christians are coming back with Him. Just as the Sons of Zadok have a special place in the Millennium, so too certain Christians will have a special blessing...and some won't.